COULD IT REALLY HAPPEN?

Also by Marvin Moore

Sunday laws,
economic boycotts,
death decrees,
religious persecution
in America…

COULD IT REALLY HAPPEN?

Marvin Moore

Pacific Press® Publishing Association
Nampa, Idaho
Oshawa, Ontario, Canada
www.pacificpress.com

Book design by Gerald Lee Monks
Cover photo CANSTOCKPHOTO.com
Inside photo dreamstime.com

Unless otherwise noted, all Scripture quotations are from the HOLY
BIBLE, NEW INTERNATIONAL VERSION, copyright © 1973,
1978, 1984 International Bible Society. Used by permission of
Zondervan Bible Publishers.
Scripture quotations credited to NKJV are from The New King James
Version, copyright © 1979, 1980, 1982 by Thomas Nelson, Inc. Used
by permission.

Library of Congress Cataloging-in-Publication Data

Moore, Marvin, 1937-
Could it really happen? : Revelation 13 in the light of history and
current events / by Marvin Moore.
p. cm.
ISBN 13: 978-0-8163-2185-8
ISBN 10: 0–8163–2185–X
1. Bible. N.T. Revelation XIII—Prophecies—Sabbath. 2. Sabbath—
Biblical teaching. 3. Bible N.T. Revelation XIII—Prophecies—Sunday
legislation. 4. Sunday legislation—Biblical teaching. 5. Seventh-Day
Adventists—Doctrines. I. Title.

BS2825.6.S22M66 2007
236'.9—dc22   2006052172

Additional copies of this book are available by calling toll-free 1-800-
765-6955 or by visiting http://www.adventistbookcenter.com.

08 09 10 11 • 5 4 3 2

Acknowledgments

I would like to thank several people who have contributed to making this a better book. Attorney Alan Reinach, the religious liberty director of the Pacific Union Conference of Seventh-day Adventists, read several of the chapters dealing with church-state issues and made valuable suggestions. Dr. John Markovic, a professor of European history at Andrews University, read my chapters dealing with European history. His comments about the history of Germany covered in chapter 5 were especially helpful and made that chapter significantly more accurate. Dr. Brian Bull, a personal friend who is a physician at Loma Linda University, kindly consented to read the entire manuscript. His suggestions made the book, as a whole, more reader friendly. Finally, I would like to thank David Jarnes, my editor, for a superb job of preparing the manuscript for publication. Even the best writing can be improved by a good editor, and David has certainly accomplished that admirably with this book.

Contents

Prologue

I like wild, foolish predictions. The more wild and foolish they are, the better I like them. Why? Because the wilder and more foolish a prediction seems when it's first given, the more of an impression it will make when it comes to pass.

Of course, there's always the possibility that my prediction won't come to pass. In that case, my prediction isn't the only thing that's wild and foolish—I am too! That's the risk anyone takes who makes a prediction. Therefore, it's always wise to be sure that our predictions have a reasonable, rational foundation in the best facts available at the time we make them.

CHAPTER I

The Adventist Prophetic Scenario

Frederick Wheeler, a Methodist Episcopal minister, was conducting a Communion service in a small church in Washington, New Hampshire, on a Sunday morning back in early 1844. Before serving the emblems, he told the congregation that "all who confess communion with Christ in such a service as this should be ready to obey God and keep His commandments in all things."

Rachel Oakes Preston, a Seventh Day Baptist, was sitting in the congregation that day. Later, when Wheeler visited her in her home, she challenged him. "You remember, Elder Wheeler, that you said everyone who confesses Christ should obey all the commandments of God?"

"Yes."

"I came near getting up in the meeting right then and saying something."

"I thought so," Wheeler replied. "What did you have in mind to say?"

"I wanted to tell you that you had better set that Communion table back and put the cloth over it until you begin to keep the commandments of God."

Wheeler was taken aback. What, he asked, did she mean? Mrs. Preston said she had in mind the fourth commandment, which she said Wheeler was violating by not observing the Sabbath on the seventh day of the week. Wheeler accepted the challenge and went home to study what the Bible said about the Sabbath. A few weeks later he kept his first Saturday Sabbath, and in March 1844, he preached his first sermon about the Sabbath.

That is how Rachel Oakes Preston introduced the seventh-day Sabbath to Adventists,* and it's how Frederick Wheeler became the first Seventh-day Adventist minister. At the time, neither Mrs. Preston nor Pastor Wheeler knew the global impact their simple exchange that Sunday morning in Washington, New Hampshire, would have.[1]

There's a bit of uncertainty about exactly what happened next. However, we do know that T. M. Preble, another preacher who lived in or near Washington, New Hampshire, became convinced of the seventh-day Sabbath, and in the summer of 1844, he began to keep it. It's most likely that he learned about the Sabbath from Frederick Wheeler or one of Wheeler's members.

William Miller was at the height of his preaching career at the time, and in February of the next year, Preble published an article on the Sabbath in *The Hope of Israel,* a Millerite publication. Joseph Bates read Preble's article and within a few days made up his mind to keep the Sabbath. From that point on, he was an indefatigable promoter of the Sabbath. In early 1846, he discussed the Sabbath with James White and Ellen Harmon, but at the time they didn't think it was important. In August 1846, Bates published a forty-eight-page tract titled *The Seventh-day Sabbath a Perpetual Sign.* James and Ellen White, who were married that same month, studied Bates's tract, became convinced that it was the truth, and began keeping the day. Thus began the long history of the Adventist observance of the Sabbath on Saturday, the seventh day of the week.

Now consider this: Over the past 150 years, the global membership of the Seventh-day Adventist Church has grown from about three thousand in 1863 to some fifteen million around the world today (2007). On the other hand, Seventh Day Baptists, who outnumbered the Adventists several to one back in the mid-1800s, have a global membership today of about fifty thousand. That's a tiny fraction of one percent of today's Adventist membership. What made the difference? Why did Seventh-day Adventists grow so dramatically during the past 150 years while the Seventh Day Baptist membership has remained more or less static? I propose that one of the primary reasons is that from the very beginning of our history, we placed the Sabbath in an eschatological

---

*It would be another seventeen years before Sabbath-keeping Adventists adopted the name *Seventh-day Adventist,* and nineteen years before they organized as a denomination.

setting, while for the Seventh Day Baptists, the Sabbath is simply the right day to keep.

The Sabbath and eschatology

Eschatology is the study of the final events of this world's history up to and including the second coming of Jesus. Eschatological themes are found throughout the Bible, but especially in the major and minor prophets of the Old Testament and in Revelation in the New Testament. Additionally, the Gospels and Epistles reveal that Jesus and the apostles were keenly aware of eschatology. The apostles all believed that the second coming of Jesus would occur within their lifetime or shortly thereafter.*

Daniel and Revelation have particularly fascinated students of prophecy for hundreds of years, and Adventists are no exception. However, our understanding of these prophecies differs significantly from that of nearly all other Catholic and Protestant interpreters, and the Sabbath is a key aspect of our unique perspective. As we understand it, the mark of the beast in Revelation 13:16, 17 is a symbol pointing to a law requiring the observance of Sunday, which will be enforced first in the United States and eventually all over the world just before the second coming of Jesus. We believe that an important issue in the world's final conflict will be whether God's people should observe the Sabbath on Saturday, the seventh day of the week, or on Sunday, the first day.

This view goes back to the very beginning of our movement, some fourteen or fifteen years before we organized as a church. Joseph Bates was the first to connect Revelation's "mark of the beast" with the observance of Sunday. In a tract he published in January 1847, he wrote, "There are tens of thousands that are looking fore [sic] Jesus, that don't believe the above doctrines, what will become of them? Consult John, he knows better than we do; he has only described two companies. See xiv 9–11, 12. One is keeping the commandments and faith of Jesus. The other has the mark of the beast. . . . *Is it not clear that the first day of the week for the Sabbath or holy day, is the mark of the beast?*"[2]

A few years later Ellen White, a cofounder of the Adventist Church in the mid-1800s, expressed the same primitive understanding of the mark

---

*See for example Romans 13:11, 12; James 5:8, 9; 1 Peter 4:7; 1 John 2:18; Revelation 22:7, 12, 20.

of the beast. In her book *Early Writings,* she said, "Then I realized, as never before, the importance of searching the Word of God carefully, to know how to escape the plagues which that Word declares shall come on all the ungodly who shall worship the beast and his image and receive his mark on their foreheads or in their hands. It was a great wonder for me that any could transgress the law of God and tread down His holy Sabbath, when such awful threatenings and denunciations were against them."[3]

While Ellen White did not specifically state the relationship between the mark of the beast and the observance of Sunday, she clearly had that thought in mind, for she contrasted the mark of the beast with the observance of the Sabbath. And she maintained this understanding throughout her seventy years of ministry. For example, in 1899, she wrote, "When the decree shall go forth enforcing the counterfeit sabbath, and the loud cry of the third angel shall warn men against the worship of the beast and his image, the line will be clearly drawn between the false and the true. Then those who still continue in transgression will receive the mark of the beast."[4]

As this statement suggests, Adventists believe that just before Christ's second coming, the world will be divided into just two camps: Those who keep the Sabbath will receive the seal of God, while those who honor Sunday will receive the mark of the beast. Ellen White wrote,

> The Lord has shown me clearly that the image of the beast will be formed before probation closes; for it is to be the great test for the people of God, by which their eternal destiny will be decided. . . .
>
> . . . All who prove their loyalty to God by observing His law, and refusing to accept a spurious sabbath, will rank under the banner of the Lord God Jehovah, and will receive the seal of the living God. Those who yield the truth of heavenly origin and accept the Sunday sabbath, will receive the mark of the beast.[5]

This is the eschatological context in which Seventh-day Adventists have placed the Sabbath. We believe God has called us not only to proclaim what the Bible says about the Sabbath but also to warn the world of the final conflict, which will revolve around the commandments of God, particularly the fourth one. As we understand it, the dividing line in the end time between those who serve God and those who do not will involve this Sabbath-Sunday controversy. At that time, Sabbath keepers will be persecuted and even martyred for their loyalty to God in observing the Sabbath on Saturday. We feel compelled to warn the world regarding what most people aren't even faintly aware of and many find unbelievable, yet which we are certain lies just ahead. This is one of the major factors that has made our proclamation of the Sabbath so much more successful than that of the Seventh Day Baptists. This is one of the primary reasons why we today have fifteen million adherents to the Seventh Day Baptists' fifty thousand.

But could it really happen?

This eschatological interpretation of the Sabbath comprises a stupendous claim, to say the least! *Audacious* is not too strong a word. Even a casual look at American political history makes it difficult to believe that the United States would ever enforce a national Sunday law, for throughout our history, we've kept church and state separate.

Back in 1970, when I was the pastor of a small Adventist church in the west Texas town of Uvalde, I made friends with a local Baptist businessman. We were chatting in his office one day about religion and prophecy, and I asked him if he would be interested in knowing what Adventists believe about the end time. He said Yes, so I shared with him what you've read in this chapter. When I was through, I asked him what he thought. He smiled and said, "I think it's stupid."

He isn't the only one to think so, nor is he the first one. Back in the early 1900s, one critic called our view that the mark of the beast will be the enforced observance of Sunday "absurd." He said that the rejection by the United States of its historic support of religious freedom would require "a greater miracle than for God to grow a giant oak in an instant."[6]

Another early critic of the Adventist prophetic scenario was D. M. Canright. A popular Adventist evangelist and leader during the early years of our movement, he severed his connection with us in 1887 and joined a Baptist congregation in Otsego, New York. In his book *Seventh-day Adventism Renounced,* Canright wrote,

> Seventh-day Adventists lay great stress upon their interpretation of this symbol [the lamblike beast of] Revelation 13:11–18. Their theory of the mark of the beast, his image, the seal of God, the Third Angel's message, and all their special work about the

Sabbath is built upon their assumption concerning that beast. If they are mistaken here, their whole system collapses. They claim that this beast is the United States, and that soon we shall have here a church and state united, the image of the beast, the papacy. The mark of the beast is Sunday-keeping. A law will enforce this upon Seventh-day Adventists. They won't obey. Then they will be outlawed, persecuted, and condemned to death! Of all the wild Advent speculations in the prophecies, this deserves to stand among the wildest.[7]

That's strong language! And while I wouldn't go so far as to say that if we are wrong in our prophetic interpretation of Revelation 13, our whole system collapses, it is true that much of what we view as our mission to the world is based on our understanding of that chapter. The critical question, then, is this: Could it really happen? Is it reasonable to suppose that the United States will ever legislate Sunday as a day of rest? Is it anything more than fantasy to suppose that at some point in the fairly near future, a global edict will require that people everywhere observe Sunday as the Sabbath and that violators will be threatened with death and perhaps even executed? Is this what the mark of the beast is all about?

My purpose in writing this book is not to *prove* to you that the answer to these questions is "Yes." It's more to present the evidence as I and many other Adventists see it and then let you decide for yourself. That's why I've titled this book *Could It Really Happen?* not *Will It Really Happen?*

Prophecy and current events

I like to compare the interpretation of prophecy to a pair of sunglasses. If you put on a pair with blue lenses, the world will look blue. A pair with amber lenses will cause the world to look amber. Green lenses will give the world a green tint. In the same way, any person's interpretation of Bible prophecy will affect the way he or she views what's happening in the world today and what's likely to happen in the future. Dispensationalists, for example, have a particular understanding of prophecy, and they interpret world events in light of that understanding. They focus their attention on the Middle East, especially Israel. They interpret events such as 9/11, the conflict in Iraq, and the clash between Israel and the Palestinians in light of their dispensationalist understanding of prophecy.

Their dispensationalist prophetic lenses also lead them to make certain predictions about the future.

The Adventist prophetic understanding differs greatly. It's like putting on a pair of sunglasses with lenses of a much different color from those that Dispensationalists wear. The world looks different through our lenses, which leads us to a much different explanation of what's happening now and what to expect in the future. While we need to be cautious about reading a prophetic implication into every news event that appears in the daily paper or on TV, *trends over a period of time* can give us an indication of where the world is headed. And our understanding of Bible prophecy influences our interpretation of those trends.

In this book you will read a detailed explanation of the Adventist understanding of Revelation 13 and how it affects our interpretation of trends in today's world. This first chapter is a brief introduction. The rest of the book examines the details. Two key questions will dominate my discussion throughout the book:

- *Is the Adventist interpretation of Revelation 13 reasonable—is it based on what the Bible actually says, or is it mere speculation?* To answer this question, we will examine Revelation 13, as well as a few other Bible prophecies.
- *Do history and current events indicate that the Adventist scenario is realistic?* To answer this question, we will review the history of Catholicism, the history of both Protestants and Catholics in America, and what both are doing in America today.

Introduction to the book

A few comments follow that should make it easier for you to understand this book. First, a word about what you can expect to find. As I suggested a moment ago, this book is largely an interpretation of Revelation 13 in the light of history and current events. I've divided it into three sections, each of which deals with a different aspect of Revelation 13:

- The first section deals with a terrible beast that arises from the sea.
- The second section deals with a beast that arises from the land.
- The third section deals with the mark of the beast.

The first two sections each begin with a chapter explaining the biblical basis for the Adventist understanding of that part of Revelation 13. The section on the mark of the beast begins with two chapters on the biblical basis for that interpretation of the prophecy. The chapters that follow each of these introductory chapters provide historical evidence—some ancient, some very modern—to show that the Adventist interpretation also has a solid basis in world events that *have* happened or that *are* happening.

Second, I'm a lifelong Seventh-day Adventist, so, obviously, I've written this book from an Adventist perspective. However, I've also written it in such a way that it should make sense to those who are not of our faith and thus not familiar with our beliefs. In fact, you will no doubt notice that the tone of the book addresses non-Adventists as much as it does Adventists. Because of this, I've explained the biblical basis for our interpretation of Revelation 13 in greater detail than many Adventists will need.

And finally, Ellen G. White is without a doubt the most influential Adventist author. She lived for eighty-eight years, from 1827 to 1915. In December 1844, when she was just seventeen years old, she received the first of some two thousand visions that she claimed God gave her throughout her lifetime. She was the most prolific female author of the nineteenth century, and perhaps of all time. During her seventy-plus years of ministry, she wrote more than a hundred thousand pages, all by hand, including more than two dozen books. And since her death, excerpts from her letters and diaries and other writings have been collected and published as books, as well.

Adventists accept Ellen White as a genuine prophet, though she preferred to be known as a "messenger of the Lord." She had a great deal to say about the end time. I shared several of her statements with you earlier in this chapter, and I will quote her occasionally in future chapters. Adventist readers will no doubt accept these citations as the word of the Lord. Non-Adventists reading this book can think of these quotations as simply representative of what Adventists believe. Most Adventists will probably agree with the majority of what I say in this book. I invite non-Adventist readers to accept what I say as well, if it makes sense. In any case, I hope that reading this book will help both Adventists and those who are not of our faith to understand our prophetic interpretation better.

1. My two sources for this story are the *Seventh-day Adventist Encyclopedia* (Hagerstown, Md.: Review and Herald®, 1966), 1019, 1020; and Arthur W. Spaulding, *Origin and History of Seventh-day Adventists* (Hagerstown, Md.: Review and Herald®, 1961), 117–119.

2. Joseph Bates, *The Seventh-day Sabbath a Perpetual Sign From the Beginning, to the Entering Into the Gates of the Holy City According to the Commandment,* 1847 edition, 59, italics added; cited in *Development of Seventh-day Adventist Theology Source Book: Maxwell Source Collection,* a private manuscript prepared by Mervyn Maxwell for students in his class on the history of Adventist theology, 271.

3. Ellen G. White, *Early Writings* (Hagerstown, Md.: Review and Herald®, 1882), 65.

4. Manuscript 51, 1899; cited in Ellen G. White, *Evangelism* (Hagerstown, Md.: Review and Herald®, 1946), 234, 235.

5. *The Seventh-day Adventist Bible Commentary* (Hagerstown, Md.: Review and Herald®, 1957), 7:976.

6. Theodore Nelson, in the introduction to Dudley M. Canright's book, *Seventh-day Adventism Renounced* (Nashville: Gospel Advocate Company, 1914), 23.

7. Canright, ibid., 89.

Chapter 2

Looking at Revelation's Big Picture

When was the last time you looked at a painting? Was it a portrait of a handsome man or a beautiful woman, or was it perhaps a landscape? And did you try getting up real close and examining the tiny details? That's not the way to appreciate the beauty of a painting, is it? The artist has to pay careful attention to each brush stroke as he paints, and even after the work is completed, art critics will look at those fine details. But up close, those individual brush strokes aren't very attractive. If you really want to appreciate the beauty of the artist's production, you have to back away and look at the whole painting. Sooner or later, even the critic has to stand back and look at "the big picture."

Revelation is full of images—pictures, if you please. You'll find more of these symbolic images in Revelation than in any other part of the Bible. In this book, we're going to be "art critics" of the images in Revelation. We're going to spend a lot of time examining the details in these images, especially in chapter 13. But just as the details in a painting don't show us the picture as a whole, so our understanding of Revelation can't be complete if we look only at the details. Consequently, in this chapter, we're going to look at Revelation's "big picture." We'll examine the details in later chapters.

The great controversy

You don't have to be a biblical scholar to understand Revelation's basic message. Even a nonreligious person reading casually through the last half of the book can recognize that the major theme is the conflict between good and evil—what Seventh-day Adventists have traditionally called the "great controversy." According to Revelation, this conflict actually began in God's own heaven several thousand years ago. Revelation 12:7 says, "*And there was war in heaven.* Michael and his angels fought against the dragon, and the dragon and his angels fought back" (italics added). Michael is the leader of heaven's loyal angels, and the dragon is Satan, the leader of the angels that rebelled against God.

This war didn't affect just heaven, though. Revelation says that the dragon "was hurled to the earth, and his angels with him" (verse 9). So, the battle between good and evil shifted to this earth, and it has been going on since shortly after God created our world. Even today, it doesn't take much to see the conflict in action. Spend a few moments reading the newspaper or watching the evening news. You'll get your fill.

The second half of Revelation focuses especially on the last few months and perhaps years of the conflict between good and evil—what I will refer to as "the final conflict." At that time, Satan will put forth the most intense efforts of his career to intimidate human beings and control them. And most people will go along quite cheerfully. Revelation says, "The whole world was astonished and followed the [evil] beast" power (13:3). It says, "All inhabitants of the earth will worship the beast—all whose names have not been written in the book of life belonging to the Lamb that was slain from the creation of the world" (verse 8).

The issue will be obedience. The question that has faced God's people throughout history and that will especially confront them in earth's final conflict is whether they will obey God or the powers of evil in the world. Adam and Eve faced the choice of obeying God or the serpent, and they chose to obey the serpent. On the other hand, Shadrach, Meshach, and Abednego, threatened with death in a burning fiery furnace, chose to obey God rather than worship a pagan king's golden image. And in the New Testament, Jesus obeyed His Father by going to the cross. The basic issue in the final conflict will be the same: Will God's people obey Him, or will they yield to political pressure and obey the end-time powers of evil in the world that are pressuring them to disobey God?

Revelation 12:17 introduces us to the obedience of God's end-time people and the conflict this sets up between them and the forces of evil on the earth: "Then the dragon [Satan] was enraged at the woman [God's people] and went off to make war against the rest of her offspring—*those who obey God's commandments* and hold to the testimony of Jesus" (italics added). And 14:12 says, "This calls for patient endurance on the part of the saints *who obey God's commandments* and remain faithful to Jesus" (italics added).

Thus, according to Revelation, God's commandments—His laws—will be a major focal point of the final conflict. God's people will remain loyal to His laws, but doing this will bring on them the wrath of earth's apostate religio-political powers. Here's how Ellen White described this aspect of the final conflict: "The last great conflict between truth and error is but the final struggle of the long-standing controversy concerning the law of God. Upon this battle we are now entering—a battle between the laws of men and the precepts of Jehovah, between the religion of the Bible and the religion of fable and tradition."[1]

However, obedience is only part of the issue in Revelation. The other part is faith. Christians often speak of "righteousness by faith." A correct understanding of righteousness by faith requires that we achieve a correct balance between faith and works. An overemphasis on faith leads to cheap grace, while an overemphasis on works leads to legalism. God's people who live during the end time will have a correct understanding of both faith and works. Revelation itself suggests this when it says, "Here are they that keep the commandments of God, *and the faith of Jesus*" (Revelation 14:12, KJV, italics added).

The two sides

The final conflict will involve deeply spiritual issues. The world will be divided into just two camps, with God's people on one side and the forces of evil arrayed against them on the other side. People need not suppose that their mere profession of Christianity will get them by. Jesus warned that when He comes the second time, many people will say to Him, " ' "Lord, Lord, did we not prophesy in your name, and in your name drive out demons and perform many miracles?" Then I will tell them plainly, "I never knew you. Away from me, you evildoers!" ' " (Matthew 7:21–23).

Notice that these people believe in Jesus. They are loyal, upstanding church members. They are faithful to their spouses, pay their tithe, and carry major responsibilities as church officers. Yet Jesus will say to them, "I never knew you." We can also turn that around and say that they never knew Him either. Their Christianity was very shallow. It consisted of assent to a set of doctrines and the performance of good deeds. They trusted that membership in "the right church" would gain them access to heaven. You probably rub shoulders with some of these people in your church and will be surprised someday to discover that they aren't with you in God's kingdom.

I propose that many of these people will be on Satan's side during the final conflict. This may sound strange to you. Just keep in mind that the final conflict will be primarily a spiritual battle over profoundly spiritual issues, and Satan will use extremely subtle arguments to keep people on his side. Jesus warned about this. He said, " 'False Christs and false prophets will appear and perform great signs and miracles to deceive even the elect—if that were possible' " (Matthew 24:24). The world will be divided into just two sides during the end time: Those who are loyal to God and those who are loyal to Satan. Unfortunately, many professed Christians will be surprised to find, when it's all over, that they joined the wrong side.

Several of Jesus' parables illustrate this division of the world into two groups. In one place He called the righteous "good seed" and the wicked "weeds." In another place He called them the sheep and the goats (Matthew 13:37–43; 25:31–33). Revelation also has symbols for these two end-time groups of people. The righteous receive the seal of God while the wicked receive the mark of the beast (see Revelation 7:1–4; 13:16, 17). God's people will keep His commandments, while the wicked will set up their own laws and rebel against God's laws. Not only that, the wicked will try to force the whole world, including God's people, to join them in their rebellion against God. This will result in a life-and-death struggle between God's people and the powers of evil in the world—*and at first it will appear that the forces of evil are winning.* Revelation 13:7 says that the beast from the sea "was given power to make war against the saints *and to conquer them*" (italics added), and verse 15 says that those who refuse to worship in the politically correct manner will be killed. Revelation 17 describes an evil woman who is "drunk with the blood of the saints" (verse 6), suggesting that the saints have been martyred.

Reading these statements in Revelation, you'd get the impression that the powers of evil will win in the final conflict. And, indeed, at first it will appear that they have won, just as they appeared to have won when Jesus died on the cross. Christians understand that by His death, Jesus gained a great victory. However, to those who witnessed His crucifixion, it looked as though He had lost. Even His disciples, mourning His death, said, " 'We had hoped that he was the one who was going to redeem Israel' " (Luke 24:21). In the same way, during the final conflict it will look as though earth's evil powers have won and God's people have lost. The world will reward the loyalty of the righteous to God and His commandments with persecution and death, and people will actually rejoice at the apparent victory of the powers of evil. Here's how Revelation describes that rejoicing: "Now when they [God's people] have finished their testimony, the beast that comes up from the Abyss will attack them, and overpower and kill them. . . . The inhabitants of the earth will gloat over them and will celebrate by sending each other gifts, because these two prophets [God's people] had tormented those who live on the earth" (Revelation 11:7–10).

The world has never appreciated God's laws. They find His moral principles too restrictive of their freedom. When God's people call attention to His laws, the world responds with ridicule. That's why, during the final conflict, "the inhabitants of the earth will gloat over" God's people who have been upholding His laws. That's why they will "celebrate by sending each other gifts."

Obviously, this will be a very stressful time for God's people. A rebellious world will be putting intense pressure on them to yield their loyalty to God and disobey His laws. What will cause them to remain faithful to God during this time? The verses we read a moment ago provide the answer:

- "Then the dragon [Satan] was enraged at the woman [God's people] and went off to make war against the rest of her offspring— those *who . . . hold to the testimony of Jesus*" (Revelation 12:17, italics added).
- "This calls for patient endurance on the part of the saints *who . . . remain faithful to Jesus*" (Revelation 14:12, italics added).

God's people will maintain their loyalty to Him because they "hold to the testimony of Jesus"; they "remain faithful to Jesus." The key is to have an intimate relationship with Jesus. That has always been the key to victory over temptation, and it will especially be so during the final crisis—what Revelation calls "the hour of trial that is going to come upon the whole world" (Revelation 3:10). Ellen White said that the intensity of the pressure that will be brought to bear on God's people during the final crisis "will show whether there is any real faith in the promises of

God. It will show whether the soul is sustained by grace."[2] You don't have to be an Adventist to understand that the relationship that you and I are developing with Jesus right now will determine whether we will remain loyal to God during the world's final crisis or will yield our convictions in the face of the world's pressure to conform.

The end of the conflict

The world will appear to have conquered God's people, but that victory will be short-lived. At the last minute, when to all appearances God's people must seal their commitment to Him with their blood, Jesus will intervene on their behalf. Here's how Revelation puts it:

- " 'They [the evil beast powers] will make war against the Lamb, but the Lamb will overcome them because he is Lord of lords and King of kings—and with him will be his called, chosen and faithful followers' " (Revelation 17:14).
- "Then I saw the beast and the kings of the earth and their armies gathered together to make war against the rider on the horse and his army. But the beast was captured, and with him the false prophet. . . . The two of them were thrown alive into the fiery lake of burning sulfur" (Revelation 19:19, 20).

These two verses are actually snapshots of the battle of Armageddon. Contrary to popular opinion, Armageddon will not be a battle between certain nations on the earth. Armageddon will be a battle between the spiritual powers of good and evil in the world. During the initial phase of the battle, it will appear that the forces of evil are winning. But at the very last minute, when all appears to be lost, Jesus will return to this earth, strike down the forces of evil, and deliver His people from their grasp.

Revelation 13

In the rest of this book we will examine Revelation 13 in detail. However, I believe you will find it helpful if you get an overview of the chapter first. To get started, I recommend that you simply read the chapter. You can read it from your own Bible if you wish, but I have also reproduced it from the New International Version on the next two pages. And because chapter 12:17 is so closely linked with chapter 13, I have started with that verse.

(Chapter 12:17) Then the dragon was enraged at the woman and went off to make war against the rest of her offspring—those who obey God's commandments and hold to the testimony of Jesus.

(Chapter 13:1) And the dragon stood on the shore of the sea.

And I saw a beast coming out of the sea. He had ten horns and seven heads, with ten crowns on his horns, and on each head a blasphemous name. (2) The beast I saw resembled a leopard, but had feet like those of a bear and a mouth like that of a lion. The dragon gave the beast his power and his throne and great authority. (3) One of the heads of the beast seemed to have had a fatal wound, but the fatal wound had been healed. The whole world was astonished and followed the beast. (4) Men worshiped the dragon because he had given authority to the beast, and they also worshiped the beast and asked, "Who is like the beast? Who can make war against him?"

(5) The beast was given a mouth to utter proud words and blasphemies and to exercise his authority for forty-two months. (6) He opened his mouth to blaspheme God, and to slander his name and his dwelling place and those who live in heaven. (7) He was given power to make war against the saints and to conquer them. And he was given authority over every tribe, people, language and nation. (8) All inhabitants of the earth will worship the beast—all whose names have not been written in the book of life belonging to the Lamb that was slain from the creation of the world.

(9) He who has an ear, let him hear.

(10) If anyone is to go into captivity,
into captivity he will go.
If anyone is to be killed with the sword,
with the sword he will be killed.

This calls for patient endurance and faithfulness on the part of the saints.

(11) Then I saw another beast, coming out of the earth. He had two horns like a lamb, but he spoke like a dragon. (12) He exercised all the authority of the first beast on his behalf, and made the earth and its inhabitants worship the first beast, whose

fatal wound had been healed. (13) And he performed great and miraculous signs, even causing fire to come down from heaven to earth in full view of men. (14) Because of the signs he was given power to do on behalf of the first beast, he deceived the inhabitants of the earth. He ordered them to set up an image in honor of the beast who was wounded by the sword and yet lived. (15) He was given power to give breath to the image of the first beast, so that it could speak and cause all who refused to worship the image to be killed. (16) He also forced everyone, small and great, rich and poor, free and slave, to receive a mark on his right hand or on his forehead, (17) so that no one could buy or sell unless he had the mark, which is the name of the beast or the number of his name.

(18) This calls for wisdom. If anyone has insight, let him calculate the number of the beast, for it is man's number. His number is 666.

You noticed, I'm sure, that Revelation 13 describes two great beasts. One arises from the sea and the other one from the earth. Thus, for the rest of our study I will call them "the sea beast" and "the land beast."

Overview of the two beasts

Who or what do these two beasts represent? Adventists, along with most other interpreters of prophecy, understand a beast in apocalyptic prophecy to represent a powerful political entity—a major world power. For example, an angel specifically told the prophet Daniel that the four great beasts of Daniel 7:1–8 represent " ' "four kingdoms that will rise from the earth" ' " (Daniel 7:17). It was no doubt the same angel who told Daniel that the ram and the goat in Daniel 8:1–8 represent the kingdoms of Media-Persia and Greece (see Daniel 8:20, 21).

The questions naturally arise, Which world powers do the sea beast and the land beast in Revelation represent? Did these political entities exist in the past, or are they present in the world today? Let's begin by getting a broad overview of both beasts—the "big picture" of Revelation 13.

Global powers. The first thing we notice about these two beasts is that both of them are religio-political powers with global influence. The sea beast clearly has global political power, because it is "given authority over

27

every tribe, people, language and nation" (verse 7). We see its religious nature in the fact that the world worships it and it "blaspheme[s] God, and slander[s] his name and his dwelling place and those who live in heaven" (verse 6). The land beast is also a global political power, because it has the authority to order the inhabitants of the earth to set up an image to the sea beast (verse 14). Its religious authority is evident in the fact that it causes "all who refused to worship the image to be killed" (verse 15).

False worship. A careful look at Revelation 13 shows clearly that both beasts promote false worship. With the exception of God's remnant, the world's entire population will worship the sea beast (verse 8), and the land beast will force the world to worship the image to the sea beast (verse 15).

Religious persecution. Another factor that is common to these two beasts is that both of them persecute those who oppose their religio-political program. The sea beast "make[s] war against the saints and . . . conquer[s] them" (verse 7), and, as noted a moment ago, the land beast forces the entire world to worship the image to the sea beast (verse 15).

End-time powers. Another immediate conclusion we can draw about the sea beast and the land beast is that they are both end-time powers. This is evident from the fact that they cooperate in enforcing the mark of the beast, which both futurist and historicist interpreters of Revelation understand to be an end-time phenomenon.

Many interpreters of prophecy are convinced that we today live in the end time. If that's true—and I've based this book on the premise that it is—then both of these horribly intolerant powers exist in the world today. Twenty, thirty, and forty years ago, some students of prophecy pointed to the communist Soviet Union as the fulfillment of at least one of these beasts—an option that ceased to exist about 1990. Today it may be tempting to think of Islamic terrorists as the fulfillment of one or both of these beasts. However, neither communism nor Islamic terrorism is the correct identification of either of them. Seventh-day Adventists have very specific ideas about the identity of each one. I will share with you our understanding of the sea beast in the next chapter. Later chapters will identify the land beast, the image to the beast, and the mark of the beast.

---

1. Ellen G. White, *The Great Controversy* (Nampa, Idaho: Pacific Press®, 1911), 582.

2. White, *Christ's Object Lessons* (Hagerstown, Md.: Review and Herald®, 1900), 412.

PART ONE

The Sea Beast of Revelation 13

CHAPTER 3

Revelation 13 and the Sea Beast

Suppose you and I are talking about a mutual friend whose name is John, and I say to you, "John's a bulldog!" You know immediately that I don't mean John is a member of the canine species. Instead, I mean that some characteristic that our culture associates with bull-dogs is also true of John, or at least of my perception of him. I probably mean that John is very aggressive and tenacious—when he gets something in his head, he goes after it and refuses to let go until he's achieved it.

When used this way, the word *bulldog* is a metaphor—a symbol, if you please. Each language and each culture has such symbols. And Revelation is full of them: beasts, stars, trumpets, crowns, and thrones, to name just a few. There's just one problem with Revelation's symbols—we can't find their meaning so easily. For the most part, Revelation doesn't tell us what they represent. There are exceptions, to be sure. For example, in chapter 12:9 we learn that the dragon represents "the devil, or Satan." But most of Revelation's symbols don't come with descriptions that help us understand what they mean.

So, how can we make sense of Revelation when we don't know the meaning of so many of its symbols? Actually, the meanings of some symbols are fairly obvious. For example, in our culture today as well as in the Roman culture two thousand years ago, a crown represents a governing authority. So does a throne. Thus, when we read about crowns and thrones in Revelation, we can be fairly certain that these symbols represent some form of government. God's throne shows up repeatedly in

Revelation, which simply means that God has a government. Earthly governments rule over a small portion of the world's land mass, but God's government rules over the entire universe!

Another way to determine the meaning of a symbol in Revelation is to look up how it's used elsewhere in the Bible and bring that meaning to Revelation. We'll also take that approach from time to time in this book.

War is one of Revelation's most pervasive symbols, and it's a rather obvious metaphor for conflict. In Revelation, war is usually a symbol of the conflict between the forces of good and evil. We began looking at this war in the previous chapter, and we learned that it actually began in heaven: "There was war in heaven. Michael and his angels fought against the dragon, and the dragon and his angels fought back" (Revelation 12:7). Michael is the leader of God's heavenly army, and in verse 9 we learn that the dragon is Satan. He lost the war in heaven, and Revelation says that he was "hurled . . . to the earth, and his angels with him" (verses 7–9). Then Revelation adds an ominous note:

"But woe to the earth and the sea,
    because the devil has gone down to you!
He is filled with fury,
    because he knows that his time is short" (verse 12).

This war has engulfed our world for thousands of years. Satan is furious that he lost the war in heaven, and his anger is driving him with bitter intensity to win the war *here* that he lost *there*. In the cases of most people, Satan has actually won the war. They're his allies! The object of his wrath today is the few people who still resist him. This book is about the part of Satan's war against God's people that will be fought on our planet just before Jesus returns. Revelation 12:17 introduces us to that final phase of the conflict: "Then the dragon was enraged at the woman and went off to make war against the rest of her offspring—those who obey God's commandments and hold to the testimony of Jesus" (Revelation 12:17).

The dragon in this verse is Satan, and the woman represents God's people. Thus, Revelation 12:17 confirms what I just shared with you—that the major participants in earth's final conflict will be Satan and God's people, and Satan's wrath will be at a fever pitch. God's people who live through this conflict will have to deal with an extremely hostile enemy! But is that all we know about the final conflict? Absolutely not! Revelation 12:17 is only an introduction. Chapter 13 fills in a large amount of detail. We took a broad look at Revelation 13 in the previous chapter of this book. It's now time to look at the details. In the rest of this chapter, we will examine the beast that arises out of the sea. This will provide the biblical-factual basis for the Adventist understanding of the sea beast and its role during earth's final crisis.

Identifying the sea beast

Most of today's students of prophecy interpret the sea beast to represent either the ancient Roman Empire (preterist interpreters) or a future secular, atheistic antichrist that will emerge during the Tribulation (futurist interpreters). But Seventh-day Adventists understand the sea beast to represent the papacy. We base our interpretation on a comparison of the sea beast with Daniel's vision of four beasts in Daniel 7, especially the little horn on the fourth beast. (If you are already familiar with the Adventist interpretation of Daniel 7 and of the sea beast as the papacy, you may wish to skip the rest of this chapter.)

In Daniel 7, the prophet described a vision that God gave him of four great beasts that rose out of the sea. I have listed these beasts in the left-hand column below. The column on the right gives the kingdom that each one represents:

A lion (Daniel 7:3, 4)	Babylon
A bear (verse 5)	Media-Persia
A leopard (verse 6)	Greece
A ferocious beast, a dragon (verses 7, 8)	Rome

John brought each of these beasts into his description of the sea beast in Revelation 13:2, as the italicized words below will show:

- The sea beast had "a mouth like that of a *lion*" (italics added).
- It "had feet like those of a *bear*" (italics added).
- The beast as a whole "resembled a *leopard*" (italics added).
- "The *dragon* gave the beast his power and his throne and great authority" (italics added).

John obviously had Daniel's vision of the four great beasts in mind when he described the sea beast in Revelation 13. *And there's more.* Going back to Daniel, we learn that the fourth beast had ten horns, and Daniel saw a "little horn" rise up among the ten, actually displacing three of them in order to make room for itself. Daniel 7:25 contains a detailed description of this little horn. Revelation 13:5–7 brings in four additional symbols from this detailed description. The chart below quotes the relevant words from each passage:

Similarities Between the Little Horn and the Sea Beast	
The Little Horn **Daniel 7**	**The Sea Beast** **Revelation 13**
Blasphemes God " 'This horn had . . . a mouth that spoke boastfully' " (verse 8); " ' "He will speak against the Most High" ' " (verse 25).	**Blasphemes God** "The beast was given a mouth to utter proud words and blasphemies" (verse 5); "He opened his mouth to blaspheme God" (verse 6).
Persecutes God's people He will " ' "oppress [God's] saints" ' " (verse 25).	**Persecutes God's people** "He was given power to make war against the saints" (verse 7).
Conquers God's people " ' "The saints will be handed over to him" ' " (verse 25).	**Conquers God's people** He will conquer the saints (verse 7).
Is given a time period " ' "The saints will be handed over to him for a *time, times and half a time*" ' " (verse 25, italics added)—that is, 1,260 years.	**Is given a time period** "The beast was given . . . [power] to exercise his authority for *forty-two months*" (verse 5, italics added)—that is, 1,260 years.

The similarities between the little horn of Daniel 7 and the sea beast of Revelation 13 leave no doubt that both symbolize the same earthly power. Some interpreters consider the little horn to represent the end-time antichrist. However, Adventist interpreters have consistently identified the little horn as the medieval papacy. If this is true, the conclusion seems evident that the sea beast of Revelation 13 also represents the papacy. On what basis, then, do Adventists identify Daniel's little horn as the papacy?

Is the little horn really the papacy?

The little horn in Daniel 7 grew up on the head of the fourth beast, which I noted a moment ago represents the Roman Empire. Let's take a closer look at this beast. Here's how Daniel described what he saw in his vision:

> "After that, in my vision at night I looked, and there before me was a fourth beast—terrifying and frightening and very powerful. It had large iron teeth; it crushed and devoured its victims and trampled underfoot whatever was left. It was different from all the former beasts, and it had ten horns.
>
> "While I was thinking about the horns, there before me was another horn, a little one, which came up among them; and three of the first horns were uprooted before it. This horn had eyes like the eyes of a man and a mouth that spoke boastfully" (Daniel 7:7, 8).

Daniel named each of the first three beasts in his vision: a lion, a bear, and a leopard. However, the fourth beast was so unusual, so different from anything he'd ever seen before, that he couldn't name it; he could only describe it. I call it a dragon. The powerful nature of this dragon makes it an apt symbol of the Roman Empire. However, we're interested in the dragon's ten horns, and especially its little horn.

The ten horns represent the barbarian tribes that overran the Roman Empire between A.D. 300 and 500. Daniel said that a "little horn" arose among the ten, uprooting three of the ten in the process. Daniel's detailed description of the little horn in verses 24 and 25 unlocks its meaning. I'll begin by quoting these two verses: " ' "The ten horns [on the dragon's head] are ten kings who will come from this kingdom. After them another king will arise, different from the earlier ones; he will subdue three kings. He will speak against the Most High and oppress his saints and try to change the set times and the laws. The saints will be handed over to him for a time, times and half a time." ' "

These verses provide us with seven specifications of the little horn that the papacy fulfilled:

1. "After them another king will arise." The barbarian tribes were well established in the Roman Empire by the middle of the fifth century (the 400s). The Western Roman Empire fell to the barbarian tribes in 476. The political power of the papacy did not begin until 538, as we will see in the next chapter. Therefore, the papacy fits the specification in Daniel's prophecy that *"after them* [after the barbarian tribes had settled in the Roman Empire] another king will arise." The papacy did indeed arise as a powerful political force in Europe *after* the ten tribes had conquered the Roman Empire.

2. It will be "different from the earlier ones." The papacy is different from the ten horns in that it is both a religious power and a political power, whereas the other nations of Europe are strictly political.

3. "He will subdue three kings." All the barbarian tribes that conquered Rome eventually converted to Christianity, but three of them— the Visigoths, the Vandals, and the Ostrogoths—adopted Arianism,* a theological view of Christ that the Council of Nicaea and subsequent church councils proclaimed to be a heresy. Clovis, king of the Franks, conquered the Visigoths in 508. At the request of the popes, the Roman emperor Justinian sent his armies to root out the other two heretical tribes: the Vandals in 534, and the Ostrogoths in 538.[1] Thus, it's reasonable to say that the papacy uprooted these barbarian tribes.

4. "He will speak against the Most High." Historicist interpreters of Bible prophecy point to several claims and teachings of the papacy that fulfill Daniel's prediction that the little horn would "speak against the Most High." One of these is the claim of the popes to be the Vicar of Christ. The word *vicar,* which means "substitute," comes from the same root as the word *vice* in vice president, which means a substitute for the president in the president's absence. Thus, in claiming to be the Vicar of Christ, the pope is saying that he is Christ's personal representative on earth during the time that Christ is in heaven and therefore absent from the earth. However, Jesus specifically said that He would send the Holy

---

*The Arians denied the doctrine of the Trinity, which affirms the full equality and divine nature of the Father, Son, and Holy Spirit. They believed Jesus to be a created Being and thus by nature inferior to God the Father. Antitrinitarians are still sometimes called Arians.

Spirit to represent Him on earth in His absence (John 16:7, 8). Thus, the pope's claim to be the Vicar of Christ intrudes on the role of the Holy Spirit.

Two other claims of the papacy will suffice to show that the papacy fulfills Daniel's prediction that it will "speak against the Most High." One is the teaching that through the confessional Catholic priests have the power to forgive sins—a prerogative that is God's alone. Second is the claim that the priest sacrifices Christ's literal body and blood on the altar in the service of the Mass. The point is not only that this teaching contradicts the message of Hebrews that Christ offered one sacrifice for all time (see Hebrews 9:25, 26); it also puts the Catholic priest in the position of bringing Christ down from heaven in order to sacrifice Him.

5. *He will "oppress his saints."* That is, the power represented by the little horn would persecute God's people. The papacy has more than fulfilled this prediction by its use of the power of the state to persecute and in many cases execute so-called heretics. Most of these "heretics" were simply pointing out what they perceived to be the doctrinal errors of the papacy and in some instances the immoral practices of the popes. The Spanish Inquisition is probably the best-known example of this persecution.

6. *He will "try to change the set times and the laws."* The Catholic claim that the church has the authority to change God's law fulfills this specification of the prophecy. The church removes the second commandment (against images) entirely from its catechisms, and by substituting the first day of the week, Sunday, for the seventh-day Sabbath of the fourth commandment, it has fulfilled Daniel's prediction that it would change times.[2]

7. *"The saints will be handed over to him for a time, times and half a time."* The Aramaic word for time in this verse is *'iddan*, which means "a year." A "time" equals one year, "times" is two years, and "half a time" is six months. According to prophetic reckoning, a year has 360 days,[*] and by the year-for-a-day principle, one symbolic year represents 360 years.

---

[*]A calendar year consists of 365 days. However, Revelation gives this symbolic time period three ways: (1) as a repetition of Daniel's "time, times and half a time," which equals three and a half years (Revelation 12:14; 3.5 × 360 = 1,260); (2) as 1,260 days (Revelation 12:6); and (3) as forty-two months (Revelation 13:5; forty-two thirty-day months equals 1,260 days).

Thus:

1 year	=	360 symbolic days, or 360 literal years
2 years	=	720 symbolic days, or 720 literal years
1/2 a year	=	180 symbolic days, or 180 literal years
Total	**=**	**1,260 symbolic days, or 1,260 literal years**

I'll provide more details in the next chapter. For now, it's enough to say that the 1,260 years began in 538, when the decree of the Roman emperor Justinian declaring the bishop of Rome, the pope, to be the head of all the churches throughout the empire went into effect. It ended 1,260 years later, in 1798, when Napoleon's General Berthier imprisoned Pope Pius VI.

One other detail about Daniel's little horn helps to confirm that it represents the medieval papacy: It arises and asserts its power at just the right time. Notice that the little horn arises on the head of the dragon, suggesting that it will be a part of the dragon. This is a good representation of how the papacy arose. Whereas Babylon, Media-Persia, Greece, and Rome each overthrew the empire that preceded it, the papacy grew out of Rome and was a part of the empire just as the little horn grew out of the head of the dragon and was a part of the dragon. When Rome fell, the papacy stepped into the political void.

Many Protestant students of prophecy interpret the little horn to represent an *end-time* antichrist. However, this leaves a gap of some fifteen-hundred-plus years between the fall of the Western Roman Empire in 476 and the final events of earth's history. But there were no long historical gaps between any of the nations represented by the previous beasts. Each one immediately replaced its predecessor. Similarly, the papacy immediately replaced the Roman Empire; no long, historical gap occurred between its rise and the empire's fall.

To summarize, the little horn of Daniel 7 is clearly a religio-political power, and the papacy is the only religio-political power that arose after the barbarian tribes overthrew the Western Roman Empire. The papacy also fulfills all the specifications of the little horn that are recorded in verses 24 and 25. Thus, it is very reasonable to understand the little horn as a symbol of the papacy.

Back to Revelation's sea beast

I think I'm safe in saying that most conservative interpreters of Revelation understand the beast from the sea to represent an intolerant power that will arise on the earth near the end of world history. Many understand the sea beast to represent atheism and secularism. Adventists have historically identified it as the end-time papacy. We have based this conclusion on the similarity between the sea beast and the little horn of Daniel 7. The little horn represents the papacy during the Middle Ages, while the sea beast represents the papacy during the end time.

If this conclusion is correct—which I believe it is—then according to Revelation 13, we can expect to see several developments in the next few years:

- *"He [the sea beast] was given authority over every tribe, people, language and nation" (verse 4).* This means that the papacy will achieve political dominance over the whole world.
- *"The whole world was astonished and followed the beast. Men . . . worshiped the beast and asked, 'Who is like the beast? Who can make war against him?' " (verses 3, 4).* The world will acknowledge the papacy's spiritual leadership and will pay it homage.
- *"He was given power to make war against the saints and to conquer them" (verse 7).* The papacy will persecute those who oppose its authority.

The question is, Could these astonishing predictions about the papacy really be fulfilled? Is it realistic to suppose that the papacy will gain universal political dominance, that the whole world will acknowledge its spiritual leadership, and that it will persecute those who refuse to obey it?

Could this really happen?

The short answer is yes. The long answer will take the rest of this book. The next three chapters will examine the political history of the papacy from the fall of the Roman Empire to the present. Following that, I will devote two chapters to a discussion of Catholic political theory. Then we will turn to an examination of the land beast and the mark of the beast in Revelation 13. Toward the end of the book, we will return to the role of the sea beast in the final days of earth's history, including its partnership with the land beast in their joint persecution of God's people.

---

1. See William Shea, *Daniel: A Reader's Guide* (Nampa, Idaho: Pacific Press®, 2005), 116, 117.

2. Ibid., 120–122. Shea provides significant documentation regarding the papacy's claim to have the authority to change the Sabbath from the seventh day of the week, Saturday, to the first day, Sunday.

CHAPTER 4

The Ancient Papacy: The Beginning and the End of Its Political Power

You'd have found it interesting, I think, being a Christian a thousand years ago. Things were done differently back then. If we did things today the way they were done then, the president of the United States would appoint the president of the Seventh-day Adventist General Conference, and he or other government officials would also appoint the presidents of the church's divisions and unions. On the other hand, the president of the General Conference would appoint the president of the United States and lead out in the swearing-in ceremony! Or, to put it the way things actually were done back then, when a pope died, the emperor approved the appointment of the next pope, and he gave his consent to the appointment of cardinals, archbishops, and other church officials. On the other hand, when an emperor died, the pope appointed the next emperor and consecrated him.

However, shortly after the beginning of the second millennium A.D., the church decided that it wanted to appoint its own popes independent of the emperor. An opportunity arose in 1059, when the church needed to appoint a new pope. A church council in Rome decreed that from that time forward all popes would be appointed by the College of Cardinals—a method of selecting popes that continues to the present. And because the emperor at the time, Henry IV, was a child, he couldn't resist the church's decision.

That went fairly smoothly. However, the appointment of cardinals, archbishops, and lesser officials was still in the hands of the emperor, and the church wanted to assume that responsibility as well. Thus, in 1075,

Pope Gregory VII decreed that the emperor would no longer appoint any church official. Henry IV, by this time a grown man, defied the pope by appointing the bishop of Milan. He also wrote Gregory a letter informing him that he was no longer pope and calling for the election of a new pope. Gregory wasn't about to take that threat sitting down! He responded with a letter in which he excommunicated Henry, deposed him as emperor, and instructed his subjects that they no longer owed him their allegiance.

The conflict might have raged for some time, but a group of German nobles, seeing an opportunity to get what they wanted from Henry, demanded that he make peace with the pope or lose their support. They also called for a meeting at Augsburg to settle the conflict, and they invited the pope to chair the session. Henry, seeing the handwriting on the wall, capitulated. He started across the Alps toward Rome in the dead of winter to make peace with Gregory.

Meanwhile, Gregory saw the invitation to preside at the council of Augsburg as an opportunity to further his cause. He quite gladly accepted and set out in the middle of the winter to cross the Alps toward Germany. Part way across, however, he received word that Henry was crossing the Alps toward Rome, and he realized that the two of them would likely meet at some point. Fearing that Henry meant to harm him, the pope took up residence in a fortified castle at Canossa.

Henry, however, had started across the Alps as a penitent, not as a warrior. Hearing that the pope was holed up in the castle at Canossa, he made his way there. The pope was not inclined to entertain the king right away, though. For three days, January 25–27, 1077, Henry stood weeping at the gate of the castle, dressed as a penitent, beseeching the pope's forgiveness. Tradition has it that the king knelt barefoot in the snow those three days. On the third day, Gregory granted him an audience, forgave him, and lifted the excommunication. However, he did also require that Henry provide him with an escort and guarantee him free and safe passage to the Diet. When Henry met these conditions, he returned to Germany with his kingship restored.

This story illustrates the relationship that existed between church and state during the medieval period of European history. The pope was a powerful political figure who was able to lord it over kings and princes. Daniel predicted that the little horn in chapter 7, representing the medieval papacy, would have power for three-and-one-half years. We saw in the previous chapter that these three-and-one-half years are a symbol representing 1,260 actual years, from 538 to 1798. The papacy gained its political control of Europe during this period, and it also lost it.

Revelation 13:3 says, "One of the heads of the [sea] beast seemed to have had a fatal wound, but the fatal wound had been healed." If the wounding of the sea beast's head represents the "wounding" of the papacy, what historical event or events fit the picture, and what does the healing of the wound mean? In this chapter we will survey very briefly the 1,260 years—how the papacy's dominance in European politics began and how it ended. Adventists understand the papacy's decline and fall in the sixteenth to the eighteenth centuries to correspond to the sea beast's fatal wound. So let's go back to the beginning and find out the origin of the church-state relationships that made possible the collision of wills between Pope Gregory VII and King Henry IV. Several details in the rest of this chapter provide a foundation for future chapters. I will mention them when we come to them, so please watch for them.

Starting at the beginning

At His trial, Jesus said to Pilate, " 'My kingdom is not of this world. If it were, my servants would fight' " (John 18:36). It was never Jesus' intention that His disciples and their spiritual heirs should achieve political power in the world. His parting command to them was not to *conquer* all nations; it was to *proclaim* to all nations the good news of salvation (see Matthew 24:14; 28:19, 20; Acts 1:8). Christianity did not enjoy legal freedom in the Roman Empire before A.D. 313, so Christians couldn't have held political power during that time. When Constantine recognized Christianity as a legal religion, almost overnight, Christianity's role in the empire changed.

Constantine's recognition of Christianity had a profound effect on the relationship of church and state. Our modern Western understanding of church-state separation was completely foreign to everyone's thinking back then. For several hundred years, the emperor had been the official head of a pagan religion that required citizens to worship the emperor. This made for a close union between religion and government. Everyone *expected* the state to play a major role in religious affairs and vice-versa. It never occurred to anyone, Christians included, that there might be a better arrangement. However, Christianity's change of legal status soon led to an important question: Which was the official state religion, paganism or Christianity? Within one hundred years, Christianity had replaced paganism as the official religion of the Roman Empire. Did Christians

41

see a problem with that? Of course not! That's how things were *supposed* to be done.

Augustine on church and state

The concept of the church as a political force gained strong theological support from Aurelius Augustinus (354–430), whom you know as Saint Augustine. He was a bishop of the church in North Africa, and he is still considered one of the greatest theologians in Christian history. In order to understand Augustine's concept of the relationship between the church and the state, we need to know something about his view of prophecy.*

For the first several hundred years after Christ left the earth, Christians were *pre*millennialists. That is, they believed that Jesus would return *at the beginning of the millennium.* The earliest Christians understood Daniel's prophecy of the stone that struck the image on the feet to represent the destruction of all earthly kingdoms at Christ's second coming, when He will establish His own eternal kingdom (see Daniel 2:44, 45). In other words, the millennium would follow the Second Coming. During most of this time, Christians also expected that Christ's return would happen at any time.

However, as time passed and Jesus didn't return, a change took place in the way people thought about His second coming. In a book called *On the City of God,* Augustine proposed that the church was the stone that struck the image on the feet. The church, which was established at Christ's *first* coming, now became God's eternal kingdom. And since in Daniel's vision of the great image the stone destroyed all earthly kingdoms, the Christian church's mission during the millennium was to destroy all earthly kingdoms, turn the whole world into a Christian society, and establish itself as God's eternal kingdom on earth. "The Church even now is the kingdom of Christ, and the kingdom of heaven," Augustine said. "Accordingly, even now His saints reign with Him."[1] *Augustine's interpretation of Daniel 2 and the implication of that interpretation for the mission of the church are important theological concepts that we will return to later in this book.*

Augustine's prophetic interpretation fit very nicely with the relationship that was developing at that very time between the church and the

---

*Leroy Edwin Froom gives an excellent overview of Augustine's prophetic interpretation in *The Prophetic Faith of Our Fathers* (Hagerstown, Md.: Review and Herald®, 1950), 1:465–491.

empire. The emperors were Christians. The empire itself was officially Christian. Furthermore, even as Augustine wrote, the Roman Empire was collapsing under the invasions of barbarian tribes from the north, and as the empire collapsed, the church stepped in to fill the political void. Also, the church was successful in Christianizing all of these tribes, which seemed to be a further indication that Augustine's prophetic interpretation was correct.

Augustine proposed that it was only a matter of time till the church Christianized all of society, conquered the world's political systems, and established the rule of God's kingdom all over the earth. Once all the nations of the world had submitted to the church's authority, Jesus would return—at the *end* of the millennium. That's why this interpretation of the millennium is called "*post*millennialism."

This doesn't mean that the church claimed to *be* the state. The church recognized that political entities were still needed to govern society, raise armies, and provide public services. The church's role was to provide the state with moral guidance and to ensure that it supported true religious belief. The church expected the state to enforce the church's moral principles and to make sure that its citizens remained doctrinally orthodox. Anyone who dared to challenge the church's authority or to disagree with its doctrines was turned over to the state for punishment as a heretic.

The 1,260 years begins

By Augustine's time, Christian churches were scattered in cities and villages all over the empire, and the churches in the large cities—those in Alexandria, Ephesus, Constantinople, Athens, Rome, etc.—had each gained a great deal of influence throughout their respective regions. A significant problem remained, though: No one church was considered to be the official head of all Christian churches throughout the empire. Christians, especially those in the western part of the Roman Empire, often looked to the bishop of Rome for leadership, but there was nothing official about this arrangement. Then in 330, Constantine moved the capital of the empire from Rome to Constantinople. This left a political power vacuum in Rome, which the church was quick to fill. Modern historians, both religious and secular, affirm that the bishop of Rome and his church stepped into the power vacuum that Constantine had left, and this led to the bishop of Rome and his church eventually becoming the head over all the churches throughout the empire. That's why the Catholic Church is officially known as the *Roman* Catholic Church. To this day, the pope is officially the bishop of the church in Rome.

However, with the capitol city of the empire now in Constantinople, the bishop in that city began to get ideas of his own about which church should represent all of Christendom. A tug-of-war ensued between the bishops of Rome and Constantinople for leadership of the Christian churches throughout the empire. The emperor Justinian settled the question in 533 with a letter confirming that the bishop of Rome was the "head of all the holy churches" and "head of all the holy priests of God."[2]

At that time, though, a barbarian tribe known as the Ostrogoths was in control of the city of Rome. The Ostrogoths were Arians; they denied the doctrine of the Trinity and were thus considered heretical by the Roman Church. Justinian's decree making the bishop of Rome head over all Christian churches was as good as void as long as the Ostrogoths controlled Rome. But Justinian took care of that problem too. He sent his army to Italy, and in 538, his soldiers pushed the Ostrogoths out of Rome.* Then Christianity had an official head who could actually function.

The significance of this is not that the pope suddenly became involved in politics for the first time. Christian bishops, and especially the bishop of Rome, had been influencing secular politics for more than two hundred years. Rather, at that point the church finally had an official head who could represent the entire body of Christians in political matters as well as religious matters. Justinian's decree gave the bishop of Rome—the pope—the authority he needed to expand his religious control over all of Christendom, and eventually his political control over all of Europe. *The events of the year 538 enabled the bishop of Rome to move toward political domination of Europe.* That's why 538 is the beginning point for the 1,260 days (the time, times, and half a time) of Daniel 7:25.

---

*The Roman general Belisarius easily occupied the city of Rome in 536, since the majority of the Ostrogothic forces were fighting the Franks in northern Italy. However, the Ostrogoths returned shortly, and with vastly superior numbers laid siege to the city. Obviously, in this situation the pope still could not exercise his authority over the Christian churches throughout the empire. However, in 538, Belisarius received reinforcements that enabled him to free Rome permanently from the power of the Ostrogoths.

Pepin's gift to the pope

The papacy received a significant advance in its political power in 752 from Pepin III (the Short). At the time, a man by the name of Childeric was officially the king of the Franks—now France—and Pepin held the title of mayor (the word didn't mean the same thing then that it does today). However, even though he wasn't the king, Pepin's position authorized him to make royal decisions. So in 752, he appealed to Pope Zacharius with a question: Who should be the official ruler of the Frankish kingdom—the person with the *title* of king or the person with the *power* of the king? The pope agreed that the power to make decisions was more important than the title. With the pope's blessing in his pocket, Pepin was elected king by an assembly of leading Frankish men, and Pope Stephan II* traveled all the way from Rome to consecrate him as king.

The significance of this incident lies in what it tells us about the pope's and the church's political power at that time: The pope was the final arbiter in a dispute over who should be king of the Franks, and when Pepin was elected, the pope officiated at his consecration service.

In 754, Pepin, wanting to express his appreciation for the pope's support, gave him an independent territory in Italy. This event is also very significant, because for the first time, the pope held political power as a temporal ruler. Now he was the head not only of a church but also of a piece of real estate—a kingdom. This made it much easier for him to interact with other secular rulers as "one of them." Succeeding popes continued to rule over the Papal States (as they came to be called) in central Italy for more than a thousand years, until 1870, when, much to the displeasure of the papacy, they were incorporated into the modern state of Italy.

The next major event in the political history of the papacy that I will discuss here is the conflict in 1075 between Pope Gregory VII and King Henry IV of Germany that I shared with you at the beginning of this chapter. Gregory, one of the greatest popes, proclaimed that "the Roman Church had never erred and never could err, that the pope is supreme judge, that he may be judged by no one, that there is no appeal from his decision, that he alone is entitled to the homage of all princes, and that he alone may depose kings and emperors."[3] That's an arrogant claim to be coming from the head of the Christian church. But again, it's indicative of the political power that the papacy had achieved by that time.

---

*Zacharius died shortly after responding to Pepin's inquiry.

It would be a mistake to suppose that from that time forward, popes always got their way in the political interplay between the church and the various rulers of Europe. The point is that increasingly, the papacy was a powerful political factor that every temporal ruler was forced to deal with.

The pinnacle of papal political power

The papacy reached the height of its political influence in European politics during the thirteenth century. Innocent III, who was pope from 1198 to 1216, continued the papal practice of crowning kings and emperors. He acknowledged Frederick as king of Sicily, and he mediated a dispute between Philip of Swabia and Otto IV over who should be emperor. He favored Philip, but when Philip was murdered, he supported Otto, who was crowned in Rome in 1209. A year later, when Otto invaded some of the papal lands in Italy and tried to gain control of Sicily, Innocent excommunicated him and promoted a man by the name of Frederick, who was crowned emperor in 1215. In terms of today's political realities, it's as though the General Conference president could unseat the American president and install the candidate of his choice in that office. *That's political power!* And I want you to notice how the pope exercised it: *He used the spiritual authority of the church and of his office—excommunication—to achieve a civil/political end.*

The same thing happened in England a few years later. When King John refused to accept Cardinal Stephen Langton as archbishop of Canterbury, the pope excommunicated him and placed England under interdict—which means that the pope forbade the church to minister the sacraments to anyone in the entire kingdom. In Catholic theology, Christians receive God's grace through the sacraments, so Catholics who are refused the sacraments are essentially cut off from the source of salvation. An interdict, then, cuts off an entire nation from the source of salvation!

Threatened by opposition from his nobles, John capitulated. He surrendered England to the pope and received it back as a papal fief. Again, this would be like the pope appointing as cardinal of New York someone whom the president of the United States dislikes and refuses to accept, so the pope tells the entire Catholic population of the United States that they can't receive the church's sacraments until their president accepts the pope's choice of a cardinal. This is essentially what took place between Pope Innocent III and King John of England in their conflict over the appointment of the archbishop of Canterbury. *That's political power. And, again, it was achieved by means of a powerful spiritual threat. This is an extremely important point to keep in mind. We will return to it later in this book.*

Innocent's political philosophy harmonized with his deeds as pope. He declared that "ecclesiastical liberty is nowhere better cared for than where the Roman church has full power in both temporal [political] and spiritual affairs."[4] He also decreed that the pope holds the right to decide whether a king is worthy of his crown.

Boniface VIII, the next great pope, ruled the church a hundred years later (1294–1303). By that time, the secular rulers in France and England were increasingly asserting their power, and the political authority of the papacy over European politics was beginning to diminish. When King Philip IV of France taxed the clergy, Boniface issued a bull stating that kings couldn't tax the clergy without the pope's consent. Philip retaliated by cutting off the French church's contributions to Rome, and, facing a major financial loss, Boniface backed down. Money talked back then too!

In a conflict with Philip in 1302, Boniface issued his famous bull *Unam Sanctam*, which stated that the pope has authority over secular rulers: "With truth as our witness, it belongs to the spiritual power [the papacy] to establish the terrestrial [secular] power and to pass judgment if it has not been good."[5] However, when Boniface excommunicated Philip, the French king called an assembly in which twenty-nine accusations were made against the pope, and five archbishops and twenty-one bishops sided with Philip. In September 1303, a band of two thousand mercenaries attacked the papal palace and imprisoned Boniface. A week later he was released and returned to his palace, but in mid-October he developed a violent fever and died.

Clearly, the political power of the papacy was beginning to wane, and it continued to decline over the next several hundred years.

Reasons for the decline

What caused this decline in the political power of the papacy? More than anything else, it was caused by a revival of learning. Greek and Roman thought was largely forgotten during the Dark Ages, from about A.D. 500 to 1000. However, the twelfth century saw a rediscovery of this ancient literature—Plato, Aristotle, Socrates, and the Greek scientists and mathematicians. This eventually led to the Renaissance, which started in the fourteenth century and continued into the sixteenth. Humanism also rose out of this revival of learning. Humanism stresses the importance of rational solutions to human problems rather than solutions dictated by religion and the church. This revival of learning started a process of secularization that has continued to the present time. More than any other factor, this secularization led to the demise of papal political power. *This is another extremely important point that we will return to several times throughout the rest of this book.*

Gutenberg's invention of the printing press in the mid-fifteenth century brought about an intellectual explosion, contributing in a major way to the secularization process. By the year 1500, printing presses had been established all over Europe. Prior to Gutenberg, the only way anyone could get a copy of a book such as the Bible was to hire a scribe to copy it a word at a time on parchment. It could take a year to produce a single copy of the Bible! Obviously, very few people owned books back then. In fact, most people couldn't even read. Suddenly, Gutenberg made it possible to produce hundreds of copies of the Bible or any other book in a matter of weeks, so that anyone with modest means could own a small collection of books, and wealthy individuals could own a sizeable library. More and more people learned to read, and knowledge began to spread rapidly.

The birth of modern science in the late fifteenth and early sixteenth centuries also impelled the secularization process. The Polish mathematician and astronomer Nicolaus Copernicus, who lived from 1473 to 1543, developed the theory that the planets orbit the sun rather than the sun and the planets orbiting the earth. The papacy opposed Copernicus bitterly because his theory contradicted a literal reading of certain passages in the Bible that suggested the earth was the stationary center of the universe around which the sun orbited.* Of course, Copernicus was correct and the church was wrong. Scholars consider his discovery to have launched the modern scientific revolution.

All this advance in learning caused people everywhere to begin thinking for themselves. When people begin to think, they question, and when they question, they start challenging authority. And religious authority is one of the first that they begin to challenge. The papacy was still a powerful force in European politics in the year 1500, but its authority was being challenged. That was secularization at work.

Then along came Martin Luther.

---

*See, e.g., Psalms 93:1; 104:5; Ecclesiastes 1:5.

Luther had no intention of starting a reformation when he nailed those ninety-five theses to the church door in Wittenberg, Germany, on October 31, 1517. He wrote those propositions in Latin, but they were immediately translated into German, and within two weeks they had been printed and scattered all over Germany. And within two months they had been translated into the various European languages, printed, and scattered all over the continent. By the time Rome realized what was happening, it was too late to stop the popular movement that Luther had inadvertently started.

Luther's break with Rome would have been impossible without the printing press, which allowed a rapid spread of information. The point is that the increase of knowledge inspired people to challenge authority; in this case, papal authority. The printing press simply enabled this movement to make a giant leap forward. And while Luther was profoundly religious, his break with Rome also contributed to the secularization process.

Pope Leo X declared Luther's views to be heretical and summoned him to Rome. However, Luther had the support of Frederick III, the elector of Saxony, who, knowing that Luther would likely be imprisoned and possibly executed in Rome, refused to send him. The pope had no choice but to send representatives to confront Luther in Germany. Several diets (meetings) were held in which Luther presented his views to papal representatives. Predictably, all of them declared his views to be heretical. In 1521, Luther was excommunicated from the Roman Catholic Church. However, Frederick protected him. This was a major departure from the way princes, kings, and emperors had dealt with heretics in the past. For several hundred years, the church had relied on the state to punish heretics, but Frederick refused to carry out the punishment the church had decreed against Luther. *Secularization was working.* The papacy's political power over European politics had taken a severe blow.

The Age of Enlightenment

As knowledge continued increasing, the papacy's political authority continued declining. During the eighteenth century, a movement developed that was called the Enlightenment (also known as the Age of Reason). Its proponents challenged the basic tenets of Christianity and promoted rationalism in philosophical, political, and economic thought. The Enlightenment pushed the secularization process into fast-forward. You may recognize some of the more prominent names associated with this movement:

- Voltaire (whose real name was François-Marie Arouet)
- Jean-Jacques Rousseau
- Baruch Spinoza
- René Descartes
- David Hume
- Immanuel Kant
- Thomas Jefferson
- Benjamin Franklin
- John Locke
- Thomas Paine

Secular humanists continued questioning and undermining the authority of the church, both Catholic and Protestant. These forces gradually brought the papacy to its political knees, leading, toward the end of the eighteenth century, to two landmark events that changed the face of Western politics for more than two hundred years: the American Revolution (1775–1883) and the French Revolution (1789–1799).

The primary result of the American Revolution was the creation of a representative form of government that was based on a constitution with a balance of power between the legislative, administrative, and judicial branches. In the American system, there is no state church. State and church are separated from each other, each operating independently within its own sphere. There is a good reason for this division between religion and government. The papal excesses of the previous thousand years, together with the persecution of dissenters in America during the colonial period, led the American founding fathers to fear that religion might once again control government. Thus, while the American government has never attacked religion, its constitution was clearly a reaction to the excessive control that religion and the church had held over European politics for a thousand years.

Several factors contributed to the French Revolution. The one that concerns us here is religion. The French Revolution was, to a large degree, a violent secular rebellion against Roman Catholicism. The church, which had been the largest landowner in France, saw its property confiscated by the French government. There was a severe repression of the clergy, including the imprisonment and massacre of priests throughout the country. The result of all this was a massive shift in political power from the Catholic Church to the secular state.

The climax came in 1798, when Napoleon's General Louis Alexandre Berthier entered Rome and demanded that Pope Pius VI renounce his temporal authority over the Papal States. When the pope refused, Berthier took him prisoner to France, where he died a year and a half later.* Thus began what Jesuit author Malachi Martin called "two hundred years of inactivity that [were] imposed on the papacy by the major secular powers of the world."[6] What Martin meant was that the papacy was no longer able to hold a dominating influence over governments the way it had during the previous twelve hundred years. This loss of the political power of the papacy to the secular state is what Adventists have always understood to be the fatal wound that Revelation 13 prophesied the sea beast would suffer.

The time, times, and half a time (1,260 days or years) of Daniel 7:25 began in 538 when the bishop of Rome was able to exercise the authority over all of Christendom that the emperor Justinian had granted him five years earlier. For the next seven hundred years, the political power of the papacy grew ever stronger until it reached its zenith in the thirteenth century. From that point on it gradually declined until, in 1798, Napoleon's general took the pope prisoner. The church's loss of political power in 1798 marked the end of the 1,260 years of papal supremacy that Daniel had prophesied.

This isn't to say that the papacy has been totally inactive in the political field during the two hundred years since 1798, as we shall see in the next chapter. It *is* to say that for two centuries a secular, democratic philosophy of government has predominated in the Western world in particular. *Secularism* in government means that civil law is the ultimate authority in the affairs of the state, as opposed to the papal and medieval idea that the authority of the church is superior to that of the state. In secular states, the power and authority of the state arise either from a secular dictator or, in the case of democracies, from the people themselves. In secular governments, whether dictatorships or democracies, religion is subordinate to civil power and has no authority over it. In a democracy, the moral principles that form the laws of the state arise from the common understanding of the people and are not based on the religious/ moral principles of the Catholic Church or of any other religion or church. The public educational institutions of Western nations are controlled by

---

*Berthier took control of the Papal States, but they were restored to the papacy two years later, and for the next seventy years the papacy held control of them on-again, off-again, until 1870, when it lost them permanently to the modern state of Italy.

the state rather than by the church. Religion and government distance themselves from each other on a principle that is commonly known as church-state separation.

It's extremely important to note that, more than anything else, *it was the secularization of government that led to the religious freedom that the Western world has known for the past two-hundred-plus years.*

However, this philosophy of government has been very distressing to the Catholic Church, which claims to be the sole repository of the moral truths on which the laws of every good state must be based. The church also claims the right to demand that governments enforce Catholic moral principles, and it opposes church-state separation of the American variety.

The fatal wound that was inflicted on the sea beast in Revelation 13:3 has been the inability of the Catholic Church these two hundred years to enforce its moral principles and its philosophy of government on secular states, both dictatorships and democracies. However, Revelation prophesied that the fatal wound would be healed and the papacy would regain political authority over the entire world. For 150 years, Adventists have predicted that this will happen. Back in the 1850s, when we began saying it, this seemed to be nonsense. The nations of Europe had stripped the papacy of the last vestiges of its political authority over them a scant fifty years earlier, and now along came Seventh-day Adventists insisting that before Christ's return the papacy would gain political authority over the entire globe! The whole idea seemed preposterous. But we said it because prophecy said it.

Could this really happen?

---

1. Leroy Edwin Froom, *The Prophetic Faith of Our Fathers* (Hagerstown, Md.: Review and Herald®, 1950), 1:483. My comments about Augustine's interpretation of prophecy are based on Froom's work.

2. Cited in *The Seventh-day Adventist Bible Commentary,* vol. 4 (Hagerstown, Md.: Review and Herald®, 1955), 827.

3. Ibid., 837.

4. Cited in C. J. Barry, ed., *Readings in Church History,* vol. 1 (Westminster, Md.: The Newman Press, 1960), 438.

5. Bull of Pope Boniface VIII promulgated November 18, 1302. Papal Encyclicals Online, *Unam Sanctam,* http://www.papalencyclicals.net/Bon08/B8unam.htm.

6. Malachi Martin, *The Keys of This Blood: The Struggle for World Dominion Between Pope John Paul II, Mikhail Gorbachev, and the Capitalist West* (New York: Simon and Schuster, 1990), 22.

CHAPTER 5

The Modern Papacy: Healing the Fatal Wound

Berthier's imprisonment of Pope Pius VI in 1798 was by no means the first time in Christian history that a pope had been taken prisoner. But before 1798, when secular rulers imprisoned popes, the papacy always bounced back; within a few years it regained much of the political authority that it had lost. This was not the case in 1798, which is why the pope's imprisonment in 1798 constituted a "fatal wound." And this fatal wound persisted throughout the nineteenth century.

When the Congress of Vienna convened in 1815, the papacy, which a couple of hundred years earlier might have been a significant player, had only a minor role through its representative, Cardinal Ercole Consalvi. The purpose of the Congress was to settle the boundaries of the kingdoms that Napoleon's wars had disrupted. When Russia, Austria, and Prussia formed a "Holy Alliance" to encourage the kingdoms of Europe to base their governments on Christian principles, most of the other kingdoms signed on.* All the pope could do was to condemn the proposal. He refused to reach an agreement with so many "heretics." *The French Revolution truly did break the papacy's power over European politics as it had functioned for the better part of a millennium.* During the rest of the nineteenth century, the Roman Catholic Church was largely on the defensive in world politics.

---

*Because at that time Europe was strongly anticlerical, most of the nations scoffed at the proposal, but they signed on anyway. In any case, the Alliance lasted only about ten years.

Democracy and the secular state

In addition to putting the final kibosh on the political power of the papacy, the American and French revolutions gave impetus to the new political paradigm that we noted in the previous chapter: democracy and secular states that kept religion separate from government. The papacy was accustomed to states in which it had a major influence—states in which Catholicism was the official religion and in which the state enforced the church's doctrinal and moral principles. The papacy was not accustomed to making its own way in a secular state in which it was an outsider to the government.

Under the old paradigm, where Catholicism was the state religion, the interplay between church and government sometimes led to disputes between the church and the state. The church was accustomed to settling these disputes with kings, emperors, and princes "by quick decision in the ante-room of a palace."[1] It was much easier for the church to cut deals with a king or an emperor than it was to have to negotiate with large bodies of elected representatives in parliaments and congresses, especially when that church wasn't even the state religion. Kings and emperors were answerable to no one but themselves. Their decision was law regardless of what the subjects might think. The representatives in parliaments and congresses, on the other hand, are answerable to their constituents, and it matters a great deal what the people think. If the constituents are largely Catholic, the papacy's interests might be protected—though there is no guarantee even of that. And Catholic interests are certainly not ensured when the citizenry is largely Protestant or nonreligious, even antireligious.

The United States and its republican form of government came on the scene a scant few years before the French Revolution, and this set the pace for the rest of the Western world throughout the nineteenth century. One monarchy and dictatorship after another fell in Europe and Latin America and was replaced with a secular, democratic government based on a constitution. Political power now resided with the people rather than with a king or the pope.

The Roman Catholic Church's primary "contribution" to this trend was to fulminate against it. Pius IX (pope from 1846 to 1878), in his "Syllabus of Errors,"[2] condemned church-state separation and the freedom of secular government from oversight by the church. Pius objected strenuously to the proposition that "in the case of conflicting laws enacted by the two powers, the civil law prevails." He protested vehemently the political concept that government leaders are exempt from the authority of the church and that the church and the state should remain separate.[3] Leo XIII (pope from 1878 to 1903), insisted that the state should protect the Catholic Church for the good of society.[4]

The historian Owen Chadwick, in his book *The Secularization of the European Mind in the Nineteenth Century*, stated the problem well:

> Church and State had always rubbed along [prior to the nineteenth century] with a measure of friction, occasionally issuing in explosive crises, usually kept within tolerable limits by luck and by compromise.
>
> Representative governments posed the problem of this frontier between Church and State in a new form. It made customary forms of compromise impossible. The old world regulated its give-and-take with less discomfort because government was avowedly and openly Christian, whether Catholic or Protestant. Churchmen accepted restrictions on liberty which government proposed because the government itself owed allegiance to the Church. But no representative government could be openly Christian in the ancient way. Even if king or prime minister were devout or saintly . . . government must be neutral, must treat all religions impartially; and to treat all religions impartially is to treat irreligion impartially.[5]

Another factor that contributed to the weakening of the church's political power during the nineteenth century was the growing divide between science and religion. Scientists never forgot—nor forgave—the church's punishment of Galileo for confirming Copernicus's theory that the earth and the other planets orbit the sun. Secular people perceived that the church had allowed dogma to rule over reason.

One of the more significant political events the papacy had to deal with in the nineteenth century was its loss of the Papal States. In the previous chapter, I mentioned that Pepin III gave this land to the pope in 754. The Catholic Church ruled the Papal States for more than a thousand years. In 1860, Italian forces that were antagonistic to papal rule conquered a large portion of the Papal States, and in 1861, King Victor Emmanuel took the first steps in establishing the modern, secular nation of Italy. Ten years later, in September 1870, Italy declared war on what remained of the Papal States, including the city of Rome. Italian forces reached Rome on September 20. Pope Pius IX put up a token re-sistance with his tiny army, but after three hours, the Italian forces en-tered Rome, and the Papal States came to an end. The pope was furious. For the next fifty-nine years, one pope after another demanded the re-turn of the Papal States, but the Italian government steadfastly refused. So, for those fifty-nine years, the popes protested by maintaining a self-imposed imprisonment inside the Vatican. This conflict between the pa-pacy and the government of Italy came to be known as "the Roman question."

However, the twentieth century saw a sea change in the Vatican's re-lationship to world politics. It would be impossible in this short chapter to delve into even a fraction of the Vatican's political activities during that century. I will illustrate with three of the more important examples: (1) The Vatican's Lateran Treaty with Mussolini's Italy in 1929, which restored the Vatican's status as a state. (2) The Vatican's concordat with Hitler's Germany in 1933. (3) The Vatican's contribution to the fall of communism in Eastern Europe and Russia during the late 1980s and early 1990s.

The Lateran Treaty

The story of the Lateran Treaty of 1929 began fifty-nine years earlier, when the Catholic Church lost the Papal States to the emerging state of Italy. At that time, Italy, along with most of the other European states, was on a roll toward liberalism, democracy, anticlericalism, and the secu-lar nation-state—a trend that the papacy opposed bitterly, for the papacy much preferred dealing with authoritarian governments that would es-tablish Catholicism as the state religion and give it a prominent role in civic life. The popes proclaimed that liberalism, democracy, and freedom of speech and the press are sinful, and declared that anyone who voted for the secular Italian state committed a sin that automatically resulted in eternal damnation.[6]

In the first decade of the twentieth century, the Vatican lifted its ban on Italians voting. In fact, because socialism—which the Vatican also detested—was rapidly gaining ground in Italy following the First World War, the Vatican allowed Catholics to organize themselves into a politi-cal party—the *Partito Populare*—as a way to counteract the socialist in-fluence. The party, led by a Sicilian priest named Don Sturzo, soon be-came a powerful force in Italian politics.

About this same time, the Italian *Partito Fascista* (Fascist Party) sprang up, and on October 22, 1922, its leader, Benito Mussolini, took control of the Italian government. Among other things, Mussolini and the Fascists fought socialism and communism with a vengeance. The Vatican, including the recently installed Pope Pius XI, noted this development with great satisfaction, for if there was anything the papacy hated more than democracy, it was socialism and communism, both of which were even more secular than democratic governments. Communism was particularly odious, because it declared, in the words of Karl Marx, that religion is "the opium of the people." The popes were well aware of the atrocities committed against the church by the communist government of Russia.

Mussolini, who was maneuvering to assume dictatorial powers, was resisted by a coalition made up of socialists and the Catholic *Partito Populare*. Pius XI, seeing in Mussolini's Fascists a powerful opponent of socialism and communism, backed the Fascists against his own Catholic party. He warned all Italian Catholics that any alliance with the socialists was a sin, and he ordered all priests who were members of the Catholic party to resign. Mussolini got his dictatorship. The *Partito Populare* was doomed.

The Lateran Treaty. The Vatican was anxious to resolve the sixty-year controversy with the Italian government over the Papal States. In October 1926, Pius XI began negotiations with Mussolini that resulted in the Lateran Treaty, which was signed by the Vatican and the Italian government on February 11, 1929.

The Lateran Treaty consisted of three documents: The treaty itself, called the "Conciliation Treaty"; a "Financial Convention"; and a "Concordat."* Article 1 of the treaty established Catholicism as the state religion. While the relationship between church and state that the treaty outlined was still not ideal by Rome's standards, it was a major step in that direction. Articles 3 and 4 of the treaty gave the Holy See complete sovereign authority over Vatican City and guaranteed that the Italian government would not intervene in the Vatican's internal affairs.

The Financial Convention stipulated that the Italian government would reimburse the Vatican 7.5 million Italian lire in compensation for its loss of the Papal States in 1870.

---

*A concordat is a formal agreement. Sometimes the term is used specifically of an agreement between a government and the Roman Catholic Church regarding their relationship.

Article 11 of the Concordat recognized the feast days established by the church, the first of which was "all Sundays." Article 34 established Catholic canon law as the basis for marriage and divorce.* Article 36 gave the Catholic Church control over all religious instruction in Italy's public schools. The Concordat also stipulated that civil marriages should be regulated by the canon law of the Catholic Church. The significance of this is that it established Catholic canon law in the matters of education and marriage as the official policy of the Italian government. In essence, Catholic canon law became Italian law. This was of extreme importance to the Vatican, for once again, some of the most important Catholic moral principles were, in theory at least, to be enforced by a civil government, albeit a secular one.

One of the primary effects of the Lateran Treaty was to restore to the Vatican its authority as an independent state. Now the Vatican, and the pope as a legitimate head of state, could again carry on business with other nations of the world, including the exchange of ambassadors.

Some Seventh-day Adventists, hearing news of the Lateran Treaty in 1929, proclaimed that the fatal wound had been healed. The treaty was indeed a major step in the healing of the fatal wound; however, the healing is still in progress.

The concordat with Germany

Germany emerged from World War I as a democratic nation called the Weimar Republic. Several parties competed for influence in the Reichstag—the German parliament or congress. Among these were the Center Party, the German Workers' Party (which Hitler later transformed into the National Socialist German Workers' Party—the Nazis), the Social Democrats, and the Communists. The Center Party, the German equivalent of the Italian *Partito Populare*, was a Catholic party.

---

*The Catholic Church forbids its members to divorce, so the church authorizes annulments for couples who are estranged. Technically, annulment differs from divorce in that it states that the marriage never existed in the first place, whereas divorce acknowledges the existence of the marriage and breaks it—something that Catholic theology forbids. In practice, however, Catholic annulments serve the same purpose as divorce, so, in effect, there's no distinction between the two.

Eugenio Pacelli. In 1920, the Vatican sent Eugenio Pacelli, one of its most gifted diplomats, as a nuncio* to the German state of Bavaria. Three years later, he was reassigned to Berlin, where he became the church's nuncio for all of Germany. In this capacity, he was able to exert a significant influence on German politics. One of Pacelli's great ambitions during the 1920s was to negotiate a concordat with the Weimar Republic. He succeeded in establishing a concordat with Bavaria, where he had gone as a nuncio in 1920, because Bavaria is largely Catholic. But Germany is one-third Catholic and two-thirds Protestant, and the democratic Weimar government wasn't interested in establishing a concordat with the Vatican that would subject Germany's Protestants to Catholic canon law, particularly one that gave the church control over public education and marriage. Thus, Pacelli was never able to establish a concordat with the Weimar Republic. He would have far greater success with Hitler.

Adolf Hitler. Nobody would have thought of Adolf Hitler as an up-and-coming world leader during his early years. He wanted to become an artist, but he was an utter failure at it. He couldn't even gain acceptance into a decent art school. Instead, he spent most of the years during World War I as a down-and-outer, barely eking out an existence in Vienna. However, he had two great assets: He was a gifted orator who could sway crowds, and he was a master politician. In 1919, he joined the German Workers' Party (soon to be the Nazi Party) and became an ardent supporter of "the cause." By 1921, he had risen to such prominence in the party that he was named its leader. Thus, about the time that Mussolini was gaining dictatorial power in Italy, Hitler was emerging as a minor force in German politics.

Two important factors contributed to Hitler's subsequent rise to power. The first was the harsh terms of the Treaty of Versailles that the Allied governments forced Germany to sign at the conclusion of the First World War. The second was the horrible economic conditions in Germany during the 1920s, culminating with the Great Depression in the 1930s. The two were closely related.

The Treaty of Versailles severely limited Germany's military forces, gave large chunks of German territory to the surrounding nations, and,

---

*A Catholic nuncio is essentially the same thing as an ambassador and serves also as the Vatican's chief liaison with the bishops in the country to which he's assigned.

most important, demanded that Germany pay huge reparations for the damage that her war had caused to the European states. The German people felt humiliated, and their economy, already reeling under the heavy burden of the cost of the war, was devastated by the reparations. Millions of people were unemployed. Inflation rose to the point that a barrel full of marks was hardly enough to buy a loaf of bread. The global economic collapse of 1929 brought Germany to her knees.

Hitler, the consummate orator, mesmerized the German people with his glowing promises to cease reparation payments, rebuild the German military, and regain the territory that had been stripped from Germany by the Treaty of Versailles. By the late 1920s, he was emerging as a powerful force in German politics.

Hitler and the Catholic Church. As Hitler gained political power in Germany, he realized that he would have to deal with the moral opposition to his policies by Germany's Protestants and Catholics, particularly his anti-Jewish policies. He also saw the concordat that the Vatican negotiated with Italy in 1929 as a model that he could use to neutralize the political power of the Catholics. Thus, early in his political career, Hitler determined that he would establish a concordat with the Vatican. First, though, he had to become the leader of the German government and turn it into a dictatorship with himself as its head.

Through the 1920s, the National Socialist party had played a minor role in German politics. But as Germany sank into economic chaos, particularly following the global economic collapse of 1929, Hitler's promise to restore Germany's military might, and especially his promise to end the crushing reparations payments and cure the nation's economic woes, were extremely popular with the German people. The result was that in a September 1930 election, the Nazis garnered 107 seats in the Reichstag, making them the nation's second largest political party. Hitler was on the way to achieving his ambition of ruling Germany. However, the majority of the Catholic people and their bishops and archbishops were still bitterly opposed to Nazi policies and condemned them publicly.

Fortunately for Hitler, he had an ally at the Vatican.

The Vatican and the Nazis. In 1930, Pope Pius XI recalled Eugenio Pacelli to Rome and named him the Vatican's secretary of state. Pacelli and Pius had one overriding ambition for German politics: a concordat. And they saw Hitler's rise to power as the means to achieve it. They also viewed Hitler as a powerful counterforce to the communists, whom they feared and hated. These were two of the dominant forces shaping the Vatican's relationship with Germany during the early 1930s. In his book *The Churches and the Third Reich*, Klaus Scholder* said, "Every German administration was judged by Rome above all on two issues: how resolutely it fought against atheistic Communism and how prepared it was to conclude a Reich concordat."[7]

However, as I mentioned earlier, the Weimar Republic wasn't interested in concluding a concordat with the Vatican. A concordat with Germany's state of Bavaria was fine, because Bavaria was largely Catholic. But two-thirds of Germany's population were Protestants, and there was no way that the democratic Weimar Republic was going to impose on them a concordat favoring Catholics.

A visit that German Chancellor Heinrich Bruening had with Pacelli in Pacelli's office at the Vatican in August 1930 indicates both the importance that the Vatican accorded to the negotiation of a concordat with Germany and the resistance of the Weimar government to such an agreement. Though a Catholic himself, Bruening was strongly opposed to a concordat, and for good reason: He knew that the German constitution wouldn't allow it, and he understood German politics. In short, Bruening knew that the Weimar government would never accept a concordat with the Vatican. However, Bruening's Catholicism on the one hand and his opposition to a concordat on the other was a dichotomy that Pacelli could not understand. Many years after his visit with Pacelli, Bruening published his recollection of their conversation. Klaus Scholder describes the impasse in detail:

> [Pacelli] raised the question of a Reich concordat. . . . Bruening, however, would have nothing to do with such a connection. As he reported on the course of the conversation: "I [Bruening] told him [Pacelli] that it was impossible for me as a Catholic Chancellor, in view of the tension in Germany, even to approach this issue at all. . . . If I had raised the question of a Reich concordat

---

*Klaus Scholder (1930–1985) was a German ecclesiastical historian and professor of history at the Eberhard Karls University of Tubingen. He is especially known for his two-volume *Die Kirchen und das Dritte Reich,* with the English title *The Churches and the Third Reich*. Most of what I say about the relation of the Vatican with Germany prior to World War II is based on Scholder's first volume.

now, I would have whipped up the furor *Protestanticus* on the one side and run into complete misunderstanding with the left on the other."

Scholder continues his analysis of the interview:

> [Bruening's rejection of Pacelli's demand] was clearly an accurate assessment. To Pacelli, however, these German difficulties were obviously unimportant. . . . For more than a decade he had devoted all his energies towards reaching this goal [of a concordat with the German government]. Now a new political situation had arisen [Hitler's rise to power] and Pacelli was determined to take advantage of it—as he had always sought to take advantage of political situations.
>
> With Bruening, however, this could not be done. Rather, the Chancellor replied firmly to the Cardinal [that] "he mistook the political situation in Germany, and, above all, the true character of the Nazis."
>
> The conversation became still more heated when the subject of the Protestant church treaties was mentioned. Pacelli thought it impossible, as Bruening noted, "that a Catholic Chancellor should conclude a Protestant church treaty. I [Bruening] answered sharply that in accordance with the very spirit of the constitution to which I had sworn an oath, I had to protect the interests of religious Protestantism on the basis of full equality. The Cardinal Secretary of State now condemned my whole policy."[8]

This exchange between the German chancellor and the Vatican secretary of state is an excellent illustration of the kind of pressure that the Vatican can bring to bear on its Catholic members who are politicians. The church *expects* its Catholic politicians to support the church's political ambitions. *This is another extremely important point that we will return to in later chapters.*

Events following Bruening's visit with Pacelli worked in Pacelli's favor. Shortly after his visit with the cardinal secretary of state, Bruening's unpopular economic policies brought his chancellorship to an end. And in an election on July 31, 1932, the Nazis more than doubled their representation in the Reichstag, from 107 members to 230. Hitler was well on his way to achieving his political ambition of ruling Germany.

The German bishops' opposition to Hitler. Interestingly, the German bishops and German Catholics didn't share the Vatican's favorable attitude toward Hitler. They were still strongly opposed to Hitler and his Nazi party. Germany's Catholic bishops held a conference in August 1932, very shortly after the election that gave the Nazis 230 seats in the Reichstag, and the minutes of that meeting record that

> all the diocesan authorities have banned membership of this party [the Nazis], first because parts of its official programme contain false doctrine in what they say and the way in which they must be understood; . . . secondly, because the declarations of numerous representatives and spokesmen for the party are of a character hostile to the faith, expressing an attitude inimical to the fundamental teachings and claims of the Catholic church. . . . Thirdly, it is the collective judgment of the Catholic clergy and of the loyal Catholic champions of the church's interests in public life that if the party achieves the monopoly of rule in Germany which it so ardently desires, the church interests of the Catholics will prove extremely bleak.[9]

Hitler's rise to power. The Vatican, however, was of a different mind altogether, and Hitler's rise to power in Germany continued to favor the Vatican's wishes. On January 30, 1933, he was named chancellor of Germany. His next ambition was to achieve dictatorial power. The Weimar Republic and its democratic constitution barred the way, but he had a solution for that problem. The republic's constitution included a clause stating that in a national emergency, an "Enabling Act" voted by a two-thirds majority in the Reichstag could grant dictatorial powers to the chancellor. So, Hitler wanted an Enabling Act. There was just one problem: His Nazi Party did not hold two-thirds of the votes in the Reichstag. In order to get an Enabling Act, the Nazis would have to collaborate with another of Germany's political parties—but which one? For Hitler, the answer was simple: the Catholic Center Party. And he had a plan to bring the party around: Offer the Vatican a concordat.

The plan worked. Eugenio Pacelli, as determined as ever to negotiate a concordat with the German government, and viewing Hitler as an ally in combating communism, readily agreed. The Catholic Center Party lent its votes to the Nazis, and on March 23, 1933, the Reichstag gave

Hitler his Enabling Act—less than two months after he became chancellor of Germany. Thus, the Vatican (not the German bishops) was a major contributing factor in Hitler's rise to power! Klaus Scholder comments, "Those who dispute a link between the acceptance of the Enabling Act and the conclusion of the Reich concordat definitely seem unconvincing."[10] And in his book *The Coming of the Third Reich*, Richard J. Evans wrote, "The [Center] party was reassured in two days of discussions with Hitler that the rights of the Church would not be affected by the Enabling Act. . . . These promises, *combined with heavy pressure from the Vatican*, proved sufficient to win the Centre Party deputies over to supporting the measure that in the long run was bound to mean their own political demise."[11]

It's important to note that the concordat was strictly between the Vatican and the German government, not between German Catholicism and the German government. Scholder comments that "Pacelli obviously saw—probably quite correctly—that his plans [for a concordat] would be endangered, if not doomed to failure, by a premature inclusion of the German bishops in the concordat negotiations. Hence in this first phase he kept everything to do with the concordat secret—evidently without considering what a triumph it must be for Hitler when the Curia had more confidence in him than in its own bishops."[12]

The distinction between the Vatican and Germany's Catholic bishops may seem irrelevant at first glance. However, it's extremely important, and it helps us understand the role of the Vatican in world politics. The concordat was an arrangement between two nation states: Hitler's German government and the government of the Vatican. It had nothing to do with German Catholics and their bishops. And because of the hierarchical structure of the Catholic Church, when the pope spoke, the bishops were obliged to follow whether or not they agreed. The Catholic *Allgemeine Rundschau* noted that "the bishops cannot fight where Rome concludes peace."[13]

Richard Evans points out that "in pursuit of the promised Concordat . . . the German bishops withdrew their opposition to Nazism and issued a collective declaration of support for the regime in May [1933]." And at a bishop's conference on June 1, they issued a pastoral letter "welcoming the 'national awakening' and the new stress on a strong state authority." At the same time, they maintained the major reservations that had concerned them the previous year—their apprehension over "the Nazis' emphasis on race and the looming threat to Catholic lay institutions."[14]

The Reich concordat. Contrary to the Lateran Treaty, the concordat between the Vatican and Hitler's Germany did not establish the Catholic Church as the state religion. This would have been impossible, since two-thirds of the German people were Protestants. However, Article 1 of the concordat guaranteed "freedom of profession and public practice of the Catholic religion," and the church was granted the freedom to "manage and regulate her own affairs independently, and, within the framework of her own competence, to publish laws and ordinances binding on her members." Article 3 provided for an exchange of ambassadors (nuncios on the Catholic side) between Germany and the Vatican. Article 4 granted the church the freedom to publish "instructions, ordinances, Pastoral Letters, official diocesan gazettes, and other enactments regarding the spiritual direction of the faithful issued by the ecclesiastical authorities within the framework of their competence . . . without hindrance."

Several articles were of extreme importance for Hitler. Article 16 stated that

> before bishops take possession of their dioceses they are to take an oath of fealty [that is, loyalty] either to the Reich Representative of the State concerned, or to the President of the Reich, according to the following formula: "Before God and on the Holy Gospels I swear and promise as becomes a bishop, loyalty to the German Reich and to the State of [the name of a German state is inserted here]. I swear and promise to honor the legally constituted Government and to cause the clergy of my diocese to honor it. In the performance of my spiritual office and in my solicitude for the welfare and the interests of the German Reich, I will endeavor to avoid all detrimental acts which might endanger it."

Hitler wanted to neutralize the political power of the German clergy, and this was achieved with Article 32 of the concordat, which stated that "the Holy See will prescribe regulations for the exclusion of clergy and members of religious Orders from membership of political parties, and from engaging in work on their behalf." One of the results of the concordat was the demise of the Catholic Center Party. Scholder stated, "The Centre Party fell apart with a speed which surprised even the National Socialists [the Nazis]."[15]

On the other hand, Article 21 was of extreme importance to the church. It provided that "Catholic religious instruction in elementary, senior, secondary and vocational schools constitutes a regular portion of the curriculum, and is to be taught in accordance with the principles of the Catholic Church." Article 21 also gave the clergy authority over the selection of textbooks for religious instruction in public schools and "the right to investigate whether pupils are receiving religious instruction in accordance with the teachings and requirements of the Church."

Most people are unaware of the crucial role that the Vatican played in assisting Hitler to power in Germany. Master politician that he was, Hitler would probably have achieved his goal of ruling Germany by some other means if not through the Vatican. Historically, however, it's a fact that the Vatican's anxiety to conclude a concordat with Germany was a key factor in bringing Hitler to power. Hitler was a throwback to the kind of autocratic ruler that the Vatican historically was accustomed to dealing with. And at that time, the world didn't know what horrible atrocities Hitler would commit in Europe.

The Vatican's relationship with the Weimar Republic and Hitler also illustrates an important shift in its policy toward democratic nations. It came to realize that fulminating against democracy and political liberalism got it nowhere. So it began seeking ways to achieve its political objectives through the democratic process. Where during the nineteenth century, the Vatican had discouraged its members from participating in the democratic process—to the point of telling them it was a sin to so much as vote—the Vatican now joined the democratic process to the point even of allowing the establishment of Catholic political parties. However, it expected the parties to toe the Vatican's political line. And as the confrontation between Bruening and Eugenio Pacelli demonstrates, the Vatican could not understand a Catholic politician who would put the constitution and laws of his country above the demands of the church. In the end, the Vatican was willing to sacrifice its own Catholic party when doing so achieved one of its major objectives, namely, a concordat with Hitler's Germany.

My purpose in sharing with you this brief account of the relationship between Hitler and the Vatican (and between Mussolini and the Vatican) has been simply to illustrate the emergence of the papacy as a significant actor in world politics during the twentieth century. It has not been my intention to put the Vatican on the spot. It's important to remember that only hindsight is 20/20. While there were warning signs of what was to come in Hitler's Germany during the early 1930s, no one at that juncture could have anticipated Auschwitz, Dachau, and the annihilation of six million Jews. Klaus Scholder noted that "as long as human beings cannot see the future, neither supporters nor opponents can very well be blamed for basing their decisions on previous experiences and standards, rather than on the figure of a man who in his own way was undoubtedly a type that appears once in a century."[16]

One more example of the Vatican's growing influence in global politics during the twentieth century will suffice.

The Vatican and the fall of communism

Monday, June 7, 1982, was a historic day at the Vatican. It was also historic for America. Most of all, it was historic for the Soviet Union and its Eastern European satellites, though it's not likely that the Soviet Union and its allies were aware of what was happening. On that day, Ronald Reagan spent fifty minutes with John Paul II in the Vatican library. They talked alone. No secretaries, no aides, no interpreters.

It was the first meeting between the president and the pope, though not the last. The topic of their conversation? "Reagan and the Pope agreed to undertake a clandestine campaign to hasten the dissolution of the communist empire."[17] They were "convinced that Poland could be broken out of the Soviet orbit if the Vatican and the U.S. committed their resources to destabilizing the Polish government."[18] They also believed that if they could bring down the communist regime in Poland, other Eastern European nations would follow, with the eventual demise of the Soviet Union a distinct possibility.

Solidarity. The strategy that Reagan and John Paul adopted was to support Poland's outlawed Solidarity Trade Union. The union had its origins in an illegal strike by the workers at Poland's Gdansk* shipyard in 1970. The communist government sent in riot police to break up the strike, resulting in more than eighty deaths. However, Lech Walesa, one of the members of the strike committee, went on to organize small underground unions all over the country. The Polish economy deteriorated rapidly in the late 1970s, leading to strikes by these independent trade unions. Another strike occurred at the Gdansk shipyard in August 1980. Walesa scaled a wall in support of the strike and in defiance of the

---

*Gdansk is the sixth largest city in Poland and its principal seaport.

government, instantly making him a national hero. Spontaneous strikes soon followed across Poland.

In September, the government signed an agreement with the strikers that allowed for the legal organization of the National Coordination Committee of the Solidarity Free Trade Union. Walesa was chosen as the committee's chairman, and membership rapidly mushroomed to nine million. However, Poland continued to sink into economic chaos, resulting in food shortages, rationing, and rising unemployment. Strikes continued, and on December 31, 1981, the government leader, General Wojciech Jaruzelski, declared martial law and suspended the union. The following October he banned it. Six thousand Solidarity leaders were arrested, and hundreds were charged with treason. However, thousands more took refuge in churches and monasteries, sheltered by priests and bishops. Six months later, Reagan met with John Paul in the pope's library.

John Paul and Ronald Reagan. Solidarity was above all a movement of the Polish people, and it did not die when it was outlawed. It simply went underground. John Paul and Ronald Reagan determined to keep the movement alive and help it grow. Solidarity would be their dagger in the heart of the communist regime. Reagan and John Paul would each make his own contribution. The United States would provide the necessary financial and technological help, John Paul would provide the moral inspiration, and the church in Poland would provide headquarters and meeting places for underground union locals throughout the country.

And so it happened. Using covert channels, the United States sent tons of equipment to the Polish underground: fax machines, printing presses, photocopiers, computers, and software. Often, the equipment was sent first to Sweden or Denmark, transferred to large shipping containers, and resent from a Scandinavian address to the Polish port of Gdansk. Dockworkers who were clandestine agents of Solidarity knew which containers contained the contraband, and, using priests and other church channels, they passed it on to secret union establishments all over Poland.

John Paul encouraged Walesa to keep his union alive underground. The church's strategy was to avoid clashing with the Polish government while cooperating with the United States in applying increasing pressure on the Polish dictatorship. Thus, John Paul instructed Walesa to pass on the word to his union members that they should avoid the open confrontations with the government that taking to the streets and striking entailed. The latter, he said, would only force the government to intervene and possibly incite the Kremlin to send in Russian troops to break up the rebellion.

In June 1979, three years before his visit with Reagan, John Paul had visited Poland to the cheers of millions of adoring Poles. In June 1983, a year after his visit with Reagan, the pope returned to his homeland, again to the cheers of millions as he toured the country, demanding human rights and praising Solidarity. This time, John Paul met for the first time with a nervous Jaruzelski, who realized that his government was on shaky ground.

The combined political pressure from America and the Vatican proved too much for the totalitarian regime. On April 5, 1989, the government signed an agreement legalizing Solidarity again and opening the way for parliamentary elections two months later. And in December 1990, Lech Walesa became the president of Poland.

The Vatican and world power

One of the primary reasons why the Vatican supported Mussolini and Hitler was the two dictators' fierce opposition to communism. But when the Vatican joined with Mussolini and Hitler to fight communism, it lost. On the other hand, when the Vatican joined with the United States, it succeeded. The Vatican-Washington alliance brought communism to its knees in John Paul's Polish homeland. By early 1990, communism was banished from all of Western Europe, and in December 1991, the communist Soviet Union collapsed. Thus, it's reasonable to say that the Vatican, which played such a central role in European politics during the Middle Ages, has again become a significant power player in world politics today.

The three examples of Vatican involvement in politics that I've shared with you in this chapter are just that—examples. There are many others. In chapter 16, you will read about the Catholic Church's current relationship to American politics. Catholic involvement in politics in the twenty-first century differs significantly from the power politics of the Middle Ages. A thousand years ago, the church didn't have to worry overly much about public opinion. It shifted its political weight around among kings and emperors according to which one seemed most likely to fulfill its ambitions. Today's Vatican has to cooperate with democracies and inspire movements among the people. And it has proved itself as adept at working with modern political realities as it was at working with political realities a thousand years ago. As Archbishop Pio Laghi told one Washington diplomat during the years that John Paul and Ronald Reagan were undermining Polish communism, "Listen to the Holy Father. We have 2,000 years experience at this."[19] The online newsletter published by Stratfor* said, "Popes know how to play power politics."[20]

In the chapter "Revelation 13 and the Sea Beast," I explained why Adventists understand the sea beast to represent the end-time papacy. Based on this interpretation, near the end of the chapter I stated several conclusions that we can reasonably draw about the end-time papacy:

- *"He [the sea beast] was given authority over every tribe, people, language and nation" (verse 7).* This means that the papacy will achieve political dominance over the whole world.
- *"The whole world was astonished and followed the beast. Men . . . worshiped the beast and asked, 'Who is like the beast? Who can make war against him?' " (verses 3, 4).* The world will acknowledge the papacy's spiritual leadership and will pay it homage.
- *"He was given power to make war against the saints and to conquer them" (verse 7).* The papacy will persecute those who oppose its authority.

Could these astounding conclusions really happen?

One hundred years ago, many students of prophecy probably viewed as truly wild and foolish the Adventist prediction, based on the sea beast of Revelation 13, that the papacy would achieve global political dominance during the end time. However, the global political influence that the papacy achieved during the twentieth century makes that prediction much more reasonable today.

What about the predictions, based on Revelation 13, that the world will acknowledge the papacy's spiritual leadership, and that the papacy will persecute those who dissent?

Could that really happen?

To answer these questions, we need more background.

---

*Stratfor stands for Strategic Forecasting. This issue of Stratfor's newsletter was a commentary on the controversial remarks about Islam that Pope Benedict XVI made in September 2006.

1. Owen Chadwick, *The Secularization of the European Mind* (Cambridge, UK: Cambridge University Press, 1975), 127.

2. "The Syllabus of Errors Condemned by Pius IX," Papal Encyclicals Online, http://www.papalencyclicals.net/Pius09/p9syll.htm. You can obtain a copy of the "Syllabus" by typing "Syllabus of Errors" into any search engine.

3. See especially part 6 of the "Syllabus" titled "Errors About Civil Society, Considered Both in Itself and in Its Relation to the Church."

4. Leo XIII, "On the Nature of True Liberty," 96.

5. Chadwick, 126.

6. Avro Manhattan, *The Vatican in World Politics* (New York: Gaer Associates, 1949), 108.

7. Klaus Scholder, *The Churches and the Third Reich*, trans. John Bowden (Philadelphia: Fortress Press, 1988), 146.

8. Ibid., 152, 153.

9. Ibid., 157.

10. Ibid., 247, 248.

11. Richard J. Evans, *The Coming of the Third Reich* (New York: Penguin Press, 2004), 352; italics added.

12. Scholder, 392.

13. No. 16, April 19, 1933; cited by Guenther Lewy in his book *The Catholic Church and Nazi Germany* (New York: McGraw-Hill, 1964), 44.

14. Evans, 363.

15. Scholder, 396.

16. Ibid., 221.

17. Carl Bernstein, "Holy Alliance," *Time*, February 24, 1992, 28.

18. Ibid.

19. Ibid., 33.

20. George Friedman, "Faith, Reason and Politics: Parsing the Pope's Remarks," Stratfor online newsletter, September 19, 2006.

CHAPTER 6

All the World Wondered

You'd never have known, reading the major newspapers and news magazines the week of John Paul's death, that secularism was in and religion was out in our Western world. Images of people weeping, praying, holding candles, and crossing themselves filled the major media, both print and broadcast. Under what other circumstances would *Time* magazine publish the words, "Jesus Christ is the answer to the question that is every human life," or *Newsweek* come out with the cover headline "Go With God"?[1]

In the weeks after John Paul's funeral, I heard Adventists everywhere saying, "All the world wondered after the beast" (Revelation 13:3, KJV). They viewed John Paul's life and the global fascination with his funeral as a fulfillment of prophecy. And for good reason.

Newsweek's Kenneth Woodward certainly was correct in his comment that John Paul II "transformed the figure of the pope from distant icon to familiar face. His face."[2] At the time of his election in 1978, when he was fifty-eight years old, John Paul was the youngest pope in 132 years. And if nothing else, he was energetic. Three months after his appointment as pope, he set out for the Dominican Republic and Mexico—the first of 104 pilgrimages that marked his twenty-six years as Pontifex Maximus.* During this time, he traveled the equivalent of three times

---

*Pontifex Maximus was originally the title of the high priest of the pagan state religion of the Roman Empire. From the time of Augustus Caesar on, the emperor held the title, and with the fall of the Western Roman Empire in A.D. 476, the title passed to the bishop of Rome, the pope.

the distance to the moon.[3] "The world was a stage," said *Time* magazine's David Van Biema, "every last inch of which the Pope appeared determined to tread."[4] And tread it he did, for during his tenure as pope, John Paul visited 129 of the world's 191 countries.* The Catholic Church's most traveled pope—he made more trips outside of Rome than all previous popes combined[5]—was seen in person by more people than any other world figure, religious or political. He viewed himself as a successor not only to Peter but also to Paul, who "could never sit still and was constantly on the move."[6]

John Paul energized people. He "knows that no one reads the encyclicals of a dead pope," said Philadelphia's Archbishop Justin Rigali. "That is why he has taken to the streets. It can last only a minute, but you'd think people had ten hours of the most intimate mystical experience. For many people, it is that one moment when they say, 'I saw another possibility in life.' "[7] Speaking personally, while I never felt mystical about John Paul (I have serious doctrinal differences with Catholics), I can say that I felt his charisma, especially in his early years as pope. I liked him as a person.

John Paul's travel schedule was enough to exhaust most people. Yet his other accomplishments were also astounding. He spoke eight languages, and when he knew the language of a questioner, he answered in that language. In 1989, when he first met with Mikhail Gorbachev, he and the Soviet premier spoke for ten minutes in the Russian language. John Paul's speeches and writings fill 150 thick volumes.[8] He also completed an enormous task begun by a predecessor of his, Paul VI: the revision of the church's massive code of canon law. He reviewed, edited, and corrected the entire document a line at a time.[9]

John Paul's impact on his church was also impressive. During his pontificate, church membership increased 41 percent—from 737 million in 1978 to 1.09 billion in 2003. Catholic growth in Africa was 168 percent, and the number of African priests increased by 237 percent![10] John Paul appointed upward of 150 cardinals during his tenure as pope, including 44 at a single stroke in February 2003. Seven months later, in September, he appointed 31 more! John Paul was famous for being doctrinally very conservative. And his conservatism is bound to dominate

---

*This is the number of independent states listed by the U.S. State Department in May 2005 on its Web site http://www.state.gov/www/regions/independent_states.html.

the church for years to come, for of the 117 cardinals from fifty-two countries who gathered in Rome on April 18, 2005, to choose his successor, he had appointed 114.[11] John Paul's conservatism lives on in Benedict XVI, for in his powerful role as prefect of the Vatican's Sacred Congregation for the Doctrine of the Faith (formerly the Inquisition), Benedict was for a quarter of a century John Paul's enforcer of doctrine.

Ecumenism

One of John Paul's passions was establishing relationships with other religious groups. While he was especially anxious to unite all Christians under the papal banner, he was also attentive to non-Christian religions. He felt a particular bond with Jews because of his acquaintance with them and their sufferings during World War II in Nazi-dominated Poland. He was the first pope to visit a Jewish synagogue in Rome. In 1993, he established diplomatic relations between the Vatican and Israel. And in 2000, he visited Israel, where he prayed at the Wailing Wall and visited with Jewish leaders. In 2004, Israel's chief rabbis returned the favor by calling on John Paul at the Vatican.

John Paul also initiated contacts with Muslims. In 1996, upon being presented with a copy of the Koran by Patriarch Raphael of Iraq, he bent down and kissed the book as a sign of respect. He also cooperated with Muslims on endeavors of similar interest. At the United Nations conference on women in 1994, John Paul worked with Muslims to push the conference to adopt language in the final resolution that protected the unborn. In 1984, he met with members of the B'nai B'rith. And in 1986, he brought together more than 270 religious leaders, both Christian and non-Christian, for a worship service at Assisi. Among the attendees were Hindu holy men, tribal shamans, and the Tibetan Buddhist, "His Holiness" the Dalai Lama, with whom John Paul sat side by side.

In addition to all of this, John Paul was a consummate political diplomat. He stood up to communism, fearlessly challenged its leaders, and brought the whole system in Eastern Europe to its knees. The Soviet Union—in its heyday one of the world's two superpowers—no longer exists, in large part because of John Paul's political skills.

Leaders of all the world's great religions viewed John Paul as a great man. Billy Graham called him "the moral conscience of the West"[12] and "the strong conscience of the whole Christian world."[13] Commenting on a meeting he had with the pope in 2002, Chief Mufti Selim Mehmed, the head of Bulgaria's large Muslim community, said, "We believe the world needs him because he speaks for peace, for the poor and the deprived."[14] And Rabbi James Rudin of the American Jewish Committee said that John Paul "understood Jews, not just with his head but with his heart. His contributions are historic, and probably in history, he's the best Pope Jews ever had."[15] And notice the headlines on a whole series of articles published by *Christianity Today*, the flagship magazine of evangelical American Protestantism:

- "Pope Gave Evangelicals the Moral Impetus We Didn't Have"
- "Pope 'Broadened the Way' for Evangelicals and Catholics"
- " 'Antichrist' No More: Evangelicals Praise Pope"
- "He Was My Pope, Too"
- "Protestants Laud Pope for Ecumenical, Social Stands"
- "Pope's Funeral Spotlights Kinship Between Catholics and Evangelicals"

John Paul's funeral

It's against this background that we must evaluate John Paul's funeral and its prophetic fulfillment. Why did four kings, five queens, and more than seventy prime ministers attend? Why did twenty-three Orthodox and eight Protestant delegations attend, along with representatives of Judaism, Islam, and other non-Christian religions? Why did three past and present American presidents kneel for five minutes in front of the pope's casket? Why did more than seven hundred thousand people stand for several hours in St. Peter's square to watch the pope's funeral? And why did an estimated two billion people around the world watch it on TV, four million of them in Rome alone?

The answer is simple: Because of who John Paul II was as a person and because of the impact he had on the world. For John Paul transformed the way the world viewed his office and his church. That's why, for days prior to his death, TV, radio, and newspapers around the world gave daily and sometimes hourly reports on his deteriorating condition. His funeral topped the news for at least a week. The death of John Paul and the selection of his successor kept the Roman Catholic Church at the top of the news throughout the entire month of April 2005. The death of previous popes *made* the news around the world, and a few political dignitaries attended. But four kings, five queens, seventy prime ministers, and twenty-three Orthodox and eight Protestant delegations *attending* his funeral? Four million people *watching* his funeral in Rome alone, and two billion around the world? I agree with those who interpret these events as a fulfillment of Revelation 13:3, that "all the world wondered after the beast" (KJV). John Paul's funeral had major prophetic implications indeed!

Revelation 13:3, 4 also says, "The whole world . . . worshiped the beast." At the conclusion of my chapter on "Revelation 13 and the Sea Beast," I suggested that this means that shortly before the end of time the world as a whole will acknowledge the papacy's spiritual leadership. That prediction may have sounded wild and foolish a hundred years ago, but developments in the world that I have outlined in this chapter and the previous one make that conclusion much more reasonable today.

Revelation 13:7 goes on to say that the sea beast will "make war against the saints and . . . conquer them." In other words, the end-time papacy will become an intolerant, persecuting power, punishing with civil penalties those who dissent from its spiritual and moral agenda.

Could this really happen?

To answer that question we need more evidence. The next two chapters will be helpful, but the complete answer will emerge toward the end of this book.

---

1. David Van Biema, "Pope John Paul II, 1920–2005: A Defender of the Faith," *Time*, April 11, 2005, 36. *Newsweek*, April 18, 2005, 1.

2. Kenneth L. Woodward, "Beloved and Brave," *Newsweek*, April 11, 2005, 35.

3. Andrew Nagorski, "Freedom Matters," *Newsweek*, April 11, 2005, 46.

4. Van Biema, 39.

5. Woodward, 42.

6. Jeffery L. Sheler, "Pope John Paul II: Pastor to the world, he led a revolution of conscience," *U.S. News & World Report*, April 11, 2005, 31.

7. Cited by Van Biema, 39.

8. Woodward, 44.

9. Ibid., 43.

10. Van Biema, 40.

11. Ibid., 42. In an April 18, 2005, Web news article, CNN put the number at 115.

12. Woodward, 39.

13. Van Biema, 36.

14. Ibid.

15. Ibid., 42.

CHAPTER 7

Catholic Political Theory Before Vatican II

At this point we need to consider the Roman Catholic view of the relationship that should exist between the church and the state. This is necessary in order to understand the aims of the papacy in today's world. I have divided this discussion into two parts. In this chapter, we will examine the Catholic theory of church-state relationships and religious freedom as they were stated by popes and theologians prior to Vatican II (1962–1965) and in some cases after Vatican II.* The next chapter examines Catholic statements about church-state separation and religious freedom by Vatican II and after.

Superiority of the Catholic Church

The Catholic view of church-state relationships and religious freedom is built on a number of major premises. The first is that Christianity is the only true religion, and the Catholic Church is the only true Christian church. Pope Pius IX stated categorically, "The religion of the Catholic Church is the only true religion."[1] In his encyclical "On Fostering True Religious Unity," issued on January 6, 1928, Pius XI said, "The Catholic Church is alone in keeping the true worship. This [the Catholic Church] is the fount of truth, this the house of faith, this the temple of God."[2]

The papacy also teaches that salvation is available only through the

---

*Vatican II was a general council of the Roman Catholic Church. It was held at the Vatican (hence the name "Vatican II") from October 11, 1962, to December 8, 1965. Vatican I was held in 1869 and 1870.

Catholic Church. The *Catechism of the Catholic Church,* second edition, published during John Paul II's pontificate, states, "The Church . . . is necessary for salvation. . . . They could not be saved who, knowing that the Catholic Church was founded as necessary by God through Christ, would refuse either to enter it or to remain in it."[3] Pius XI said, "If any man enter not here, or if any man go forth from it, he is a stranger to the hope of life and salvation."[4] The Catholic author George La Piana, himself a critic of the church, said that the church considers itself to be "the exclusive divine agency of salvation, the exclusive organ of divine grace, the exclusive channel of the divine spirit."[5]

Catholics aren't the only ones to claim that theirs is the only true church. Some Protestant churches have made the same claim. There are a number of problems with this assertion, not the least of which is the arrogance and exclusivity that it often leads to. The problem I'll focus on in this book is the detrimental effect that arises when the Catholic "true church" idea is combined with other aspects of Catholic political theory, which we will examine in the next few pages.

Supreme authority of the pope

The next major premise of Catholic political theory is that the pope is the supreme authority in both religious and temporal affairs. Nobody will question the pope's right to authority in Catholic affairs. But the Catholic Church insists that the pope has supreme authority over political rulers as well. We noted in a previous chapter that Innocent III, who was pope from 1198 to 1216, said, "Ecclesiastical liberty is nowhere better cared for than where the Roman church has full power in both temporal [political] and spiritual affairs."[6] One hundred years later, in 1302, Boniface said in his Bull *Unam Sanctam,* "With truth as our witness, it belongs to the spiritual power [the papacy] to establish the terrestrial [political] power and to pass judgment if it has not been good."[7]

The papacy bases its claim to authority over temporal rulers on Romans 13:1. In this verse, Paul, speaking of the authority of political rulers, said, "The authorities that exist have been established by God." In Leo XIII's 1881 encyclical "On Government Authority," he picked up on this idea. He said, "As regards political power, the Church rightly teaches that it comes from God."[8] But the papacy carries the principle a step further, claiming that God exercises His authority over kings and kingdoms through the church, and that since the pope is the head of the church, he has authority over political rulers. Writing in the thirteenth century, Thomas Aquinas said, "Secular [political] power is subject to the spiritual power as the body is subject to the soul," and "In the pope the secular power is joined to the spiritual. He holds the apex of both powers."[9] Pope Leo XIII echoed this thought in his 1888 encyclical "On the Nature of True Liberty." He pointed out that since secular and religious authorities share the same constituencies, their interests sometimes coincide. Then he said, "There must necessarily exist some order or mode of procedure to remove the occasions of difference and contention, and to secure harmony in all things. This harmony has been not inaptly compared to that which exists between the body and the soul."[10]

The point that Aquinas and Leo were making is that both political and religious powers are ordained of God, but the religious power, being spiritual, is superior to the political, which is secular. Thus, the pope has authority over the king, and any time the two conflict, the authority of the pope predominates. Popes can tell kings what to do and where to go. This was the philosophy of church-state relationships that dominated European politics during the Middle Ages. Kings didn't always bend to the will of the popes. However, as we saw in a previous chapter, the popes held the power of excommunication and the interdict, by which they could put intense pressure on secular rulers to submit to the church.*

As the papacy sees it, protecting the church is one of the most important functions of the state. Pope Pius XI, whose papacy extended from 1922 to 1939, said, "The royal power was given not only for the governance of the world, but *most of all* for the protection of the Church."[11] In a very real sense, our modern democratic governments are also responsible for protecting religion, churches, synagogues, and mosques. But this simply means that the state is responsible to create a safe environment in which religion can flourish. Pius and other popes meant something quite different when they said that "the royal power was given . . . most of all for the protection of the church." They meant that in an ideal state, the Catholic Church is the only official religion, and the state is responsible for protecting the Catholic Church against all others.

Church-state union

Obviously, the papacy also prefers a union of church and state and quite objects to the modern political principle of church-state separation.

---

*Regarding the papal interdict, see pages 46 and 47.

Furthermore, in the view of the papacy, since the Catholic Church is the only true religion, Catholicism should be the state religion, and ideally, it will be the only religion that the state allows. Thus, Pius IX, whose papacy extended from 1846 to 1878 (making him one of the longest-reigning popes in Catholic history) said that one of the principal errors of our times is the idea that "in the present day it is no longer expedient that the Catholic religion should be held as the only religion of the State, to the exclusion of all other forms of worship."[12]

In America and most other Western countries today, the state is purposely nonreligious. In other words, it is secular. The secular state is not hostile to religion; indeed, it protects religion, as I said a moment ago, by providing freedom for all churches and all religions to carry out their mission as they see fit without any interference from the state. However, according to Catholic political theory, it's essential for the state to provide "means and opportunities whereby the community may be enabled to live properly, that is to say, according to the laws of God. For, since God is the source of all goodness and justice, it is absolutely ridiculous that the State should pay no attention to these laws or render them abortive by contrary enactments."[13] *The point is that the state should be overtly religious, enforcing God's laws, not just secular laws.* This is a key point that we will return to in later chapters. Thus Pius XI, who was pope from 1922 to 1939, said that Christ's "kingly dignity demands that the State should take account of the Commandments of God and of Christian principles, both in making laws and in administering justice."[14] And, since the Catholic religion is the only true religion, the commandments of God and the moral principles on which government is based should be in harmony with the Catholic understanding. Leo XIII, who was pope from 1878 to 1903, earnestly exhorted rulers "to defend religion, and to consult the interest of their States by giving that liberty to the [Catholic] Church which cannot be taken away without injury and ruin to the commonwealth."[15]

In other words, because the church's spiritual authority is superior to that of the state, it has the right to dictate the true moral laws that will govern nations and their people. A state that enacts laws that disagree with the church's moral teaching is wrong, and for the common good of society, it must change its laws to conform to the church's moral understanding.

This is why the Catholic Church opposes church-state separation so strongly. Pius IX stated that another of the "principal errors of our time" is the idea that "the Church ought to be separate from the State and the

State from the Church."[16] Leo XIII considered the idea of church-state separation to be "a fatal principle."[17] George La Piana said that the Catholic Church condemns church-state separation "as an offense of God's law and a fatal source of evil."[18]

Opposes freedom of conscience

It follows naturally that the church rejects the ideas of freedom of religion, freedom of conscience, and freedom to worship as one chooses. Pius IX considered one of the principal errors of our times to be the idea that "every man is free to embrace and profess that religion which, guided by the light of reason, he shall consider true."[19] Gregory XVI, pope from 1841 to 1846, stated that "this shameful font of indifferentism [liberalism and democracy] gives rise to that absurd and erroneous proposition which claims that *liberty of conscience* must be maintained for everyone."[20] Pius IX called it an "erroneous opinion, most fatal in its effects on the Catholic Church and the salvation of souls, called by Our Predecessor, Gregory XVI, an insanity, vis., that 'liberty of conscience and worship is each man's personal right, which ought to be legally proclaimed and asserted in every rightly constituted society.' "[21]

Of course, freedom of conscience for every citizen is one of the foundational principles of the secular democratic state that adopts church-state separation as a basic principle of government. *The papacy's opposition to freedom of conscience is another key point that we will return to later in this book.*

Opposes government by the people

Since people can't be trusted to choose their own religion or follow their own conscientious convictions, it follows that neither can they be trusted to choose their own government. After all, the authority to rule comes from God, not from the people. Thus, the papacy strongly opposes "government of the people, by the people, for the people" (to quote Abraham Lincoln's famous Gettysburg Address). In his encyclical "On Government Authority," Pope Leo XIII said, "Indeed, very many of more recent times, walking in the footsteps of those who in a former age assumed to themselves the name of philosophers, say that all power comes from the people; so that those who exercise it in the State do so not as their own, but as delegated to them by the people, and that, by this rule, it can be revoked by the will of the very people by whom it was delegated. But from these, Catholics dissent, who affirm that the right to rule is from God, as from a natural and necessary principle."[22] Leo went on to say that when "the law determining what is right to do and avoid doing is at the mercy of the majority, . . . this is simply a road leading straight to tyranny."[23]

I pointed out a few paragraphs back that the papacy bases its theory of government on Romans 13:1, where Paul said, "The [governing] authorities that exist have been established by God." The Catholic Church interprets this to mean that a government that is elected by the people has not been appointed by God. However, Paul did not say *how* a government authority should come into existence. Historically, governments have gained control of states by a variety of means: through line of descent, as in a monarchy; through election by the people; through revolution; through conquest; etc. By whatever means it comes to exist, the purpose of every governing authority is to maintain order in society, and to fulfill that purpose, citizens must obey its laws so long as they do not conflict with God's laws. The unstated assumption in the Catholic theory of a divinely appointed government is that the highest authority on earth is the pope, and since he is God's representative, any government desiring legitimacy must have his blessing. And popes prefer kings over elected presidents and parliaments. Elected governments, after all, are harder for popes to control.

To be fair, I should mention that in recent times some popes have given qualified approval to democracy as a legitimate form of government. The first pope to do so was Leo XIII. In his 1881 encyclical "On Government Authority," he said, "It is of importance, however, to remark in this place that those who may be placed over the State may in certain cases be chosen by the will and decision of the multitude, without opposition to or impugning of the Catholic doctrine."[24]

Notice that he allowed that under certain circumstances people may choose their own rulers "without opposition to or impugning of the *Catholic doctrine*." Any such ruler, to be legitimate, would have to be chosen on the basis of his agreement with Catholic doctrines and moral principles. Ideally, the ruler would be willing to submit his authority to that of the pope. And suddenly, what looked like a change of the papal heart, giving modern democracy a clean bill of health, turns out not to be such a ringing affirmation after all. Democracy is just fine, so long as it is on the pope's terms! But that, of course, is not democracy at all—at least of the secular American variety.

World rule

Finally, the papacy's ultimate goal is to rule the world someday and impose its view of church and state on the entire human race. In his encyclical "On the Feast of Christ the King," Pius XI wrote,

> Thus the Empire of our Redeemer embraces all men. To use the words of our immortal Predecessor, Pope Leo XIII: "His empire includes not only Catholic nations, not only baptized persons who, though of right belonging to the Church, have been led astray by error, or have been cut off from her by schism, but also all those who are outside the Christian faith; so that truly the whole of mankind is subject to the power of Jesus Christ." Nor is there any difference in this matter between the individual and the family or the State; for all men, whether collectively or individually, are under the dominion of Christ. In Him is the salvation of the individual, in Him is the salvation of society.[25]

The following summary of Leo's words will perhaps make the point clear:

- "The Empire of our Redeemer embraces *all men*," not just Catholics or Christians.
- "*The whole of mankind* is subject to the power of Jesus Christ."
- "*All men* . . . are under the dominion of Christ."

In one sense it is correct to say, as Pius did, that "the whole of mankind is subject to the power of Jesus Christ" and "all men . . . are under the dominion of Christ." But Pius meant more than that *God* is the ultimate Ruler of the world. He meant more than that at Christ's second coming every human being "will give an account of himself *to God*" (Romans 14:12). He meant more than that a day is coming when *Christ* will "strike down the nations" and " 'rule them with an iron scepter' " (Revelation 19:15). Since the laws of nations must be based on Scripture correctly understood, since the Catholic Church is the only true Christian church and the ultimate authority on the meaning of Scripture, and since the pope's authority supersedes that of secular rulers, it follows logically that all human beings and all nations are subject to the authority of the pope as God's representative on earth *now*.

I pointed out in an earlier chapter that Augustine radically changed the church's interpretation of Daniel's prophecy of the great image. For three hundred years the church had understood the stone that struck Nebuchadnezzar's image on the feet to represent Christ's second coming, when He will " 'crush all [of earth's] kingdoms and bring them to an end' " (Daniel 2:44). Augustine reinterpreted the stone to represent Christ's first coming; therefore, the church is God's eternal kingdom, and it is the instrument that will conquer all of earth's kingdoms. This was the scriptural, prophetic rationale that led the church during the medieval period to lord it over kings and kingdoms. And that rationale is still alive and well in papal thinking, for Pius XI—writing in the twentieth century—went on to declare, "If the Kingdom of Christ [that is, the Catholic Church], then, receives, as it should, all nations under its sway, there seems no reason why we should despair of seeing that peace which the King of Peace came to bring on earth."[26]

Pius also fulminated against modern, secular democracy that stripped the church of its temporal power. Speaking of the "plague of anticlericalism" with its "errors and impious activities"—in other words, the freedom of religion provided by secular democracy that has existed in the world for the past two hundred years—Pius said,

> This evil spirit, as you are well aware, Venerable Brethren, has not come into being in one day; it has long lurked beneath the surface. The Empire of Christ over all nations [i.e., the political power of the papacy over Europe during the medieval period] was rejected. The right which the Church has from Christ Himself, to teach mankind, to make laws, to govern peoples in all that pertains to their eternal salvation, that right was denied. Then gradually the religion of Christ [Catholicism] came to be likened to false religions and to be placed ignominiously on the same level with them. It was then put under the power of the State [instead of the state being put under the power of the church] and tolerated more or less at the whim of princes and rulers.[27]

To this day, the Catholic Church does not approve of the modern secular state. It will work with secular states because it has no choice but to do so. But the secular state with its separation of religion from government never has been and today still is not the papacy's preferred form of government. In the Catholic Church's ideal state, Catholicism is the official religion of the state, and the state enforces Catholic dogma and morality.

The Catholic author George La Piana summed up the papal ambition: "By its own claim," he said, "the Roman Catholic Church, . . . [is] a totalitarian church expecting to conquer the world on the principle that it is the exclusive divine agency of salvation, the exclusive organ of divine grace, and the exclusive channel of the divine spirit."[28]

In summary

Prior to Vatican II, the papal theory of the relationship that should exist between the church and the state included the following concepts: Christianity is the only true religion, and Catholicism is the only true Christian church. The pope has supreme authority in both spiritual and temporal affairs; therefore, kings, presidents, and prime ministers are subject to him—at least in spiritual/moral issues. Church and state should be united, with the state enforcing Christian moral/spiritual principles as they are understood by the Catholic Church. People must submit to the doctrinal authority of the church; they don't have the right to believe and worship as they please. God is the Author of the state's authority, and the Catholic Church, as God's true representative on earth, should assist the state in governing its citizens. The Catholic Church, being the only true religion, should dominate the world politically in order to establish Christ's kingdom all over the world.

I do not hesitate to say that if the papacy had its way, its totalitarian system would dominate the politics of every nation on earth right now. For the most part, the papal sources I have cited do not date back to the medieval period. They are the statements of popes and knowledgeable Catholics during the past two hundred years, some of them speaking within the twentieth century.

However, there may be those who wonder whether perhaps Vatican II, in the early 1960s, might have changed all of that. After all, the council did make some remarkable statements regarding religious freedom. Let's examine the evidence.

---

1. Pius IX, "Syllabus of Errors Condemned by Pius IX," No. 21; "Papal Encyclicals Online," http://www.papalencyclicals.net/Pius09/p9syll.htm.

2. Pius XI, encyclical, January 26, 1928, "On Religious Unity" (*Mortalium Animos*), par. 11; Papal Encyclicals Online, http://www.papalencyclicals.net/Pius11/P11MORTA.HTM.

3. *Catechism of the Catholic Church*, second edition, English translation from the Latin (Vatican City: Libreria Editrice Vaticana, 1994), No. 846.

4. Pius XI, "On Religious Unity," par. 11.

5. George La Piana and John Swomley, *Catholic Power vs. American Freedom* (Amherst, N.Y.: Prometheus Books, 2002), 20.

6. Cited in *Readings in Church History*, ed. C. J. Barry (Westminster, Md.: The Newman Press, 1960), 1:438.

7. Boniface VIII, bull promulgated November 18, 1302, *Unam Sanctam*, http://en.wikipedia.org/wiki/Unam_Sanctam.

8. Leo XIII, encyclical, June 29, 1881, "On the Origin of Civil Power" (*Diuturnum Illud*), par. 8; Papal Encyclicals Online, http://www.papalencyclicals.net/Leo13/l13civ.htm.

9. Cited in Dino Bigongiari, ed., *The Political Ideas of St. Thomas Aquinas* (New York: Hafner Publishing Company, 1953), xxiv.

10. Leo XIII, encyclical, June 20, 1888, "On the Nature of Human Liberty" (*Libertas Praestantissimum*), par. 18; Papal Encyclicals Online, http://www.papalencyclicals.net/Leo13/l13liber.htm.

11. Pius IX, encyclical, December 8, 1864, "Condemning Current Errors," also called "Forbidding Traffic in Alms" (*Quanta Cura*), par. 8; Papal Encyclicals Online, http://www.papalencyclicals.net/Pius09/p9quanta.htm; italics added.

12. Pius IX, "Syllabus of Errors," No. 77.

13. Leo XIII, "On the Nature of Human Liberty," par. 18.

14. Pius XI, encyclical, December 11, 1925, "On the Feast of Christ the King" (*Quas Primas*), par. 32; Papal Encyclicals Online, http://www.papalencyclicals.net/Pius11/P11PRIMA.HTM.

15. Leo XIII, "On the Origin of Civil Power," par. 25.

16. Pius IX, "Syllabus of Errors," No. 55.

17. Leo XIII, "On the Nature of Human Liberty," par. 38.

18. La Piana and Swomley, 51.

19. Pius IX, "Syllabus of Errors," No. 15.

20. Gregory XVI, encyclical, August 15, 1832, "On Liberalism and Religious Indifferentism" (*Mirari Vos*), par. 14, Papal Encyclicals Online, http://www.papalencyclicals.net/Greg16/g16mirar.htm; italics in the original.

21. Pius IX, "On Current Errors," par. 3; italics added.

22. Leo XIII, "On the Origin of Civil Power," par. 5.

23. Leo XIII, "On the Nature of Human Liberty," par. 16.

24. Leo XIII, "On the Origin of Civil Power," par. 6.

25. Pius XI, "On the Feast of Christ the King," par. 18.

26. Ibid., par. 20.

27. Ibid., par. 24.

28. La Piana and Swomley, 20.

CHAPTER 8

Catholic
Political Theory
After Vatican II

Several statements in the Vatican II "Declaration on Religious Freedom" are quite surprising in view of the Catholic Church's history of intolerance and its understanding of church-state relationships that I shared with you in the previous chapter. In fact, some Adventists have questioned the validity of our interpretation of Revelation 13 because of positive statements from Vatican II on religious freedom such as the two that follow:

> This Vatican Council declares that the human person has a right to religious freedom. This freedom means that all men are to be immune from coercion on the part of individuals or of social groups and of any human power, in such wise that no one is to be forced to act in a manner contrary to his own beliefs, whether privately or publicly, whether alone or in association with others within due limits. [1]

> All men should be at once impelled by nature and also bound by a moral obligation to seek the truth, especially religious truth. They are also bound to adhere to the truth, once it is known, and to order their whole lives in accord with the demands of truth. However, men cannot discharge these obligations in a manner in keeping with their own nature unless they enjoy immunity from external coercion as well as psychological freedom. Therefore the right to religious freedom has its foundation not in the subjective

disposition of the person, but in his very nature. In consequence, the right to this immunity continues to exist even in those who do not live up to their obligation of seeking the truth and adhering to it and the exercise of this right is not to be impeded, provided that just public order be observed.[2]

Coming from an institution with such a long history of persecution of dissenters, these statements are truly remarkable affirmations about religious freedom. However, a closer look shows that these positive statements in the Vatican II document on religious freedom include qualifying phrases and sentences that could, under certain circumstances, be used to negate what they appear so clearly to affirm. I don't mean that the bishops who framed these Catholic statements about religious freedom had sinister motives. I prefer to attribute to them the best of intentions. My concern is for the use that could be made of their statements under circumstances in the future that differ widely from those that exist in the world today.

Analyzing the statements

The first statement begins with the declaration that "the human person has a right to religious freedom" but concludes by stating that this freedom is "within limits." Of course, the idea that there are limits to religious freedom is not necessarily bad. The United States Supreme Court has also taken the position that under certain circumstances government is justified in preventing people from acting in harmony with their religious beliefs. To use a common hypothetical example, a person cannot act upon the religious belief that it is his duty to punch other people in the nose. An actual example is the practice of handling poisonous snakes during religious services, which American courts have consistently held that the government can forbid.

Thus the question relative to the phrase "within due limits" in the Catholic document on religious freedom is not whether this is a wrong principle. Rather, the question is, Who will set those "due limits"? In a democratic, secular government that isn't controlled by religious presuppositions about moral right and wrong, the chances are fairly good that those limits will be defined very narrowly, and religious freedom will be largely protected. However, in a state where the Catholic philosophy of church-state union prevails, the church will be the entity that defines those limits, and the religious freedom of those who disagree could very easily be curtailed.

The second statement begins by affirming that all men are "bound by a moral obligation to seek the truth, especially religious truth," and "they are also bound to adhere to the truth, once it is known." The question arises, of course, as to what constitutes "truth," and for that the Catholic Church has a ready answer: As Christ's only true church on earth, it has the exclusive right, as we have seen, to define the truth that all men are "bound by a moral obligation to seek" and "to adhere to . . . once it is known."

The statement goes on to say, however, that "men cannot discharge these obligations in a manner in keeping with their own nature unless they enjoy immunity from external coercion as well as psychological freedom." Furthermore, "the right to this immunity continues to exist even in those who do not live up to their obligation of seeking the truth and adhering to it." In other words, people have a right to be wrong! Coming as it does from a Catholic Church council, that is indeed a remarkable statement that we can surely applaud!

The qualifying phrase in the second statement is the one that says "provided just public order be observed." We can understand this to mean simply that no one has the religious right to harm another person. The real question, as with the previous statement, is Who gets to define what constitutes a "just public order"? And on that question, a statement later in the Vatican II declaration on religious freedom is sobering:

> Furthermore, society has the right to defend itself against possible abuses committed on the pretext of freedom of religion. It is the special duty of government to provide this protection. However, government is not to act in an arbitrary fashion or in an unfair spirit of partisanship. Its action is to be controlled by juridical norms which are in conformity with the objective moral order. These norms arise out of the need for the effective safeguard of the rights of all citizens and for the peaceful settlement of conflicts of rights, also out of the need for an adequate care of genuine public peace, which comes about when men live together in good order and in true justice, and finally out of the need for a proper guardianship of public morality.[3]

Notice that "it is the special duty of government" to defend society against "possible abuses committed on the pretext of freedom of religion." Again, that's fine, as long as we understand it to mean that nobody has a religious right to harm another person or to jeopardize public health and safety. Terrorism, for example, cannot be countenanced, even if the terrorists firmly believe their actions to be fulfillment of their religious duty. But the Vatican statement goes beyond that. It says that the government's action in defending society against abuses committed in the pretext of religious freedom is to be "controlled by juridical norms which are in conformity with the objective moral order," and that "arise out of . . . the need for a proper guardianship of morality."

We have already seen that the Catholic Church considers its spiritual authority to be superior to the authority of the state in the same way that the soul is superior to the body. Thus, in situations where the Catholic Church is favored by government, the church will take to itself the responsibility of defining the moral principles of the "objective moral order" that the state is to protect. This is a major qualification to the very positive statements about religious freedom that we read a moment ago. Given the proper circumstances, it could easily be interpreted as giving the church the same authority over civil government that it had during the Middle Ages.

Another important point to remember is that, for all its laudable statements in support of the individual's religious freedom, the papacy has never renounced its preference for church-state union. In a country where it can do so, it would still like to be the state church, with the state legislating and enforcing Catholic moral principles. But of course, church-state union is a key factor in nearly all persecution. In a government where there is a union of church and state, religious freedom is in danger of being curtailed to some degree.*

The Catholic catechism

The *Catechism of the Catholic Church*, the English translation of which was published in 1994, contains a statement that is relevant to our discussion: "The teaching of the [Catholic] Church has elaborated the principle of *subsidiarity*, according to which "a community of a higher order should not interfere in the internal life of a community of a lower order, depriving the latter of its functions, but rather should support it in case of need and help to co-ordinate its activity with the activities of the rest of society, always with a view to the common good."[4]

---

*Some countries, such as England, have an established church yet also extend full religious freedom to all citizens.

This statement is quite in harmony with the church's medieval philosophy of church-state relationships. It describes two communities—one of a higher order, which is the church, and the other of a lower order, the state. The word *subsidiarity* in the opening sentence is a sociological term. It means that those functions that a subordinate organization can perform effectively should not be assumed by a higher organization, since the subordinate organization is closer to local situations.

Roman Catholic church-state philosophy, of course, considers the state to be subordinate to the church. Thus, the principle of subsidiarity means that those functions that the state can best perform should be left to it. That sounds good at first glance, especially the statement that "a community of a higher order [the church] should not interfere in the internal life of a community of a lower order [the state], depriving the latter of its functions." However, the statement goes on to say that the community of the higher order (the church) should "support it [the community of a lower order—the state] in the case of need and help to coordinate its activity with the activities of the rest of society, always with a view to the common good."

This could be understood to mean that the community of the lower order (the state) is still dependent on the "support" and "coordination" of the community of the higher order (the church). Interpreted in this way, the church would be free to intervene in the affairs of the state "in case of need." And the question of "need" would obviously be decided by the community of the higher order—the church. While dressed in terms that are considerably more modern, the medieval theory of the church's superiority to the state is contained in this statement, ready to be implemented without apology when circumstances permit.

Malachi Martin

A number of years ago I purchased a book called *The Keys of This Blood.* The author, Malachi Martin, was a priest who at one time had served as a professor at the Vatican's Pontifical Biblical Institute in Rome. His best-selling book, which was published by Simon and Schuster in 1990, is of major significance for our discussion.

Martin begins his book with the bold statement that "willing or not, ready or not, we are all involved in an all-out, no-holds-barred, three-way global competition." The competition, Martin says, is about who will control the coming one-world government, which anyone age forty or less in 1990 will live to see. He then says, "The chosen purpose of John

Paul's pontificate . . . is to be the victor in that competition, now well underway."[5] According to Malachi Martin, John Paul's highest ambition was for him and his church to rule the coming one-world government. And given the global influence that John Paul developed for himself and his church during his pontificate, it's easy to believe that Martin knew what he was talking about.

Later in his book, Martin makes a number of other statements that are sobering when viewed in light of the Catholic philosophy of church-state relationships that we have been examining: "It is axiomatic for John Paul that no one has the right—democratic or otherwise—to a moral wrong; and no religion based on divine revelation has a moral right to teach such a moral wrong or abide by it."[6]

Interesting! You and I don't have a right to believe—much less to practice or teach—something that is morally wrong! The key question, of course, is, Who gets to decide what's morally right and wrong? Here is Martin's answer: "The Roman Catholic Church has always claimed—and under John Paul claims today—to be the ultimate arbiter of what is morally good and morally bad in human action."[7]

Notice that the Catholic Church claims today, as it always has, to be "the ultimate arbiter," not of what's morally good or bad for *Catholics*, but what's morally good or bad "*in human* action"—that is, for *all* human beings.

So, what does John Paul's church propose to do about people who choose to teach and abide by a moral wrong? Martin's answer and his church's answer to that question is sobering to contemplate. The statement below is loaded with long, unfamiliar words that tend to obscure Martin's meaning to the casual reader, so I have interpreted his meaning at certain points. I have also italicized a couple of key words that I will analyze for you. Here is what Martin says: "The final prerequisite for georeligious capability [religious domination of the world] is authority. The institution [Roman Catholic Church], in its organizational structures and undertakings, must have a unique authority [political control]: an authority that is . . . *autonomous* vis-à-vis all other authority on the supranational [global] plane; an authority that carries with it such *sanctions* as are effective in maintaining the unity and aims of the institution [Roman Catholic Church] as it goes about its business of serving the greatest good of the community as a whole and in its every part."[8]

On careful analysis, these words have somber implications. Martin said at the beginning of his book that John Paul's goal was for him and his church to rule the coming world government. Then he tells us that in order for any organization to have this "georeligious capability," it must have an authority that is "*autonomous* vis-à-vis all other authority on the supranational plane." What he means is that the Roman Catholic Church must have authority that is independent of, and superior to, any other authority in the world so that it is in control and can't be overruled.

He says further that the Roman Catholic Church must have the ability to put in place "such *sanctions* as are effective in maintaining the unity and aims of the institution as it goes about its business of serving the greatest good of the community as a whole and in its every part." *Sanctions* are what happen when a higher authority slaps restrictions on a subordinate authority's policies and actions until the subordinate authority submits to the higher authority's demands. A case in point is the import and export restrictions (sanctions) that the United Nations imposed on Iraq following the Gulf War in 1991 in an effort to force Saddam Hussein to disclose his program of weapons of mass destruction.

Malachi Martin said that "the institution"—that is, the Roman Catholic Church—must have the authority to impose its moral agenda on the rest of the world (he called it "the supranational plane") and to impose sanctions on any nation that refuses to bend to the papacy's demands. Martin chose his language very carefully, making sure to be somewhat ambiguous with his long words. But on careful examination, his meaning is obvious: The Roman Catholic Church must have the authority to stop anyone who interferes with its global ambition of serving what *the church* perceives to be "the greatest good of the community as a whole and in its every part." In other words, the church wants control over every element of human society all over the world! That's the same philosophy of church-state relationships that existed during the Middle Ages! It's the philosophy of church-state relationships that papal encyclicals have advocated for the past two hundred years, even though the church has been prevented from applying it in most countries.

Some Catholics would no doubt argue that Malachi Martin, who died in 1999, represented a very conservative element of Catholicism that is not accepted by the majority of Catholics today, especially in North America and western Europe. That certainly is true. However, John Paul II was a strong conservative in both his religious and his political outlook, and his successor, Benedict XVI, is equally conservative if not more so. Martin's conservative view is alive and well in Catholicism today, and given the right conditions, it could regain dominance in any one country, and, in the right circumstances, over the whole world.

Revelation 13:7 says the sea beast will be "given authority over every tribe, people, language and nation." That's political domination. Revelation 13 describes Roman Catholicism at the end time. Therefore, Revelation is predicting that the fatal wound will be completely healed and that the Roman Catholic Church will achieve political domination of the whole world during the final days of earth's history.

Could this really happen?

This conclusion seemed wild and foolish in the past, and in today's climate of religious tolerance and political correctness, I'm sure it still seems wild and foolish to many people. However, our examination of Roman Catholicism's political philosophy in this chapter and the previous one leads me to the conclusion that, in a global crisis, *it really could happen.*

In light of our prophetic understanding, Adventists believe it *will* happen.

---

1. Vatican II "Declaration on Religious Freedom," #2; http://www.vatican.va/archive/hist_councils/ii_vatican_council/documents/vat-ii_decl_19651207_dignitatishumanae_en.htm.

2. Ibid.

3. Ibid., #7.

4. *Catechism of the Catholic Church*, second edition, English translation from the Latin (Vatican City: Libreria Editrice Vaticana, 1994), No. 1883, italics in the original.

5. Malachi Martin, *The Keys of This Blood: The Struggle for World Dominion Between Pope John Paul II, Mikhail Gorbachev, and the Capitalist West* (New York: Simon and Schuster, 1990), 15, 17.

6. Ibid., 157.

7. Ibid., 287.

8. Ibid., 157, italics added.

PART TWO

The Land Beast of Revelation 13

Chapter 9

Revelation 13, the Land Beast, and the Image to the Beast

In order to interpret Revelation 13:11–18 properly, we have to understand the meaning of three symbols: the beast that arises from the land, an image that it sets up, and a mark that it requires every human being to receive. In this chapter and several that follow, we will examine the land beast and the image to the sea beast. We will examine the mark of the beast in several later chapters.

For a century and a half, Seventh-day Adventists have identified the land beast as the United States of America and the image to the beast as Protestantism. These conclusions seem very strange, for the land beast is extremely intolerant. Given the freedom of religion that has characterized America and American Protestantism for more than two hundred years, it seems incredible that the land beast and its image should symbolize this country and its Protestant churches. Nevertheless, that is what we have said and continue to say. This chapter will analyze the scriptural basis for our conclusion that the land beast represents the United States and that the image to the sea beast represents Protestantism.

IDENTIFYING THE LAND BEAST

Four characteristics of the land beast support the conclusion that it represents the United States of America.

The land beast is a *beast*

It sounds simple enough—almost redundant—to say that the land beast is a *beast*. Nevertheless, that is a significant point, for a beast in

Bible prophecy represents a nation—a major political power in the world. Daniel 7 describes a dream Daniel had in which he saw four great beasts arise out of the sea: a lion, a bear, a leopard, and a nondescript beast that I call a dragon. The angel who interpreted Daniel's dream told him that these four great beasts represented " ' "four kingdoms that will rise from the earth" ' " (Daniel 7:17; Babylon, Media-Persia, Greece, and Rome).

The land beast also represents a political power, and the United States is a political power. However, people could argue that the land beast represented the Roman Empire in John's day or any major political power of the two thousand years since. We need additional evidence in order to conclude that it represents the United States.

The land beast has global authority

Revelation 13 provides several clues that the land beast has global political authority:

- *"He exercised all the authority of the first beast on his behalf " (verse 12).* We saw in a previous chapter that the first beast of Revelation 13 is a global political power. Therefore, the land beast, which "exercise(s) all the authority of the first beast," must also be a global political power.
- He *"made the earth and its inhabitants worship the first beast" (verse 12).* The land beast has the political clout that is required to enforce false worship, not just within its own borders but also on "the earth and its inhabitants."
- *"He deceived the inhabitants of the earth"* and *"ordered them to set up an image in honor of the beast who was wounded by the sword and yet lived" (verse 14).* The land beast has the power to order the whole world to set up this image to the sea beast.

To put it in today's terms, the land beast is a global superpower. However, the fact that the land beast is a global superpower still doesn't identify it as the United States, because at the time John wrote Revelation, Rome was a superpower. Within the past several hundred years, France and England have been major world superpowers. And in the twentieth century, the Soviet Union was a global superpower. So Rome, France, England, the Soviet Union—the land beast, as a global superpower, could represent any of these. We need additional evidence in order to identify the land beast as the United States.

The land beast is an end-time power

Revelation 13:16, 17, says that the land beast will force all classes of people to "receive a mark on [their] right hand or on [their] forehead, so that no one could buy or sell unless he had the mark, which is the name of the beast." In Revelation 16, the first of seven plagues falls on "the people who had the mark of the beast and worshiped his image" (verse 2). These seven plagues are the last events to happen in the world before the second coming of Christ. Thus, the mark of the beast is clearly an end-time phenomenon, and therefore the land beast that enforces the mark must be an end-time superpower. The nations other than the United States that I mentioned in the paragraph above are no longer superpowers, so they do not match Revelation's description of the land beast. This book takes the position that we today live in the end time. The United States, then, is an end-time superpower, and thus fulfills this specification of the prophecy.

One other very significant point of evidence clearly establishes the United States as the land beast of Revelation 13:11–18.

The land beast is a Christian power

The word *lamb* occurs thirty-one times in Revelation, and in every instance but one it is a symbol of Christ. The one exception is Revelation 13:11, which describes the land beast as having "two horns like a lamb." The land beast is not Jesus Christ—it couldn't possibly be, the way it persecutes Christ's true worshipers. Nevertheless, it is "*like* a lamb." Applying this to a nation, we can say that the nation represented by the land beast is a professedly *Christian* nation.

When we put together the four characteristics of the land beast, it becomes very evident that it represents the United States:

- The land beast is a political power in the world, a nation.
- It has global authority—it is a global superpower.
- It is an end-time superpower.
- It is a Christian nation.

Only one nation in the world during the past two thousand years fits all of these specifications: the United States of America. *There is no other candidate.*

Some other conclusions

If the land beast describes the United States during the end time, we can draw several other significant conclusions about the future of this country. During most of American history, these conclusions have seemed incredible, and most of them probably still seem incredible to most people. That's why critics of the Adventist prophetic scenario have called our prediction for the future of the United States of America "wild" and "foolish." However, before you finish reading part 3 of this book, I believe you'll see that these conclusions really aren't so incredible after all.

The enforcement arm of the papacy. The medieval period in European history was a time of papal supremacy. The pope had the power to set up kings and remove kings, and the governments of Europe were expected to enforce papal doctrine and moral order. Most people are aware of the severe persecutions that took place because of the Inquisition, including the execution of heretics by such cruel methods as burning alive at the stake. However, the papacy itself didn't usually execute heretics. The papacy's religious courts heard the charges against the accused and passed sentence on those who were found guilty, but the church then handed the accused to the secular authority for punishment. Thus, *the state was the enforcement arm of the church.*

This is precisely the relationship that exists between the land beast and the sea beast in Revelation 13. Verse 12 says that the land beast "made the earth and its inhabitants worship the first beast." Verse 15 says that the land beast "was given power to give breath to the image of the first beast, so that it could both speak and cause all who refused to worship the image to be killed." In other words, the land beast enforces the worship and teachings of the sea beast.

A union of church and state. The United States Constitution requires that religion and government remain separate from each other. While Christianity is the dominant religion in America, it has never been the nation's official, legal religion. However, if the land beast of Revelation 13 is the United States, we can conclude that this nation's historic separation between government and religion will end someday. Christianity—and particularly, certain aspects of the Catholic form of Christianity—will become the official religion of the United States. This is clearly evident in

Revelation's description of the land beast, for it says that the land beast will set up an image of the sea beast, and this image will "cause all who refused to worship the image to be killed." This kind of religious persecution can happen only when religion and government are closely linked. *So, according to Revelation 13, church and state will be united in the United States someday.*

A persecuting power. Revelation says that the land beast will enforce its false worship with an iron fist. Anyone who refuses to receive the mark of the beast will be barred from carrying out any economic activity, for such people will not be allowed to buy or sell. And those who refuse to worship in the politically correct manner will be threatened with death! I know that it sounds incredible today to suggest that the United States will persecute religious dissenters someday, but keep reading. For now, let's identify the image to the beast.

Identifying the image to the beast

Revelation says that the land beast will set up an image to the sea beast and force the entire world to worship it. Anyone who refuses to worship the image can be killed, or at the very least, can be forbidden to carry on economic activity. What is this "image"? Adventists have historically identified it as Protestantism. Let's examine the evidence.

An image is a concrete representation—typically a statue, a painting, or a photograph—of something else. We should probably understand the image in Revelation 13 to be a statue. Several chapters back I pointed out that Revelation13 draws quite heavily on Daniel for its symbolism. The same is true of the image. You will recall that following King Nebuchadnezzar's vision of a metal image (Daniel 2), he built an image entirely of gold (chapter 3). Then he brought together all the leaders of the kingdom of Babylon and ordered them to bow down to his image or suffer death in a burning fiery furnace. It seems obvious that in describing the image that the land beast sets up, Revelation is borrowing from this story in Daniel.

While an image is a concrete representation of something else, it is not the same thing as what it represents. In order to be an image, it must be both similar and at the same time distinctly different from that which it represents. Fortunately, Revelation identifies the object that the image represents: It's an image of "the beast who was wounded by the sword and yet lived" (verse 14)—that is, the beast that arises out of the sea. We have already identified the sea beast as the papacy, so the image must duplicate the papacy in certain key respects. We need not expect that the image to the beast will be a literal statue; it represents an entity that has some of the chief characteristics of the papacy. I will mention five.

1. The papacy is an organization of human beings. Therefore, the image will be a human organization of some kind.
2. The papacy is a religious organization, so we can expect the image also to be a religious organization.
3. The papacy is a Christian religious organization, so this also should be true of its image.
4. The end-time papacy represented by the sea beast in Revelation 13 is very intolerant: It "make[s] war against the saints" (verse 7)—that is, it persecutes dissenters. In view of the fact that the land beast that sets up the image to the sea beast is horribly intolerant, we can reasonably conclude that the image it sets up will also be intolerant of dissenters.
5. The papacy throughout its history has been a very political organization, and we have seen that the end-time papacy will have global political power. Therefore, we can expect that its image will also have global political power.

Thus, if America is to set up an image to the beast, it seems safe to conclude that the entity the image represents will be a Christian religious organization that has great political power and is also very intolerant. Today's Christianity is divided into three major branches: Roman Catholic, Eastern Orthodox, and Protestant. The image of the sea beast will almost certainly be one of these. Obviously, we can exclude Catholicism since it is the original of which the image is a copy. This leaves us with Eastern Orthodox and Protestant Christianity. We can rule out Orthodox Christianity, since the United States is predominantly a Protestant nation. Therefore, the image that the land beast sets up will be Protestantism. That has been the historic Adventist interpretation of Revelation's image to the sea beast.

In conclusion, is it possible that at some point in the future the United States government will persecute religious dissenters? Is it conceivable that American Protestantism could come to reflect the political nature of the papacy and its intolerance? Or is the Adventist scenario of the end time simply wild, foolish speculation?

Could this really happen?

Keep reading!

Chapter 10

Church-State Separation in American History

Captain Kemble had just returned from a three-year voyage on the high seas. During that entire time, he hadn't seen his wife even once. So, when she threw open the door to welcome him home, his first impulse was to grab her, hold her tight, and give her a kiss. Which he did. Unfortunately, not everyone was as enthusiastic about Captain Kemble's outburst of affection for his wife. That "indecent" act cost Captain Kemble two hours in the stocks for "lewd and unseemly behavior." After all, he had kissed his wife "publicquely" on the Sabbath day!

You guessed it. Captain Kemble lived in the New England of the mid-seventeenth century, a time when the culture was dominated by Puritan notions of proper Sabbath (Sunday) observance, which the civil government enforced.

A traveler named Burnaby met an even worse fate. The Sabbath code in his colony stipulated that "whosoever shall prophane the Lords daye by doeing any seruill [*servile*—that is, ordinary] worke or such like abuses shall forfeite for euery such default ten shillings or be whipt." So when Burnaby kissed his wife on the street of his New England town on a Sunday, he was whipped soundly.

Following are some of the other Sabbath offenses that drew a punishment in Puritan New England:

- Captain Dennison of New Haven, Connecticut, was fined fifteen shillings for failing to attend church.

- A soldier was fined five shillings for "wetting a piece of an old hat to put in his shoe" to protect his foot.
- Elizabeth Eddy of Plymouth was fined ten shillings for wringing and hanging out clothes.
- Another Plymouth man was hauled before the court because he drove a yoke of oxen "without need" on the Sabbath.
- In 1670, John Lewis and Sarah Chapman were accused and tried for "sitting together on the Lord's Day under an apple tree in Goodman Chapman's Orchard."[1]

Not everyone was happy about this strict New England theocracy though. Roger Williams, for one, believed that religion should be totally voluntary. It was wrong, he claimed, for the civil government to enforce religious doctrine and practice.

Williams was one of the earliest advocates of church-state separation, not only in American history but also in world history. In 1635, Williams was the acting pastor of a church in Salem, Massachusetts, but his views were so controversial that on October 9, the colony voted to banish him the following January. Church-state union was still too strong in the colonies, and the idea of a secular state was too radical for the sensibilities of the Puritan leaders.

Fearing that he might be returned to England, Williams fled Salem in the middle of winter in spite of the fact that he had just recovered from a serious illness. For the next several months, he lived in the wilderness with Indian friends. Later he wrote, "I was sorely tossed for one fourteen weeks, in a bitter winter season, not knowing what bread or bed did mean."[2]

The following June, Williams negotiated with the Indians for land on which to establish a colony. He named his colony Providence, because he believed that God cared for him and his followers and had provided them the land they had obtained from the Indians. The charter that Williams drew up for his colony provided for liberty of conscience and a separation between civil and ecclesiastical authority. Eventually, Rhode Island united with Providence, with complete freedom of religion a basic part of the colony's charter. Many people came to Rhode Island seeking the freedom to practice their religion according to the dictates of their own consciences. Among these were Baptists, Quakers, and Jews. Williams was baptized as a Baptist in 1639, and he organized the first Baptist church in America.

Williams vs. the Puritans

Roger Williams and the Puritans reflect two opposing views of the relationship that should exist between religion and government, between the church and the state. Williams, as we have seen, was one of the early visionaries for the secular state with its separation of religion and government. The Puritan view dominated the colonial years. One of the darker sides of the Puritan view of church-state relationships occurred in Salem, Massachusetts, between January 1792 and January 1793. Most people have heard of the Salem witch trials. These trials were not a church-state issue in the strictest sense, because the charges against the "witches" were brought by individuals, not by any church. Nevertheless, the charges, the trials, the convictions, and the resulting executions reflected Puritan notions of proper religion and of government enforcement of that religion. The trials occurred in the context of community hysteria over alleged satanic activity on the part of the accused. By the time the hysteria had subsided, nineteen people had been executed—six men and thirteen women.

Fortunately, some people recognized and condemned the madness. A Puritan clergyman, Increase Mather, published a document in October titled "Cases of Conscience Concerning Evil Spirits," in which he argued that "it were better that Ten Suspected Witches should escape, than that the Innocent Person should be Condemned."[3] Mather's statement reflects the concept of "innocent until proven guilty" that has become a basic principle of American jurisprudence. The online Wikipedia encyclopedia noted that the impact of the Salem witch trials "was so profound that it helped end the influence of the Puritan faith on the governing of New England."[4]

However, the idea that the state should support religion was still alive and well in the New England of the eighteenth century. At the time of the American Revolution in 1776, seven of the thirteen original colonies had established churches whose pastors were paid by the colonial or state governments.* When these colonies became states, they maintained their established churches, but by 1840, they had all abandoned their support of religion. Thus, Williams's view of church-state relationships has predominated throughout most of American history.

---

*Connecticut, Georgia, Massachusetts, New Hampshire, North Carolina, South Carolina, and Virginia.

The Puritan view has always had the support of a minority though, and that minority is rapidly gaining influence in the United States. While very few people today would favor a return to a Puritan theocracy, a growing minority wants to change the historic secular government with its separation of church and state that has largely characterized the United States since 1776. Thus, it's important that we examine the foundation of religious freedom in America today and seek to understand the basis on which it is being challenged.

The uniqueness of the American system of government

Most Americans probably take their system of government so much for granted that they never pause to think about the principles on which it is based. The foundational principle is this: *Government exists by the consent of the governed.* In other words, the people create the government. This was a radical innovation in the history of nations. For hundreds of years, European governments had been imposed on people by kings and popes. Authority flowed from the top down; the ruler made the laws and enforced them. The people had no choice regarding who would be their king, because, for better or for worse, when a king died, his son, or occasionally his daughter, succeeded him—either that, or a usurper managed to take the throne by force. If the people didn't like their king and the laws he made, there was little or nothing they could do about it. As Richard Viguerie and David Franke put it in their book, *America's Right Turn*, "In the beginning America was just an extension of the Old World idea that the establishments—whether Puritan, Anglican, or agents of the British crown—set the rules, usually under the pretense of divine right. It was up to the rest of society to work and live within those rules."[5]

The uniqueness of the American system is that *the people create their own government and choose its rulers.* Here, a constitution that defines the responsibilities of the rulers and the rights of the people spells out the relationship that exists between the governed and those whom they elect to govern them. And rulers hold their office for a limited time only, after which they must face reelection by the people. If the people don't like how a particular ruler has governed, they can replace him or her at the next election. Leonard W. Levy summarized it well: "The majestic opening of the preamble [to the American Constitution], 'We the People,' summons forth the still radically democratic idea that the government of the United States exists to serve the people, not the people to serve the government. . . . American citizens have the duty as well as the right to keep government from falling into error, not the other way around."[6]

Separation of church and state is another basic principle of the American government. This concept means at least three things. First, it means that religion and government are to operate in separate spheres. The church can't control the government and the government can't control the church—neither can tell the other what to do. Second, it means that government won't finance religion. It won't pay the salaries of the clergy, and it won't pay for the promulgation of religious doctrines. And third, separation of church and state means that the laws of the state will be based on secular moral principles, not the moral principles of any church or holy book. When legislators frame laws dealing with moral issues, they will consult the common sense of the citizenry, not the Bible or the Koran or the teachings of a particular religion or church. Any civil government that has a form of church-state separation that includes these three characteristics is likely to be fairly free of persecution.

When the U.S. Constitution was presented to the nation by the Framers for ratification, it contained no statement about the relationship between government and religion. The delegates to the constitutional convention didn't believe that such a statement was necessary. They said the government couldn't act on any issue that wasn't mentioned in the Constitution, and since religion wasn't mentioned, the government couldn't act in that sphere. But several of the states refused to ratify the Constitution until they received assurance that a bill of rights would be added that included the right to religious liberty. When that assurance was granted, the last of the necessary nine states ratified the Constitution, and it has been the law of the land in the United States ever since.

The Bill of Rights is made up of ten amendments to the Constitution, the first of which states: "Congress shall make no law respecting an establishment of religion, or prohibiting the free exercise thereof; or abridging the freedom of speech, or of the press; or the right of the people peaceably to assemble, and to petition the government for a redress of grievances."

The reason for the First Amendment

Our interest is in the first two clauses of this amendment, which deal with religious freedom: "Congress shall make no law respecting an establishment of religion, or prohibiting the free exercise thereof." Why was religious freedom so important that it became the very first freedom mentioned in the Bill of Rights?* The answer is very simple: *The memory of religious persecution by both Catholics and Protestants was still fresh in the minds of America's citizens.*

Protestants were still smarting from Catholic persecution in Europe. And minority religions such as the Baptists and the Quakers were even closer to the Puritan persecution that they had endured during the colonial period. Several Quakers had been hanged in Massachusetts in the late 1650s and early 1660s, including Mary Dyer, who was executed on the Boston Common in Massachusetts on June 1, 1660, because she refused to give up her faith.[7] In the late seventeenth century, the Anglicans of Virginia succeeded in getting laws passed that refused the Quakers the right "to baptize their children, prohibited their assembly, and provided for their execution if they returned after expulsion."[8] And, of course, there were the hysterical Salem witch trials that I mentioned a few paragraphs back.

Even as late as the Revolutionary era itself, the Baptists in Massachusetts were frequently fined, whipped, and locked in jail for "crimes" related to their faith.[9] Between 1765 and 1778, clergy in Virginia had to get a license from the state in order to preach, and Baptists were refused licenses. Upwards of fifty Baptist ministers were jailed during this period simply because they preached without a license. Five Baptist ministers were jailed in Fredericksburg, Virginia, in 1768, because, as the prosecutor said, "These men are great disturbers of the peace; they cannot meet a man upon the road, but they must ram a text of scripture down his throat." The judge offered to withhold the sentence on the condition that the Baptist ministers swear off preaching for a year and a day. "Refusing to accept the condition placed on their freedom, instead they chanted hymns all the way from the courthouse to the jail."[10]

Religious dissenters were persecuted in medieval Europe and during the American colonial period because government supported religion financially and enforced its doctrines and moral codes. Also, religious leaders had a major hand in drafting laws and appointing rulers. So, the

---

*The original Bill of Rights as presented by Congress to the states had twelve amendments, the first two of which failed the ratification process. That's how the religion amendment became the first.

laws of the religion became the laws of the civil government. Government and religion were intertwined in a relationship that we call "union of church and state." This inevitably led to the persecution of dissenters and to conflicts between the interests of the state and the interests of the church.

All of this was on the minds of the Framers of the American system of government when they wrote the Declaration of Independence, the Constitution, and the Bill of Rights. It explains the importance to them of the foundational principle enshrined in the First Amendment's two religion clauses: *Government and religion are to be kept separate.* America's citizens and their leaders in the late eighteenth century wanted to avoid the persecution of dissenters and the conflicts between religion and government that had characterized European history and their own colonial period, so they created a system in which government and religion were split from each other. Religion was to keep its hands off government, and government was to keep its hands off religion. This principle is summarized in the well-known phrase "separation of church and state." It's an extremely important principle that Americans and other Western countries simply must not forget if they want to maintain the free societies that we have today.

The French Revolution was a bitter rebellion against all religion. The French Parliament actually banned religion and proclaimed an atheist state—a condition that existed for several years during the 1790s. The American Revolution, which occurred ten to fifteen years prior to the French Revolution, was far different, for in keeping church and state separate, the Framers were not motivated by any hostility toward religion. Indeed, they acknowledged that their experiment in democracy could succeed only in a nation where the people were essentially religious. James Madison wrote, for example, that "belief in a God All Powerful wise and good is essential to the moral order of the world."[11] George Washington said, "Reason and experience both forbid us to expect that national morality can prevail, in exclusion of religious principle."[12] And John Adams wrote, "Our Constitution was made only for a moral and religious people. It is wholly inadequate to the government of any other."[13]

This is not to say that the Framers were devout, Bible-thumping Christians who attended church every week. They were a unique brand of secularists who appreciated the positive contribution that religion

could make to the life of the nation. Thomas Jefferson was a Deist*
who at one time spent several evenings in the White House with a Bible in one hand and a razor in the other, cutting out the passages from the Gospels that contradicted his understanding of Jesus' teachings. Yet in the introduction to the Declaration of Independence, which he authored, he could speak of "the laws of nature and of nature's God," and in the preamble, he said, "All Men are created equal . . . *by their Creator.*" Benjamin Franklin also was a Deist who attacked religious dogma. However, he also said, "If men are so wicked with religion, what would they be if without it?"[14] And the thirteenth on his list of virtues to be practiced was to "imitate Jesus [religion] and Socrates [secular]."[15]

The Framers of the American Constitution recognized the *importance* of religion, but they also were convinced that their new government couldn't *sponsor* religion. James Madison summed up this principle in one short sentence: "Religion flourishes in greater purity without than with the aid of government."[16] He also said, "The number, the industry, and the morality of the Priesthood, & devotion of the people have been manifestly increased by the total separation of the Church from the State."[17] The state should stay out of the way of religion—turn it loose, let it go its own way. The state's role is to *protect* religion, not to *promote* it. The state should especially protect religion's freedom to teach, to persuade, and to evangelize. But the state shouldn't become involved in preaching, teaching, or leading out in any acts of public worship, nor should it finance any of these activities. This is what the expression "separation of church and state" means.

The secular and the religious in America: separate but cooperative

It's crucial to understand that *the American brand of church-state separation was the result of a unique cooperation between secularism and religion.* In communist countries, secularism so predominates that religion is tightly controlled. At the other extreme, the church has had a dominant influence over the state throughout most of Spain's history. Only in America was the government founded on cooperation between the two. And the credit for this goes to both religious and secular people at the time of the founding of the Republic.

---

*Deists hold something of a "watchmaker" view of God: He created the world and then left it unattended to run on the laws He had established.

Not all religious people were happy about church-state separation. The two majority religious groups in the country, Episcopalians and Congregationalists, didn't like giving up the support they received from the state. However, Baptists, Quakers, and members of other minority religions that had been severely suppressed during the colonial period were strong supporters of church-state separation. And on the secular side, Founders such as Jefferson, Franklin, Madison, and others were secular people who recognized the good in both secularism and religion. In his book *American Gospel*, Jon Meacham, the managing editor of *Newsweek*, said: "Neither conveniently devout nor wholly unbelieving, Jefferson surveyed and staked out an American middle ground between the ferocity of evangelizing Christians on one side and the contempt for religion by secular *philosophes*[*] on the other. The right would like Jefferson to be a soldier of faith, the left an American Voltaire. He was, depending on the moment, both and neither; he was, in other words, a lot like many of us."[18]

Two forces in the eighteenth century contributed to this cooperation between religion and secularism. On the religious side, from the time that the first colonists settled on the North American continent, the country has always been religious. A striking manifestation of this—a revival called the Great Awakening—occurred under the leadership of Jonathan Edwards and George Whitfield early in the eighteenth century. At the same time, during most of that century, a secular movement called the Enlightenment was taking place all over Europe and America. These two forces blended in the formation of the American government. The point is that *historically, in America, religious people have appreciated secularists and secularists have appreciated religious people.* Each has been willing to give and take and compromise in order to reach an accommodation that gave to each side most of what they wanted. Each accepted a certain amount of public expression of the other's views as the price to pay for peace between them.

Civil religion

The public expression of religion in America has traditionally been called "civil religion" or "ceremonial deism." Jon Meacham, in his book

---

[*]The *philosophes* (French for philosophers) were French intellectuals of the eighteenth-century Enlightenment who believed in the supremacy of human reason and questioned religious authority. Many of them were Deists, and some were quite critical of Christianity. See http://en.wikipedia.org/wiki/Philosophes.

American Gospel, calls it "public religion."[19] Public or civil religion is the recognition by government of a Supreme Being while leaving the promotion of religion and the framing of its doctrines to the churches and the individual believer. For example, in the Declaration of Independence, Jefferson could speak of a Creator and "the laws of nature and of nature's God." Civil or public religion allows us to have "In God We Trust" on our coins and "one nation, under God" in the Pledge of Allegiance. It allows us to have chaplains in the United States Congress and the military. There's always been tension between the secular and the religious. Historically, some people have wanted more religion in government and others less. But the nation's presidents, legislators, and judges have managed to frame a balance through most of our history that has kept the majority of us reasonably satisfied, if not totally happy.

Americans owe a debt of gratitude to the secularists of the eighteenth-century Enlightenment, who fostered the secular state with its separation of religion and government. We owe a debt of gratitude to the fervently religious people exemplified by the eighteenth-century Great Awakening, who recognized the value of a secular government with its separation of church and state. It would be difficult to say who has made the greater contribution to the grand experiment, the secular or the religious.

We also owe a debt of gratitude to our nation's Founders, who were wise enough to frame a constitution that incorporated a balance between the secular and the religious. And finally, we owe a debt of gratitude to both the political leaders and the common people who, for more than two hundred years, made this balance between the secular and the religious actually work in the life of the nation. It's because of this delicate balance that we have enjoyed so much freedom of religion throughout our history. Jon Meacham said, "A tolerant, pluralistic democracy in which religious and secular forces continually contend against one another may not be ideal, but it has proven to be the most practical and enduring arrangement of human affairs—and we must guard that arrangement well."[20]

Church-state separation in United States history

By and large, Americans have supported the principle of church-state separation from the very beginning of the nation's history. A moment ago, I noted a statement by James Madison that "the number, the industry, and the morality of the Priesthood, & devotion of the people have been manifestly increased by the total separation of the Church from the

State." In a letter dated January 1, 1802, Thomas Jefferson wrote to the Danbury Baptist Association in Virginia, "I contemplate with sovereign reverence that act of the whole American people which declared that their legislature should 'make no law respecting an establishment of religion, or prohibiting the free exercise thereof,' thus building a wall of separation between church and State."[21] The French historian and political thinker Alexis de Tocqueville, after traveling around America in the early nineteenth century and talking with many American clergymen, said that "all attributed the peaceful dominion that religion exercises in their country principally to the complete separation of church and state."[22]

President Andrew Jackson spoke of "the security which religion now enjoys in this country in its complete separation from the political concerns of the General Government."[23] President John Tyler "offered his thoughts on religion and freedom: 'The United States have adventured upon a great and noble experiment, . . . that of total separation of church and state.' "[24] President Ulysses Grant said, "Leave the matter of religion to the family altar, the church, and the private school, supported entirely by private contributions. Keep the church and state forever separate."[25] And more recently, on the religious side, evangelist Billy Graham said, "In America any and all religions have the right to exist and propagate what they stand for. We enjoy the separation of church and state, and no sectarian religion has ever been—and we pray God, ever will be—imposed on us."[26]

Challenges to separation

This is not to say that there have been no challenges to the concept of church-state separation in our history. In 1863, the Covenanters, a small, breakaway Presbyterian group in Allegheny, Pennsylvania, proposed an amendment to the preamble of the United States Constitution. The words of the proposed amendment are in italics between brackets: "We, the People of the United States [*recognizing the being and attributes of Almighty God, the Divine Authority of the Holy Scriptures, the law of God as the paramount rule, and Jesus, the Messiah, the Savior and Lord of all*], in order to form a more perfect union . . ." etc.[27]

This proposal went nowhere, but the Covenanters merged with other interested parties to form, in 1864, the National Reform Association (NRA—not to be confused with today's National Rifle Association!). The NRA's primary objective was to amend the American Constitution to acknowledge God as the nation's divine authority and establish Christianity as the nation's official religion. The preamble to the NRA's constitution, though a bit lengthy, is instructive in light of similar efforts that are being made in America today:

> Believing that Almighty God is the source of all power and authority in civil government, that the Lord Jesus Christ is the Ruler of Nations, and that the revealed Will of God is of Supreme authority in civil affairs;
>
> Remembering that this country was settled by Christian men, with Christian ends in view, and that they gave a distinctly Christian character to the institutions which they established;
>
> Perceiving the subtle and persevering attempts which are made to prohibit the reading of the Bible in our Public Schools, to overthrow our Sabbath laws, to corrupt the Family, to abolish the Oath, Prayer in our National and State Legislatures, Days of Fasting and Thanksgiving and other Christian features of our institutions, and so to divorce the American Government from all connection with the Christian religion; . . .
>
> Believing that a written Constitution ought to contain explicit evidence of the Christian character and purpose of the nation which frames it, and perceiving that the silence of the Constitution of the United States in this respect is used as an argument against all that is Christian in the usage and administration of our Government;
>
> We, citizens of the United States, do associate ourselves under the following ARTICLES, and pledge ourselves to God and to one another, to labor, through wise and lawful means, for the ends herein set forth:[28]

The document went on to list several articles of incorporation. Article II is particularly significant:

> The object of this Society shall be to maintain existing Christian features in the American Government, to promote needed reforms in the action of the government touching the Sabbath, the institution of the Family, the religious element in Education, the Oath, and Public Morality as affected by the liquor traffic and other kindred evils; and to secure such an amendment to the

Constitution of the United States as will declare the nation's allegiance to Jesus Christ and its acceptance of the moral laws of
the Christian religion, and so indicate that this is a Christian nation, and place all the Christian laws, institutions and usages of
our government on an undeniable legal basis in the fundamental
law of the land.[29]

The NRA actually succeeded in getting its proposed constitutional
amendment submitted to the Senate Judiciary Committee in late 1864.
However, the committee refused to pass it on to the full Senate.

My reason for sharing this rather lengthy bit of information about the
National Reform Association is to call attention to the fact that it went
basically nowhere. Most readers of this book probably have never even
heard of the National Reform Association. *The point is that the principle
of keeping government and religion apart from each other—church-state
separation, if you please—won the day, and it did so very easily.*

Anti-Catholicism and church-state separation

A strong anti-Catholicism pervaded American public opinion
throughout the nineteenth century, especially during the latter part of
the century when immigrants were flocking to our shores from the
Catholic countries of Europe, particularly Ireland, Italy, and Poland.
This anti-Catholicism resulted in some unfortunate incidents of persecution, which I will mention in a later chapter. However, American
anti-Catholicism during this period was prompted in part by a fear that
the Catholic principle of church-state *union* might be imposed on the
United States. As recently as 1960, when John F. Kennedy, a Catholic,
was the Democratic candidate for president of the United States,
America's conservative Protestants, including Southern Baptists and
most charismatic groups, were so fearful of the danger that his Catholicism posed to church-state separation that they refused to support
him in the election until he took a vow endorsing that constitutional
principle. Kennedy took that vow at a meeting of the Houston, Texas,
ministerial association in September 1960. He said:

I believe in an America where the separation of church and
state is absolute—where no Catholic prelate would tell the President (should he be Catholic) how to act, and no Protestant minister would tell his parishioners for whom to vote—where no

church or church school is granted any public funds or political preference—and where no man is denied public office merely because his religion differs from the President who might appoint him or the people who might elect him.

I believe in an America that is officially neither Catholic, Protestant nor Jewish—where no public official either requests or accepts instructions on public policy from the Pope, the National Council of Churches or any other ecclesiastical source—where no religious body seeks to impose its will directly or indirectly upon the general populace or the public acts of its officials—and where religious liberty is so indivisible that an act against one church is treated as an act against all.[30]

My point is that as recently as 1960, the majority of America's fundamentalist and evangelical Protestants were strong supporters of the principle of church-state separation. Unfortunately, a significant number of fundamentalists and evangelicals are strongly criticizing church-state separation today. How that trend has developed in the United States is the topic of the next several chapters.

---

1. The information about Puritan Sabbath keeping in this chapter comes from the online book by Alice Morse Earle, *The Sabbath in Puritan New England* (Project Gutenberg Literary Archive Foundation, 2005), chapter 10. See http://www.gutenberg.org/dirs/etext05/8sabb10h.htm#17.

2. "Roger Williams (theologian)," Wikipedia, http://en.wikipedia.org/wiki/Roger_Williams_%28theologian%29.

3. "Salem witch trials," Wikipedia, http://en.wikipedia.org/wiki/Salem_Witch_Trials.

4. Ibid.

5. Richard Viguerie and David Franke, *America's Right Turn: How Conservatives Used New and Alternative Media to Take Power* (Chicago: Bonus Books, 2004), 20.

6. Leonard W. Levy, *Original Intent and the Framers' Constitution* (Chicago: Ivan R. Dee, 1988), x.

7. "Mary Dyer," Wikipedia, http://en.wikipedia.org/wiki/Mary_Dyer.

8. Mark R. Levin, *Men in Black: How the Supreme Court Is Destroying America* (Washington, D.C.: Regnery Publishing, 2005), 36.

9. Forrest Church, ed., *The Separation of Church and State: Writings of a Fundamental Freedom by America's Founders* (Boston: Beacon Press, 2004), 17.

10. Ibid., 3, 4.

11. Jon Meacham, *American Gospel: God, the Founding Fathers, and the Making of a Nation* (New York: Random House, 2006), 228.

12. *Address of George Washington, President of the United States . . . Preparatory to His Declination* (Baltimore: George and Henry S. Keatinge, 1796), 22, 23.

13. Charles Frances Adams, ed., *The Works of John Adams, Second President of the United States* (Boston: Little, Brown and Company, 1854), 9:229.

14. In a letter to Thomas Paine; see "Benjamin Franklin's Letter to Thomas Paine," WallBuilders, http://www.wallbuilders.com/resources/search/detail.php?ResourceID=93.

15. "Benjamin Franklin," Wikipedia, http://en.wikipedia.org/wiki/Benjamin _Franklin#Public_life.

16. James Madison in a letter to Edward Livingston, July 10, 1822, cited in "Pure Religion," *Liberty*, December 2005, 13.

17. Cited in *Church and State*, April 2006, 24.

18. Meacham, 4.

19. Ibid., 25.

20. Ibid., 33.

21. Ibid., 264.

22. Ibid., 78, 80.

23. Ibid., 111.

24. Ibid., 134, 135.

25. Ibid., 143.

26. Ibid., 214.

27. "The NRA (National Reform Association) and the Christian Amendment," http://candst.tripod.com/nra.htm.

28. Ibid.

29. Ibid.

30. Cited in George J. Marlin, *The American Catholic Voter: 200 Years of Political Impact* (South Bend, Ind.: St. Augustine's Press, 2004), 254.

CHAPTER 11

The Rise of
the Conservative
Movement in America

I still remember the presidential election in the United States in November 1964. At the time, I was the pastor of the very small Adventist church in the wind-blown town of Mojave, California. My wife and I went to the polls shortly before they closed in the late afternoon. By then it was obvious from the news reports that Lyndon Johnson had won by a landslide. I joked with a friend that it was almost pointless to vote. In the most lopsided election since 1824, Goldwater received 38.5 percent of the vote to Johnson's 61.1 percent. Barry Goldwater lost big time! For those who are familiar with American politics, Goldwater garnered 52 electoral votes to Johnson's 486. Goldwater carried only his home state of Arizona and five states in the Deep South: Alabama, Mississippi, Georgia, North Carolina, and Louisiana.

However, what most people took to be a tremendous loss was to a few people a huge success. The story started about ten years earlier, back in the mid-1950s. At the time, Eastern liberal politicians controlled both the Democratic and the Republican parties. However, a small conservative movement began to grow, fueled by the growing threat of communism. The few hardheaded conservatives in the country objected to what they perceived as the liberal establishment's accommodation to communism, and they began to talk among themselves. They wrote some books and published several magazines, the most influential of which were *Human Events* and William F. Buckley's *National Review*.

In the late 1950s, Barry Goldwater emerged as the leader of this conservative movement. By the time of the 1960 presidential campaign, the

117

conservatives had gained enough strength that at the Republican National Convention, they managed to get the name of their standard-bearer placed in nomination for president. Goldwater didn't win the nomination, but he energized his troops when he took the stand to make a speech. He said, " 'This country, and its majesty, is too great for any man, be he conservative or liberal, to stay home and not work just because he doesn't agree. Let's grow up, conservatives! We want to take this party back, and I think someday we can. Let's get to work!' "[1]

That statement was, to say the least, a portent of things to come.

By 1964, the conservative movement had gained sufficient strength that conservatives managed to get Barry Goldwater nominated as the Republican candidate for president. However, with the conservative movement in its infancy and with both political parties and the print and broadcast media overwhelmingly controlled by liberals, Goldwater was lucky to have carried six states.

Far from being discouraged by their standard-bearer's overwhelming defeat, though, conservatives were elated—not by the loss but by the fact that they had managed to get one of their own *nominated* to the highest office in the land. This was *victory*, and it encouraged the troops to keep pushing on. Hadn't Goldwater himself told them, "We want to take this party back, and I think someday we *can*"?[2] The troops determined that someday they *would.* They had, after all, just persuaded more than twenty-seven million American voters to support their candidate.

There was no way, however, that conservatives could get their message across to the American public through the print and broadcast media. These were tightly controlled by liberal publishers and politicians. So the conservatives turned to direct mail to "sell" their product. And there was an advantage to this: It was "under the radar." The conservatives could build their movement without the liberal establishment realizing what was going on.

Turning the tide

And victory did come. During the 1970s, Ronald Reagan replaced Barry Goldwater as the conservatives' favorite politician, and the movement continued to grow, especially through the use of direct mail. By 1980, the movement had evolved to the point where Ronald Reagan was nominated as the Republican Party's presidential candidate, and he won by a landslide: 50.7 percent of the popular vote to Jimmy Carter's 41 percent. Even more significantly, Reagan won the election in all but six states, which meant that he garnered 489 electoral votes to Carter's 49.

Four years later, Reagan won every state except Minnesota, the home state of his Democratic opponent, Walter Mondale. In that election, Reagan won 525 electoral votes to Mondale's 13! Part of Reagan's success was Reagan himself. He deserved his nickname, the Great Communicator. However, it was the conservatives who gave him a national platform. For all his communication skills, it's doubtful that he would ever have been elected president of the United States without the tireless efforts of the conservative movement.

George H. W. Bush (Bush I) was elected president in 1988, again with the help of conservatives. However, Bush was only a conservative of sorts. He never did have the warm support of the majority of conservative voters, and when a charismatic Bill Clinton came along in 1992, he defeated Bush easily.

With Bush's defeat, some political pundits wrote the epitaph for the conservative movement. The midterm election in 1994 shocked them out of their complacency. The Democrats had held a virtual lock on both houses of Congress for the previous sixty years, but in 1994, it was the Democrats out and the Republicans in, both in the Senate and in the House of Representatives! In the Senate, the Democrats lost eight seats to the Republicans, giving the Republicans a four-seat majority. The Democrats' catastrophe was even worse in the House of Representatives, where they lost fifty-four seats to the Republicans, giving the Republicans a twenty-six-seat majority. And pundits of all stripes agreed that it was the conservatives who made the difference. Republicans continued to dominate the House of Representatives for the next twelve years, and with the exception of the 108th Congress between 2002 and 2004, they dominated the Senate as well.

Even more significant was the election of George W. Bush, the son of George H. W. Bush, as president of the United States in 2000.* Bush II was—and is—a true conservative. Far more than his father and Ronald Reagan, he toed the conservative political line. In one of the most significant decisions of his career as president, Bush nominated two conservative judges to the United States Supreme Court: John Roberts as chief justice, and Samuel Alito as an associate justice. With

---

*George W. Bush actually garnered fewer popular votes nationally than did his Democratic challenger, Al Gore, but he won more electoral votes. The key state was Florida, where the vote was so close that the Democrats challenged it in court. After several back-and-forth battles, the United States Supreme Court upheld Florida's votes, giving the election to Bush.

these appointments, conservatives held a dominant influence in all three branches of the United States government. *Conservatives had finally come into their own!*

Talk radio

Another powerful political force in the United States today is conservative talk radio. It began with Rush Limbaugh, whose daily program, *The Rush Limbaugh Show,* lampoons liberal people and causes. Limbaugh began broadcasting in Sacramento, California, in 1984. Several years later, he moved to New York City, and in 1988, he syndicated his program. As of this writing, Limbaugh's audience is estimated at between fourteen and twenty million listeners per week, making it the largest radio talk show audience in the United States.[3] Other conservative talk show hosts during the first decade of the twenty-first century are Sean Hannity, Bill O'Reilly, Michael Savage, and Laura Ingram. O'Reilly's cable TV program, *The O'Reilly Factor* on the Fox News Channel, attracts an estimated 2.2 million viewers. These talk shows push a conservative political philosophy and jab the liberal left. There is no question in my mind that Limbaugh and his fellow commentators are a powerful force that is pushing the American electorate toward a conservative political philosophy that will influence elections in this country for years to come.

However, the rise of the conservative movement in America during the last half of the twentieth century is only part of the story. Even more significant for our study is the influence of religion in the conservative movement during this time. As Timothy Byrne put it in his book *Catholic Bishops in American Politics,* "The alliance between religious leaders and political operatives that burst on the scene in the late 1970s was the result of a carefully implemented strategy to mobilize new voters, build new political coalitions, and effect a lasting realignment of the American electorate."[4]

The success of this strategy is history, as we shall see.

---

1. Cited by Richard A. Viguerie and David Franke in *America's Right Turn: How Conservatives Used New and Alternative Media to Take Power* (Chicago: Bonus Books, 2004), 67.

2. Ibid. Italics added.

3. "Rush Limbaugh," Wikipedia, http://en.wikipedia.org/wiki/Rush_Limbaugh.

4. Timothy Byrne, *Catholic Bishops in American History* (Princeton, N.J.: Princeton University Press, 1991), 90.

CHAPTER 12

The Rise of the Religious Right in America

George Rappleyea was the manager of a mining outfit, the Cumberland Coal and Iron Company, down in the backwaters of Tennessee in 1925. George liked publicity; he had a flair for the dramatic that could stir it up; and he saw an opportunity in a law—the Butler Act—that the Tennessee state legislature had just passed. The law stated, "It shall be unlawful for any teacher in any of the Universities, Normals and all other public schools of the State which are supported in whole or in part by the public school funds of the State, to teach any theory that denies the story of the Divine Creation of man as taught in the Bible, and to teach instead that man has descended from a lower order of animals."[1]

You're probably wondering what kind of opportunity for a publicity stunt George Rappleyea saw in Tennessee's antievolution law. Precisely this: The American Civil Liberties Union had offered to defend anyone who violated the new law.

George approached the town fathers with a proposal: Why not arrange for a local high school teacher to teach evolution in his classroom, get him arrested and charged, and then call in the American Civil Liberties Union to defend him? The controversy that the trial generated would put the town of Dayton on the map.

The locals liked the idea, and they commissioned George to make the arrangements. So George pitched the idea to John Scopes, a substitute science teacher in the local high school. Scopes agreed, and a few days later he devoted a class period to the theory of evolution. On May 25, he was arrested and charged with violating Tennessee's new Butler Act.

Then the American Civil Liberties Union made good on their promise, and you know the rest of the story.

"The Scopes monkey trial," as it became known, would almost certainly have been a minor blip in the history of American jurisprudence were it not for one simple fact: It pitted conservative religion against liberal secularism. The publicity was enormous. The nation's major newspapers sent more than a hundred reporters to cover the trial, and they telegraphed back more than 165,000 words *per day* to their home offices. For days, the trial made the front page of nearly every major newspaper in the country and many smaller ones. Chicago's WGN radio station and its announcer, Quin Ryan, reported on the proceedings live each day—the first on-the-scene coverage of a trial in the history of broadcasting.[2] George Rappleyea's publicity stunt paid off big time! Dayton, Tennessee, has been a famous name in American culture ever since. Books have been written about the trial; Hollywood has produced a film about it; and little old Dayton is guaranteed a secure place in world history books till the Lord comes.

By now you're probably wondering what on earth the Scopes monkey trial in the early 1920s had to do with the rise of the Religious Right in America during the second half of the twentieth century. After all, the ridicule that America's conservative Christians suffered from the trial pushed them underground for the next several decades. They hunkered down, backed out of politics, and held themselves aloof from social controversy. How could that have helped the emergence of the Religious Right fifty years later?

Allow me to give you a bit of background.

The rise of America's conservative religions

Liberal theology made deep inroads into mainstream American Protestantism during the second half of the nineteenth century and continuing on into the twentieth century. Liberal theologians denied the supernatural, including the miracles of Jesus, His virgin birth, and His bodily resurrection. They also denied the inspiration and authority of the Bible as God's Word, and they increasingly abandoned the biblical account of Creation, replacing it with the theory of evolution. Early in the twentieth century, conservative religious leaders struck back with a four-volume set of books called *The Fundamentals*. These books upheld the traditional Christian teachings that liberalism denied. The movement that sprang up from their publication came to be known as *fundamentalism*, and people who held to these beliefs were known as *fundamentalists*.

The jury ruled that John Scopes was guilty of the crime with which he was charged. Thus, fundamentalists won in the court of law. But they lost in the court of public opinion. To this day, the Scopes monkey trial is viewed as a major gain for science and secularism and a huge setback for conservative religion. Secular people heaped ridicule on fundamentalism and fundamentalists. That's why, following the trial, fundamentalists backed almost completely away from politics and involvement in social issues. Their job, they said, was the proclamation of the gospel and the salvation of souls, not political action.

However, while in one sense the trial was a huge and embarrassing loss, it did hand religious conservatives a major benefit: It gave them the perfect cause around which to rally their troops.* The issue wasn't just the creation-evolution controversy, important as that was. The issue was the whole liberal agenda, including its rejection of the supernatural, its denial of Christ's virgin birth and His resurrection, its treating the Bible like any other piece of secular literature rather than as the inspired Word of God, etc. All of these issues were challenging Christianity at the time, especially Protestantism.** So fundamentalists rolled up their sleeves and went to work winning souls to their conservative brand of religion. Between 1926 and 1940, Southern Baptists grew by almost 1.5 million members, and the Assemblies of God quadrupled their membership. Kevin Philips, in his book *American Theocracy*, commented that "evangelical, fundamentalist, and Pentecostal religion, far from evaporating or stagnating in a backwater during the early twentieth century, seem to have been a gathering force, like an incoming tide."[3]

During this same period, mainstream Protestantism shrank about as significantly as conservative Protestantism expanded. But here is an important point to note: In spite of their declining numbers, the pastors, priests, and members of the mainline Protestant denominations were the educated elite in the nation, and they dominated its politics during the first three-fourths of the twentieth century. Evangelical and fundamentalist

---

*Another benefit that fundamentalists gained from the Scopes monkey trial was the reluctance of school textbook publishers for the next three decades to deal with evolution, lest they be challenged in court. Not till the 1960s did public school textbooks deal at length with evolution.

**Seventh-day Adventists share the basic convictions of conservative Christians, including the reliability of the Genesis account of Creation and the Flood, the supernatural, the virgin birth and resurrection of Christ, and the inspiration of the Bible.

Protestants weren't interested. They were too busy winning souls. *They were busy growing.*

But fundamentalist Protestants were growing "under the radar." Very few social scientists paid them any attention whatsoever. After all, the elite presumed, they were simpletons, ignoramuses—useful as servants and laborers perhaps, but not much more. So, most of the upper class were cheerfully unaware of what was happening just outside their own backdoor. *They failed to realize that the decline in the membership of their own mainstream denominations and the dramatic rise in the membership of the fundamentalist and evangelical denominations was bound, in time, to translate into a significant shift in political power.*

The rise of the Religious Right

It's probably reasonable to say that the Religious Right was born on a snowy day in January 1979. Ed McAteer, Paul Weyrich, Howard Phillips, and Robert Billings were leaders in America's conservative movement who were intent on bending American politics toward a more conservative stance. The four of them braved a winter snowstorm to meet with Jerry Falwell at the Holiday Inn in Lynchburg, Virginia.[4] The meeting was scheduled to last an hour. It ended nine hours later.

The purpose of the meeting was to enlist Falwell as a general in the conservative army. Introducing the conversation, Weyrich said, "Out there is what one might call a moral majority in our country that agrees on the principles in the Ten Commandments. The key to any kind of political impact is to get these people united."[5]

Falwell stopped him. "What was that you said?"

Weyrich repeated what he had said, including the words *moral majority.*

"That's it!" Falwell exclaimed. "That's the name of the organization!"

And with that, the Moral Majority was born.

I pointed out in the previous chapter that the conservative movement in America began about 1955, and that by 1964, the conservatives had gained enough strength and political savvy to be able to get the Republican Party to nominate Senator Barry Goldwater as the party's presidential candidate in that year's election.

Goldwater lost, of course; but this didn't discourage the conservatives. Their goal was to take over the American government. Goldwater's nomination gave conservatives a small taste of victory. However, they soon came to realize that their only hope for gaining control of the American government was to expand their constituency. *They needed more people to join their cause.* But where could they find them? They settled on two key segments of the population that they believed they could win to their side: Southern Democrats and religious conservatives. Goldwater's sweeping of five states in the Deep South—traditionally a Democratic stronghold—proved that Southern Democrats could be brought around to vote Republican. And indeed, the Democrats largely lost the South to the Republicans during the last quarter of the twentieth century.

Political conservatives also saw in religious conservatives the potential for a powerful block of voters who could be inspired to rally to their cause. Religious conservatives held many of the same values that energized political conservatives. Southern Baptists and Pentecostals in particular had been quietly building their strength for half a century, while membership in the more liberal Protestant denominations had been declining. Liberal Protestantism had dominated American politics throughout most of the nation's history, but with its decline and the rise of conservative Protestantism, sooner or later, a political change was inevitable. One conservative political operative remarked that evangelical and fundamentalist Christians were "the greatest tract of virgin timber on the political landscape."[6] Ed McAteer, Paul Weyrich, Howard Phillips, and Robert Billings decided that the time had come to start harvesting the timber. That explains the urgency of their meeting with Jerry Falwell. One could call it a proposal for marriage.

It wasn't an easy courtship. Religious conservatives had insisted throughout most of the twentieth century that their job was spiritual, not political—that God had called them to evangelize, not politicize. Falwell himself had disdained political involvement as late as March 1965, declaring in a sermon at his Thomas Road Baptist Church that "preachers are not called to be politicians, but to be soul winners."[7] In 1976, Billy Graham insisted that he was "opposed to organizing Christians into a political bloc."[8] And as late as 1980, Pat Robertson declared that "active partisan politics is the wrong path for true evangelicals."[9] However, the sexual revolution of the 1960s jolted religious conservatives into the conviction that America was on a downward moral slide. Among the factors contributing to the decline, they felt, were the Supreme Court decisions in 1962 and 1963 that banned prayer and Bible reading in public schools. Suddenly, political involvement seemed not such a bad idea after all! Yelling and screaming weren't likely to bring about much change. If the religious conservatives were serious about reversing the country's moral decline through legislation, they'd have to roll up their sleeves and jump into the political ring.

Jimmy Carter

Religious conservatives were understandably thrilled when Jimmy Carter was nominated as the Democratic candidate for president in July 1976. Carter was a Southern Baptist. He understood the religious conservative mind. Here was one of their own to fight their battles! So, they rallied around his banner.

However, Carter failed to deliver. In the first year of his presidency, he supported (or at least was blamed for supporting) an IRS regulation stipulating that private schools that failed to meet certain standards of racial integration would have their tax-exempt status revoked. Carter also called for a White House Conference on the American Family that religious conservatives opposed. Carter wanted the conference to represent a broad spectrum of views, and he took steps to ensure that the conservative voice would be heard. But that wasn't enough for conservatives. They wanted their views to dominate, or at least to equal the volume of the liberal voice. They feared, correctly as it turned out, that the conference would promote a mostly liberal agenda. When the conference convened in the summer of 1980, one of the topics was family planning that included abortion, and homosexuals were allowed to express their version of family. Thus, conservatives felt very strongly that the delegates to the conference were, as one conservative attendee put it, "a liberal stacked deck."[10]

The final blow to the conservative support for Carter came at a meeting he had with several conservative religious leaders, including Jerry Falwell, James D. Kennedy, Tim LaHaye, and Oral Roberts. LaHaye asked the president why he supported the Equal Rights Amendment when it would be so detrimental to the family, and Carter "gave some off-the-wall answer that the Equal Rights Amendment was good for the family."[11] Following the meeting, LaHaye said a silent prayer, "God, we have got to get this man out of the White House and get someone in here who will be aggressive about bringing back traditional moral values."[12] The other ministers, he learned later, felt the same, and they worked hard to defeat Carter. This is one of the primary reasons why Carter lost his 1980 bid for reelection

The Moral Majority

The 1973 Supreme Court *Roe v. Wade* decision hit the Roman Catholic Church like a ton of bricks, and the bishops immediately set to work to reverse it. For that very reason, however, many fundamentalist and

Evangelical Protestants were initially wary of the antiabortion movement, considering it largely a Catholic issue. In 1971, two years prior to
Roe v. Wade, the Southern Baptist Convention voted almost unanimously
in support of a resolution affirming a woman's right to have an abortion
if giving birth would pose physical or emotional danger.[13] Falwell didn't
preach a sermon about abortion until 1978.[14]

Falwell got his first taste of political activity in 1979, when he helped
Anita Bryant with an antigay crusade in Florida. However, his real involvement began with the establishment of the Moral Majority that same
year. This was a total shift in his view of Christians and politics. Ed Dobson, one of Falwell's associates, explained that traditionally, fundamentalists had felt that "the political world—the public square—should not
be a part of a Christian's priority. Our priority is to love God and to love
our neighbor. Forget about politics. That pietistic idea was predominant
in the mind of the average person in the average pew in a fundamentalist
church in America. The miracle of the Moral Majority was that, in just a
matter of months, that whole concept was shattered, and [fundamental-
ists] began registering to vote and getting involved."[15]

For the next several years, Falwell spent far more time traveling and
promoting the fundamentalist/evangelical political agenda than he did
pastoring his Thomas Road Baptist Church. Some years he traveled as
much as three hundred thousand miles, often speaking several times a
day at churches and pastors' meetings, and helping to set up chapters of
his Moral Majority around the country.

Falwell was willing to join hands with anyone who would support a
conservative political agenda, regardless of whether the person was a Jew,
a Mormon, or a Catholic. Some conservative leaders were shocked. Dr.
Bob Jones of Bob Jones University thought it was "the most heretical
thing he'd ever heard." However, Falwell had an answer: "It is not a violation of your convictions, nor does it displease the Lord," he said, "for
you to work with people who don't agree with you theologically, if in so
doing you improve your country, improve your society, help families,
and accomplish things collectively that you could not have accomplished
apart from each other."[16] And it worked. "After a year of Moral Majority's
explosion," he said, "our people realized that this is what the opposition
had been doing all along. To move them away from single-issue politics
into collective negotiating and bargaining was about a one-year process,
but it's been done, and it doesn't have to be done again."[17]

When political conservatives set out to wed themselves to religious conservatives, they tapped into a huge reservoir of political power that has revolutionized American politics. One of the first success stories to come from that marriage was the election of Ronald Reagan as president of the United States in 1980.

Ronald Reagan

At first, Religious Right leaders were not enamored with Ronald Reagan. That changed on August 21, 1980. On that day, the Religious Roundtable sponsored a meeting in Dallas, Texas, that filled the city's seventeen-thousand-seat Reunion Arena. All the heavyweights of the conservative and Religious Right movements were there: Paul Weyrich, Ed McAteer, James Robison (who led out), Phyllis Schlafly, Tim La-Haye, Jerry Falwell, and Pat Robertson, to name a few. Ronald Reagan, the Republican candidate in the presidential election that year, was the featured speaker. Also present were twenty-five-hundred preachers from forty-one states.

James Robison made a powerful speech just before Reagan stood up. "The stage is set," Robison said. "We'll either have a Hitler-type takeover, or Soviet domination, or God is going to take over this country. It is time to crawl out from under the pews and stop looking through the stained-glass windows."[18] Those fiery words are characteristic of the Religious Right's militant approach to politics.

Reagan sat on the platform behind Robison, clapping at every word. And the people noticed. When Reagan stood up to speak, he said, "You can't endorse me, but I endorse you."[19] With these words, the presidential candidate gave his backing to their conservative agenda. Nor was it lost on the leaders and the people that Reagan supported tuition tax credits, complained that the Supreme Court had kicked God out of the classroom, and endorsed the teaching of biblical creationism in public schools as an alternative to evolution. Everyone present was also aware of Reagan's cryptic comment that "everybody in favor of abortion has already been born."[20]

And so Reagan was sworn into office on January 20, 1981.

However, to the disappointment of religious conservatives, Reagan was more a political conservative than he was a religious conservative. On the campaign trail, he gave lip service to conservative religious hot button issues such as abortion, tuition tax credits for parochial education, and prayer in public schools, but once in office he delivered almost nothing. Religious Right operatives were also disappointed that Reagan appointed few of their own to top cabinet posts,* but the president probably had little choice. Fundamentalist and evangelical Christians had kept themselves out of the political loop for more than fifty years, and very few of them had the experience necessary to hold down a major political appointment in the national government.

Reagan was reelected in 1984 with an overwhelming majority.** Thus, political conservatives had "their man" in the White House for most of the 1980s. Religious conservatives still had a few years to wait.

Pat Robertson

During the 1988 primary campaign, Pat Robertson made a bid to become the Republican candidate for president that fall. His two main rivals were Reagan's vice president, George H. W. Bush, and Senator Robert Dole. Bush was considered the front runner in Michigan, but conservatives ran a quiet, well-organized campaign in favor of Robertson that cut significantly into Bush's showing in that state's primaries.† Because of careful organization of his troops, Robertson actually beat Bush in the Iowa caucus, coming in second to Dole, with Bush in third place. Robertson also came in either first or second in the primaries and caucuses in Hawaii, Nevada, Alaska, Minnesota, and South Dakota.[21] Suddenly, whether they liked it or not, the liberal, left-wing media had to pay attention to a religious conservative.

Robertson lost to Bush in the super-Tuesday primaries, and Bush went on to win the nomination at the Republican convention the following August. Nevertheless, Robertson made the Religious Right's point: Conservative religious candidates could make a decent electoral showing, *and they intended someday to win.*

By the mid-1980s, the Moral Majority had lost its influence, and it disbanded in 1989. This, together with Robertson's failed presidential bid in 1988, caused the liberal talking heads to read the obituary on the

---

*James Watt, secretary of the Interior, was a member of the Assemblies of God.

**The Republicans carried every state but Minnesota, the home of Reagan's Democratic opponent, Walter Mondale. And Mondale won his own state by less than five thousand votes!

†Robertson claimed that he won Michigan, "but the 'old guard' was there and they stole it away from us"; see William Martin, *With God on Our Side: The Rise of the Religious Right in America* (New York: Broadway Books, 1996), 285.

conservative movement in America. They couldn't have been more wrong, for Pat Robertson picked up where the Moral Majority left off. His presidential campaign had left him with a huge mailing list of thousands of donors who had supported him. In addition, his aides had created a major political machine with organized groups in precincts all over the country, and these people were ready to go to work. One friend told Robertson in early 1989, "Hundreds of thousands of people, whom you have brought into politics for the first time in their lives, are looking to you for leadership. You've got to *do* something."[22]

Robertson had already started doing something.

---

1. Tennessee Sixty-Fourth General Assembly, 1925, House Bill No. 185, http://www.law.umkc.edu/faculty/projects/ftrials/scopes/tennstat.htm

2. For details of the trial, see "Scopes Trial," Wikipedia, http://en.wikipedia.org/wiki/Scopes_trial.

3. Kevin Philips, *American Theocracy* (New York: Viking, 2006), 115. Philips is the source for the statistics about the growth of fundamentalist Protestantism and the decline of mainstream Protestantism in this chapter.

4. See Connie Paige, *The Right to Lifers* (New York: Summit Books, 1983), 155. William Martin said this meeting occurred in May 1979; see his book *With God on Our Side: The Rise of the Religious Right in America* (New York: Broadway Books, 1996), 200.

5. William Martin, *With God on Our Side: The Rise of the Religious Right in America* (New York: Broadway Books, 1996), 200.

6. Ibid., 191.

7. Ibid., 70.

8. Ibid., 153.

9. Ibid., 259.

10. Ibid., 181.

11. Ibid., 189.

12. Ibid.

13. Ibid., 156.

14. Ibid., 195.

15. Ibid., 202.

16. Ibid., 204.

17. Ibid.

18. Ibid., 216.

19. Ibid., 217.

20. Ibid.

21. Ibid., 2.

22. Ibid., 299.

CHAPTER 13

The Success of the Religious Right in America

George H. W. Bush had scarcely lowered his hand from taking the inaugural oath in January 1989, when Pat Robertson sat at a banquet table with Ralph Reed, the founder and president of an organization called Students for America. The two fell into conversation about Robertson's failed presidential campaign, and Reed told Robertson very frankly what he thought Robertson had done right and what he thought he had done wrong. Robertson was impressed. Here was a young man he hardly knew who nevertheless had the courage to say what was on his mind. Furthermore, what Reed said made political sense, for by now the Religious Right was beginning to realize that getting one of their own into the White House would be only a partial success. Other battles, many of them even more important, were yet to be fought.

Falwell's Moral Majority had focused most of its attention on getting leaders elected at the national level. But Reed pointed out to Robertson that "it was going to be necessary to shift the focus of the 'pro-family' or religious conservative movement out of Washington and away from the Oval Office and get down to the grassroots—school boards, city councils, county commissions, and so forth."[1] As Paul Weyrich put it, "The only way you take Washington is by taking the countryside."[2]

Before the evening was over, Robertson had invited Reed to lead out in establishing a new organization that would replace the Moral Majority and would also change the focus of Religious Right politics from electing presidents to electing county commissioners and school-board members. The result was the Christian Coalition, which was without question the most successful Religious Right political organization during the last decade of the twentieth century and which continues to have a significant influence in conservative religious politics in the first decade of the twenty-first century.

The Christian Coalition

Few people today are aware that the Christian Coalition started out very, very small. Robertson chipped in a thousand dollars of seed money, and Reed charged the deposit on the organization's first phones to his own credit card. Their initial effort was to send a mailing to everyone who had donated to Robertson's presidential campaign. Reed took the letters to his Wednesday evening Bible study group, and after the meeting, folks stayed and helped to stuff and seal the envelopes. As money came in, they purchased full-page ads in the *New York Times, Washington Post*, and *USA Today*, demanding that Congress pass legislation barring the National Endowment for the Arts from using federal money to support pornography and other works of art that would be offensive to their religiously conservative constituents. "If you continue to vote for these things," the ads warned Congressional representatives, "you're going to face the voters in November 1992."[3]

Reed also traveled the country, setting up political action groups and training people how to get involved in local politics. And it worked. As one Religious Right political operative put it, "There were people all over America who had been involved politically for the first time [in Robertson's presidential campaign], and they had been bitten by the bug. They wanted to keep going."[4] Paul Weyrich summarized Robertson's and Reed's approach: They "learned what all those other [Religious Right] leaders never understood, and that is, if you want to have an influence on politics in this country, then elect people at the local level. Grow the movement from the bottom up. Don't worry about the presidency; the presidency will take care of itself in due course." Robertson and Reed, he said, "took seriously my injunction that they should be active in local politics first."[5]

By the end of 1991, the Christian Coalition had signed up more than eighty-two thousand members. Shortly after that came their first big political test. George H. W. Bush had nominated the politically conservative Clarence Thomas, a Black judge, to replace Supreme Court Justice Thurgood Marshall, also a Black, who was retiring. The left-wing media and the liberal political establishment were horrified, not because Thomas was Black, but because of his political conservatism. They pulled out all the stops to make sure he wasn't confirmed. But the Christian Coalition also was pulling out all their stops to be sure that he *was* confirmed. Guy Rogers, Ralph Reed's assistant, summed up what they did:

> We knew the vote [on Thomas] was going to be very close, so we did what any good grassroots organization would do. We identified [the senators] we thought were the swing votes and we mobilized our people in those states to make phone calls. We made tens of thousands of phone calls, and we made the right kinds of phone calls. [When Thomas was confirmed], that really impressed our people at the grassroots. It hit home that when we told them, "This is how you do it," we were saying, "You have feelings about this. Now you can do something about it. Your voice won't be one voice crying in the wilderness; it will be a collective voice that will ring very loud on Capitol Hill." [Judge Thomas] was the target of a tremendous smear campaign by the liberal establishment. They didn't realize that there was a sleeping giant out there that would take this man on as a champion.[6]

The Religious Right was learning that they could win at the national level by working at the local level.

The next big challenge for the Christian Coalition came in 1992, the year George H. W. Bush was up for reelection. While Bush had failed to deliver on the Religious Right's conservative agenda, they realized that he would almost certainly win the nomination at the Republican convention. Bush was also far preferable to the Democratic nominee, Bill Clinton. So religious conservatives switched from trying to get a more conservative candidate nominated to getting conservative issues such as antiabortion into the Republican platform. Reed made an impassioned plea to the party's platform committee, warning them that they would lose the votes of religious conservatives unless they included pro-family language in the Republican platform. Several religious conservatives made speeches during the convention, including Pat Robertson and Pat Buchanan. Buchanan in particular gave a militant speech in which he warned, "There is a religious war going on in this country. It is a cultural war as critical to the kind of nation we shall be as the Cold War itself.

This war is for the soul of America. And in that struggle for the soul of America, Clinton and Clinton are on the other side, and George Bush is on our side."[7]

Republican liberals were horrified at Buchanan's speech. However, the next day's polls reflected its impact. As is usually the case during political conventions, the presidential nominee's standing grows with each passing day. In Bush's case, the greatest increase came the day after Robertson's and Buchanan's speeches.

Unfortunately for Bush, it wasn't enough. In the November election, he lost to Bill Clinton, who would sit in the Oval Office for the next eight years. However, even in the bad news, conservatives saw a bit of good news. Guy Rogers, Ralph Reed's assistant, said, "What the American people don't know is that they just elected an openly pro-abortion, pro-gay rights liberal to the presidency for the first time in the history of this country. Now you are going to have a face on modern liberalism, and everybody is going to be able to see it in a way they haven't seen it before." Another Religious Right operative observed, "What better way to galvanize your troops than to have Bill Clinton to fight against?"[8]

The new winners

From this point on, thanks in large part to Ralph Reed's political skills, religious conservatives began winning elections all over the country. One of the first was a special election in which Paul Coverdale became the second Republican senator to represent Georgia in the United States Congress since Reconstruction. The Christian Coalition rallied their troops in Georgia to distribute more than a million voter guides and phone every person in their registry of conservative voters. Coverdale won the election.

However, the real success of the Christian Coalition and Religious Right forces came in the November 1994 midterm elections. While it is common for the party that holds the White House to lose Congressional strength in the midterm elections, the 1994 election was an absolute disaster for the Democrats. As I pointed out a couple of chapters back, the Democrats lost eight seats in the Senate, giving the Republicans a four-seat majority, and in the House of Representatives, they lost fifty-four seats, giving the Republicans a twenty-six-seat majority! The Republican Party also picked up eleven governorships and 472 seats in state legislatures around the country. And there's clear evidence that the Christian

Coalition had a major influence on that Republican success. Twenty-six senators and 114 Congressional representatives were incumbents who received a perfect rating on the Christian Coalition's Congressional Scorecard or were freshmen who had received the Coalition's strong approval. [9]

Political experts everywhere, many of whom had predicted the demise of the Religious Right five years earlier, now acknowledged their power. Six months after the 1994 election, *Time* magazine published an issue with Ralph Reed on the cover along with the words, "The Right Hand of God: Meet Ralph Reed. His Christian Coalition is on a crusade to take over U.S. politics—and it's working."[10] The article on the inside described the Christian Coalition as "formidable" and "one of the most powerful grassroots organizations in American politics."[11] The article quoted Bob Dole's chief strategist William Lacy as saying, "Without having significant support of the Christian right a Republican cannot win the nomination or the general election."[12] *Time* concluded its article with the statement that "the religious right is moving toward center stage in American secular life."[13] Religious conservatives were finally getting a hearing—and a grudging respect—from the liberal secular press!

A group of conservative Congressional representatives succeeded in angering the American public during their first two years in office by holding Bill Clinton's 1996 federal budget hostage to their narrow demands, and many of them were voted out of office in the 1996 election. The lackluster Bob Dole was Clinton's opponent in 1996, and Clinton won again. Nevertheless, throughout the rest of the 1990s, the Republicans held control of both houses of the United States Congress.

It's not likely that any American will soon forget the presidential election in 2000, when the contest between George W. Bush (the son of former president George H. W. Bush) and Al Gore was finally settled by the Supreme Court in favor of Bush. The significance of the Bush presidency is that he is the first president to treat religious conservatives as his core constituency, whom he had to please above all else. While it isn't loudly proclaimed in the press, it's no secret to political insiders that Bush confers on a weekly basis with both Catholic and Protestant conservatives, either in person or through his advisers. During his tenure as president, Bush has promoted a number of issues that are dear to the Religious Right, including a marriage amendment to the U.S. Constitution, school prayer, vouchers for parochial school students, and limiting abortion.

However, Bush's most lasting contribution to the Religious Right cause is without a doubt the two Supreme Court appointments he made during his second term: John Roberts to replace William Rehnquist, who died; and Samuel Alito to replace Sandra Day O'Connor, who retired. Roberts and Alito are both conservative, and both are Catholics. With their appointment, five of the nine Supreme Court justices are Catholics. I believe that Bush's appointment of these two Catholics was no accident. The Catholic lobby in the United States is very powerful, and today's Religious Right Protestants view Catholics as allies in the American culture war. Thus, Bush's appointment of two Catholics kept both sides very happy.

So what does all of this have to do with Bible prophecy? Keep reading!

---

1. William Martin, *With God on Our Side: The Rise of the Religious Right in America* (New York: Broadway Books, 1996), 300.

2. Ibid., 331.

3. Ibid., 304.

4. Dick Weinhold, cited in Martin, 306.

5. Martin, 308.

6. Ibid., 317.

7. Ibid., 325.

8. Ibid., 329.

9. Ibid., 339, 340.

10. Jeffrey H. Birnbaum, "The Gospel According to Ralph," *Time*, May 15, 1995, 1.

11. Ibid., 28, 30.

12. Ibid., 30.

13. Ibid., 35.

CHAPTER 14

The Attack on Church-State Separation

I mentioned in chapter 10 that when John F. Kennedy was running for president back in 1960, he faced the Houston Ministerial Association in September of that year to defend his stand on church-state separation. "I believe," Kennedy said, "in an America where the separation of church and state is absolute—where no Catholic prelate would tell the President (should he be Catholic) how to act, and no Protestant minister would tell his parishioners for whom to vote."[1] *Now please note this, because it's extremely important:* In saying this, Kennedy, a Catholic, went against the teaching of his own church. In fact, some Catholics were quite unhappy with him for saying it. But Kennedy knew that he was facing a large Protestant constituency—especially Southern Baptists and charismatics—who feared that his Catholicism would cause him, as president, to compromise church-state separation. Thus, Kennedy had no choice but to make that bold statement.

Yet today, America's Southern Baptists and charismatics have done a complete about-face. These same groups are now at the forefront of the battle *against* church-state separation. In the following paragraphs, I will quote some of their more forceful statements.

> *Pat Robertson:* "They [liberals and secularists] have kept us in submission because they have talked about separation of church and state. There is no such thing in the Constitution. It's a lie of the left, and we're not going to take it anymore."[2]

137

"We have had a distortion imposed on us over the past few years by left-wingers who have fastened themselves into the court system. And we have had a lie foisted on us that there is something embedded in the Constitution called separation of church and state."[3]

"[The courts] are taking our religion away from us under the guise of separation of church and state."[4]

Jerry Falwell: "Separation of Church and State has long been the battle cry of civil libertarians wishing to purge our glorious Christian heritage from our nation's history. Of course, the term never once appears in our Constitution and is a modern fabrication of discrimination."[5]

W. A. Criswell, former senior pastor of the Dallas First Baptist Church: "There is no such thing as separation of church and state. It is merely a figment of the imagination of infidels."[6]

D. James Kennedy, Presbyterian pastor in Fort Lauderdale, Florida: "If we are committed and involved in taking back the nation for Christian moral values, . . . there is no doubt we can witness the dismantling of not just the Berlin wall but the even more diabolical 'wall of separation' that has led to secularization, godlessness, immorality, and corruption in our country."[7]

Francis Schaeffer, prominent Christian philosopher of the late twentieth century: "Today the separation of church and state in America is used to silence the church."[8]

And religious leaders aren't the only ones leading the attack on church-state separation. Note the following examples.

William Rehnquist, at the time, associate justice of the United States Supreme Court. He served as chief justice of that court from 1986 to 2005: "The 'wall of separation between church and state' is a metaphor based on bad history, a metaphor which has proved useless as a guide to judging. It should be frankly and explicitly abandoned."[9]

Antonin Scalia, associate justice of the United States Supreme Court: The Web site TheocracyWatch calls attention to a speech Scalia made on January 12, 2003, at a Religious Freedom Day event, in which he said that the principle of church-state separation was not imbedded in the Constitution and therefore should be added democratically, which means through a constitutional amendment. TheocracyWatch points out, correctly, that an amendment to the Constitution on church-state separation would be impossible to achieve in the current political climate, so the argument is pointless.[10]

Tom DeLay, former U.S. House majority leader, in a speech on the floor of the House of Representatives: "To claim that our Founding Fathers were for separation of church and state is either re-writing history or being very ignorant of history."[11]

Jay Alan Seculow, chief counsel for the American Center for Law and Justice: "I've had it with the ACLU's outrageous attacks on our nation's religious heritage and our right to express our faith publicly. . . . What's frustrating about this is that their entire argument is based on the utterly false principle of 'separation of church and state.' . . . There is no 'wall' of separation!"

"The fact is, the phrase 'separation of church and state' is not found in the U.S. Constitution, the framework of our freedom. . . . Too often, the 'separation of church and state' phrase is allowed to take the place of our actual constitutional provisions."[12]

These Religious Right and political leaders claim that church-state separation is a lie of the radical left. They claim that secularists borrowed it from the constitution of the Soviet Union and imposed it on Americans. Do they have amnesia? Have they forgotten what conservative religious leaders demanded of John F. Kennedy when he was running for president?

The truth is that church-state separation has been a principle of American legislation and jurisprudence since the nation's founding. It is the radical religious right who are the radical revisionists. Back in 1960, Southern Baptists were some of the strongest *supporters* of church-state separation. Today, conservative Southern Baptists are at the forefront of the *opposition* to church-state separation. And many of America's evangelical and fundamentalist leaders are so diametrically opposed to church-state separation that they are fighting to see it defeated.

Why the change

What happened? What brought about this dramatic change in such a short time? Several factors are responsible. I'll mention three; I'm sure there are others.

COULD IT *REALLY* HAPPEN?

Secularism vs. conservative Christianity. Americans have always been a nation of both religious and secular people who have gotten along well with each other in spite of their religious and spiritual differences. However, a significant shift in the balance of power occurred during the twentieth century. On the one hand, secularism largely gained control of the major institutions of the nation, including education, entertainment, and the print and broadcast media. On the other hand, as I pointed out in chapter 12, a large proportion of the American people accepted conservative religion with its conservative moral values.

A clash between these two cultural forces was inevitable. It began with conservative political activists. In the 1970s, these activists, who were themselves largely secular, were looking for significant blocks of people in the country who might be willing to join them in their effort to gain political dominance over the American government. And conservative Christians, who for the previous fifty years had avoided political involvement—and whose numbers had been growing by leaps and bounds—were ripe for the picking. It took only a little persuasion to win over Jerry Falwell, Pat Robertson, and others on the Religious Right.

If these conservative Christians had adopted the agenda of secular conservatives, church-state separation wouldn't have been threatened, for, as I pointed out in chapter 10, the American version of church-state separation is the result of a unique blend of the religious and the secular. However, Christian conservatives have taken the whole conservative movement in a significantly different direction. They want the American government and its leading institutions to be controlled by more than a conservative *political* philosophy. They seek a conservative *religious* agenda. D. James Kennedy said, "Our job is to reclaim America for Christ, whatever the cost. As the vice regents of God, we are to exercise godly dominion and influence over our neighborhoods, our schools, *our government*, our literature and arts, our sports arenas, our entertainment media, our news media, our scientific endeavors—in short, over every aspect and institution of human society."[13] Church-state separation is especially threatened by the Religious Right's effort to "exercise godly dominion and influence over . . . *government*."

The civil rights legislation of the 1950s and 1960s, which at first glance would seem to be quite unrelated to church-state separation, has actually contributed significantly to the Religious Right's changed attitude toward that principle. Here's why.

During the nineteenth century and much of the twentieth, Protestant support for church-state separation included refusing to provide government funds for parochial religious education, which was largely Catholic at the time. Catholics had established their church-school system so their children wouldn't be exposed to the Protestantism that tended to permeate public education. They objected (rightly) that they were being forced to pay for their children's education twice: once through the property taxes that supported the public schools, and a second time through the tuition and subsidies that they had to pay to maintain their own parochial schools. Protestants replied that this was the price churches that maintained parochial school systems had to pay in order for the country to maintain church-state separation. Protestants found it easy to say this, because they weren't running very many parochial schools.

Then came the civil rights legislation of the 1950s and 1960s, and the Supreme Court decisions that mandated the integration of public schools even if it meant bussing students from one part of a city to another. And Caucasian parents were furious! They didn't want their children bussed out of their school districts merely to achieve racial balance. White Southerners, who still held many of their prejudices against Blacks, felt particularly incensed. The result was a widespread parochial school movement among evangelical Protestants. Churches everywhere began establishing their own schools. These schools provided two benefits: They kept children near their homes, and they made it possible for children to study the Bible and biblical concepts of Creation, human sexuality, and other moral issues in their schools.

And suddenly, the shoe was on the other foot. Now conservative Protestants began to realize the financial pinch of paying twice for their children's education,* and the church-state-separation argument against public funding for parochial education lost its luster. This is an important factor in the conservative Protestant about-face on church-state separation.

Supreme Court decisions. Several decisions by the United States Supreme Court during the second half of the twentieth century, and one decision by the Massachusetts Supreme Judicial Court, have also had a powerful influence on the Religious Right's attitude toward church-state separation. The first, *Everson v. Board of Education*, was handed down by the Supreme Court in early 1947. One sentence in this decision has

---

*It isn't correct to say that parents who send their children to parochial schools have to pay twice for their children's education. Everyone pays the property taxes that support public education, including people who have no children: singles, young married couples, seniors, etc.

especially incensed Religious Right conservatives. Justice Hugo Black, writing for the majority, said, "In the words of [Thomas] Jefferson, the clause against establishment of religion by law was intended to erect 'a wall of separation between church and state.'" Religious conservatives have responded vehemently, "There is no *wall* of separation!"

Two Supreme Court decisions in the early 1960s also angered religious conservatives: one in 1962 that forbids school-initiated prayer in public schools,* and another in 1963 that forbids state-mandated Bible reading in public schools.** Ralph Reed, the executive director of the Christian Coalition, called the school prayer decision "a nationwide search and destroy mission for student religious practices."[14] Two other United States Supreme Court decisions that have angered the Religious Right are *Roe v. Wade* in 1973, which allows women the right to have an abortion, and a 2003 decision decriminalizing homosexual intimacy between consenting adults.[†] Finally, there is the 2004 decision of the Massachusetts Supreme Judicial Court that permits homosexual couples to marry.[15] Roberta Combs, the president of the Christian Coalition, called that ruling "reprehensible" and a "disregard of the will of the overwhelming majority of the American people who believe that marriage is only the union of one man and one woman."[16]

These Supreme Court decisions raised the wrath of the Religious Right against church-state separation to a fever pitch.[††] And Michael Newdow's lawsuits against the words "under God" in the Pledge of Allegiance and "In God We Trust" on American money have only intensified the fears of Religious Right activists that, in the name of church-state separation, the Supreme Court will also banish from the public square these symbols of civil religion.

The Religious Right solution

The Religious Right's solution to these rulings of the Supreme Court is troubling. Please allow me to overwhelm you with the evidence.

Engel v. Vitale.

**Abington School District v. Schempp.*

†*Lawrence v. Texas.*

††The Supreme Court decision permitting homosexual intimacy between consenting adults and the Massachusetts court ruling that allowed homosexual marriage are not church-state issues, but they were among a string of decisions by American courts in recent years that angered Religious Right Protestants and Catholics who oppose church-state separation.

Religious conservatives accuse so-called "activist judges" on the Supreme Court and certain lower courts of "legislating from the bench" and ignoring the original intent in the minds of the Founders of the American republic when they wrote the Constitution. According to Mark Levin in his book *Men in Black*, "Judicial activists are nothing short of radicals in robes—contemptuous of the rule of law, subverting the Constitution at will, and using their public trust to impose their policy preferences on society. In fact, no radical political movement has been more effective in undermining our system of government than the judiciary."[17]

That's quite a statement! But Levin isn't the only one attacking the courts. On March 14, 2006, I received an e-mail from an organization called ConservativeAlerts.com. The e-mail was headlined "High Crimes and Misdemeanors: Activist Judges Need to Be Removed NOW!" It went on to accuse liberals of "subverting the Constitution by loading the federal courts with liberal ideologues," and it followed up with examples of "some of the most outrageous justices and their unbelievable rulings."

On his *700 Club* television program, Pat Robertson said, "The fact that [the courts] are trying to ignore this country's religious heritage is just horrible. They are taking our religion away from us under the guise of separation of church and state. There was never any intention that our government would be separate from God Almighty. Never, never, never in the history of this land did the founders of this country or those who came after them think that was the case."[18] According to Tony Perkins, the president and CEO of the Washington, D.C., Family Research Council, the Supreme Court "has become increasingly hostile to Christianity. It represents a greater threat to representative government than any other force—more than budget deficits, more than terrorism."[19] And Donald Wildmon, the founder and chair of the American Family Association, claims, "Anti-prayer/Anti-Christian groups—like the ACLU and Americans United for Separation of Church and State—have teamed up with liberal judges on the U.S. Supreme Court and are stripping away our religious freedom."[20]

On March 29, 2005, I received an e-mail from Conservative Petitions inviting me to an April 7 and 8 conference titled "Confronting the Judicial War on Faith." William Greene, president of RightMarch.com and sponsor of the conference, claimed in the e-mail that "activist judges are *undermining* democracy, *devastating* families and *assaulting* Judeo-

Christian morality." He concluded the e-mail by saying, "This will be an action-oriented conference seeking . . . a broad-based effort to save America from the judges."

Even President George W. Bush has weighed in on the judiciary. "We need commonsense judges," he said, "who understand that our rights are derived from God. Those are the kind of judges I intend to put on the bench."[21] He got his chance in 2005, which raised the rhetoric of the Religious Right to a shrill call to war. Reporting on the situation, *Newsweek*'s Debra Rosenberg said, "Lately the animosity [against judges has] . . . reached fever pitch." And with speculation at the time about a possible vacancy on the Supreme Court (as it turned out, there were two), Rosenberg said, "The stakes and the vitriol are higher than ever."[22] As tensions against the Supreme Court increased, some justices received death threats, prompting them to request increased protection from the U.S. Marshal's Service.[23]

Focus on the Family's James Dobson has compared black-robed Supreme Court justices to white-robed Ku Klux Klan members.[24] And in a taped speech to a Religious Right conference in Washington, D.C., that was aimed at getting rid of "renegade judges who exceed their constitutional authority," House Majority Leader Tom DeLay railed against "a judiciary run amok." He told attendees at the conference that Congress needs to "reassert our constitutional authority over the courts."[25]

At the same conference, Edwin Vieira, author of the book *How to Dethrone the Imperial Judiciary*, said, "The fifth fool on the Supreme Court decides the issue and then according to them . . . everyone else in the world is bound by this decision." Vieira also blasted the court for promoting "Marxism-Leninism-Stalinism."[26] The conference concluded with an attack on church-state separation as "a phrase not found in the Constitution and a concept foreign to constitutional law prior to 1947."[27]

A fund-raising letter I received from Jerry Falwell complained about "runaway liberal courts." The Christian Coalition's Roberta Combs has asserted, "The branch [of government] which the Founding Fathers intended to be the weakest of the three branches, has been dictating to the American people what they think is best for them for decades."[28] And in another fund-raising letter, one that I received shortly after Terri Schiavo was finally put to rest, Combs said that Schiavo's death "focused national attention on the threat to life and liberty posed by out-of-control federal judges."

Religious Right activists have proposed several radical methods to "rein in" the "out-of-control" courts and their justices. One is the impeachment of judges whose decisions they don't like. Another is to give Congress the authority to overturn any federal court ruling by a two-thirds vote and a vote of two-thirds of the state legislatures. A third suggestion is for Congress to limit funding for the courts. A fourth is for Congress to pass a law denying the federal courts the right to hear certain types of cases, especially religious cases.[29] For example, D. James Kennedy, a Presbyterian pastor in Fort Lauderdale, Florida, demanded that the courts be restricted from ruling on "any matters pertaining to God."[30] That "solution" would, of course, render the First Amendment null and void.

What it means

The implication of all this hostile Religious Right rhetoric against America's courts, and especially against the Supreme Court, is sobering to contemplate. Words have power, and as the voices saying them multiply, these words translate into a tidal wave of political power that is threatening to wash over the American political landscape and destroy many of our most basic freedoms.

For more than 225 years, the Supreme Court has been the guardian of America's religious freedom. The Religious Right claims that the courts are stripping the nation of its religious freedom because it bars Congress and the various state legislatures from enacting the Religious Right's religious and moral vision. Unfortunately, if the Religious Right gets its way, our First Amendment protections against religious laws will be but a dim memory, and all manner of religious initiatives will become the law of the land.

For more than one hundred years, Seventh-day Adventists have stood at the forefront of the effort to preserve religious liberty in America. Our motivation has been our unique understanding of the land beast of Revelation 13, which we believe represents the United States of America. This beast, which looks benign when it arises out of the earth—it has "two horns like a lamb" (verse 11)—will nevertheless speak "like a dragon." Verse 15 says that the land beast will "cause all who refused to worship the image to be killed." It will also demand that every human being receive a loyalty mark on the forehead or the hand, and those who refuse will be subjected to an economic boycott—that is, they will be refused the right to buy or sell (verses 16, 17). And the ultimate threat in the demand for religious conformity will be death.

145

Could this really happen?

One hundred years ago, our non-Adventist critics claimed that for the United States to renounce its historical support of religious freedom would require "a greater miracle than for God to grow a giant oak in an instant."[31] But religious conservatives gained tremendous political power in the United States during the last quarter of the twentieth century and the early years of the twenty-first. Pat Robertson said, "We want freedom in this country, and we want power." He meant that Religious Right conservatives want freedom and power to enact their brand of religion into law. I propose that the present demand by America's Religious Right conservatives to void church-state separation and gut the Supreme Court of its authority to consider cases dealing with religion is leading this country toward a direct fulfillment of the Adventist interpretation of the intolerant land beast of Revelation 13.

I'm sure there are those who will argue that the Adventist interpretation of Revelation 13 is incorrect. They can no longer argue that it is unrealistic.

---

1. Cited in George J. Marlin, *The American Catholic Voter: 200 Years of Political Impact* (South Bend, Ind.: St. Augustine's Press, 2004), 254.

2. From a November 1993 address by Pat Robertson, cited in Anti-Defamation League, *The Religious Right: The Assault on Tolerance and Pluralism in America* (New York: Anti-Defamation League, 1994), 4.

3. Pat Robertson on October 12, 2002, at the Christian Coalition's "Road to Victory" Conference; cited on the Web site of Americans United for Separation of Church and State, "They Said It! Religious Right Leaders in Their Own Words," http://www.au.org/site/DocServer/They_Said_It.pdf?docID=221.

4. Pat Robertson on his television program *The 700 Club*, July 19, 2005; cited by Rob Boston in "Religious Right Power Brokers: The Top Ten," *Church and State*, June 2006, 10.

5. Jerry Falwell, cited by Rob Boston in "Religious Right Power Brokers: The Top Ten," *Church and State*, June 2006, 14.

6. From a CBS interview of September 6, 1984, taped the day after he delivered the benediction at the Republican National Convention, cited in Anti-Defamation League, *The Religious Right: The Assault on Tolerance and Pluralism in America*, 4.

7. Cited in "They Said It! Religious Right Leaders in Their Own Words."

8. Francis A. Schaeffer, *A Christian Manifesto* (Westchester, Ill.: Crossway Books, 1981), 36.

9. William Rehnquist in *Wallace v. Jaffree*, 1984.

10. "Biblical Law," http://www.theocracywatch.org/biblical_law2.htm.

11. Cited in *Signswatch*, Winter 2001, 3.

12. *Ministry Magazine* (not the Adventist one), Fall, 2004; cited in "Religious Right Power Brokers: The Top Ten," 13.

13. Cited in The Rise of the Religious Right in the Republican Party, http://www.theocracywatch.org; italics added.

14. Ralph Reed, *Contract With the American Family* (New York: Random House, 1995), 6.

15. *Goodridge vs. Department of Public Health*.

16. U.S. Newswire, "Christian Coalition Condemns Massachusetts Supreme Court's Approval of Homosexual Marriage," http://releases.usnewswire.com/GetRelease.asp?id=23507.

17. Mark R. Levin, *Men in Black: How the Supreme Court Is Destroying America* (Washington, D.C.: Regnery Publishing, Inc., 2005), 22.

18. Pat Robertson on his *700 Club* television program; cited by Boston, 10.

19. Jerry Falwell at the "Confronting the Judicial War on Faith" conference, March 7, 2005; cited by Boston, 13.

20. Donald Wildman in a Fall 2000 fund-raising letter; cited by Boston, 12.

21. Cited in an e-mail I received from Lou Sheldon with the subject line, "Help Take Back Our Courts from the Anti-God Left" and with the headline, "OUR BATTLE PLAN: To Take Back Our Courts."

22. Debra Rosenberg, "The War on Judges," *Newsweek*, April 25, 2005, 23.

23. Ibid., 23, 24.

24. Ibid., 23.

25. Rob Boston, "Judge Not," *Liberty*, September/October 2005, 6, 22; can be viewed at http://www.libertymagazine.org/article/articleview/519/1/85/.

26. Ibid.

27. Ibid.

28. Roberta Combs in the Christian Coalition of America's "Washington Weekly Review" March 26, 2005.

29. Boston, "Judge Not," 6, 22.

30. Daniel Eisenberg, "The Posse in the Pulpit," *Time*, May 23, 2005, 32, 33.

31. Theodore Nelson in the introduction to Dudley M. Canright's book, *Seventh-day Adventism Renounced* (Nashville Tenn.: Gospel Advocate Company, 1914) 23.

Addendum: Reflections on Church-State Separation

Because of the attacks that are being waged against church-state separation, it's important that we have a correct understanding of that principle. I discussed church-state issues at some length in the previous chapter and in chapter 10. Here I will comment on three reasons the Religious Right gives for objecting to church-state separation. Please keep in mind two things as you read this addendum: First, entire books have been written on this topic, so what I say here is admittedly extremely sketchy. Second, I am not a constitutional lawyer. What you read here will be my reflections as I have considered the arguments on both sides over several years.*

1. Church-state separation isn't in the Constitution. Jerry Falwell said that the term *church-state separation* "never once appears in our Constitution,"[1] and Pat Robertson said, "There is no such thing [as separation of church and state] in the Constitution."[2] Technically, Falwell, Robertson, and others who make this charge are correct. You can read the American Constitution from beginning to end, and you won't find the expression "separation of church and state" anywhere in the document. But that doesn't mean the concept is unconstitutional any more than the fact that the words *Trinity, incarnation,* and *millennium* aren't in the Bible means that those concepts are unbiblical. Americans use often and believe in very strongly several other political terms that aren't found in the Constitution, among them

_____

*In appendix A, I've provided additional reflections on "original intent" and "judicial activism"—two more concerns of political and religious conservatives.

"fair trial," "innocent until proven guilty," and the "right against self-incrimination."* The *principles* that these terms express *are* found in the Constitution, even though the terms themselves are not.

So, what principle does *church-state separation* express?

The persecution of Protestants by Catholics in medieval Europe was still fresh in the minds of the Founders of the Republic, as was the persecution both of Protestants by Catholics and of Catholics by Protestants during the Reformation era. Still closer to the Founders' time was the persecution of dissenters by the Puritans during the early colonial period. Even at the time of the American Revolution, Baptists, Quakers, and other minority religions were marginalized by the established churches—in most cases, the Episcopal and Congregational churches. The state granted subsidies to these larger churches, while forbidding Baptist and Quaker ministers to even preach and imprisoning some who dared to preach anyway.

This problem was in the minds of the Founders of the Republic when they wrote the Constitution. But how to solve it? They came up with a radical idea that had never before been tried: They proposed creating a *secular government* that would be free of entanglement with religion.

During the Middle Ages, secular governments were unknown. Catholic political theory held then—and still holds today—that government and religion should be united. Not only that, the papacy claimed that spiritual power is superior to civil power, and in any disagreement between the two, the spiritual power (the church) should prevail. On the other hand, during that same period, the civil power sometimes forced its will onto the church, much to the church's distress. All this created a lot of hot words and endless feuds.

To solve this problem, the Founders said, We'll keep religion and government separate so that neither can control the other. The church won't tell the government what to do, and the government won't dictate to the church. The government won't enact religious laws, nor will it finance religion. And it won't favor one religion over another; it will be neutral toward all religions, protecting them all equally, and giving each one free rein to carry out its mission as it sees fit. The government will stay out of the business of religion altogether. That is the meaning of the two religion clauses of the First Amendment to the Constitution: "Congress shall make no law respecting an establishment of religion, or prohibiting the free exercise thereof."

---

*For a long list of these terms, see Leonard W. Levy, *Original Intent and the Framers' Constitution* (Chicago: Ivan R. Dee, 1988), 351.

To summarize, in America, separation of church and state means, very simply, that government and religion will not mix. A secular government is one that is not controlled or even directly influenced by religion. Its laws are not based on the laws of any religion. Church-state separation makes this possible.

2. *Church-state separation bans the public expression of religion.* Every now and then, I get a passionate postal mailing or an e-mail from some Religious Right organization protesting that separation of church and state is taking away the freedom of Christians to express their religion publicly. They claim that church-state separation is destroying the very thing it was designed to protect! But I notice something interesting when I read these letters and e-mails. In every single case, what the Religious Right activists really mean is that they are forbidden to express their religion *on government property and in government institutions.* But the word *public* is much broader than that. When I take a walk around my neighborhood, I see yellow Ten Commandments signs stuck in front lawns here and there. When I drive down the street, I see bumper stickers on the backs of cars that say "Jesus is Lord," and driving down the highway, I sometimes see a sign stuck on a fencepost that says "Jesus saves." Each of these is a public expression of religion, and I have yet to hear of anyone trying to stop people from posting them, *except on government property.*

Why do the courts order the removal of the Ten Commandments from public schools and courthouses? Because public schools and courthouses are government buildings, and government is supposed to be neutral to religion. If Christians and Jews can't post quotations from their sacred writings in public schools and on courthouse lawns, neither can Muslims, Hindus, and Wiccans. Separation of church and state prevents all people from expressing their religion *on government property and in government institutions*—but it doesn't prevent them from expressing their religion publicly. It's a specious argument to claim that it does. Don't let anyone fool you with it!

3. *Church-state separation is a historical myth.* As I noted in chapter 14, United States Supreme Court Chief Justice William Rehnquist once said, "The 'wall of separation between church and state' is a metaphor based on bad history," and in the same vein, Congressman Tom DeLay said, "To claim that our Founding Fathers were for separation of church and state is either rewriting history or being very ignorant of history." These statements are simply not true! The expression "separation of church and state" goes back to the time of the Founding Fathers. In a

letter to the Danbury Baptist Association, Thomas Jefferson said, "I contemplate with sovereign reverence that act of the whole American people which declared that their legislature should 'make no law respecting an establishment of religion, or prohibiting the free exercise thereof,' thus building *a wall of separation between church and State.*"[3]

Please notice that Jefferson's comment about "a wall of separation between church and state" followed immediately after his citation of the religion clauses of the First Amendment. This is a clear indication that Jefferson—who was a Founder of the American republic if there ever was one—understood the religion clauses to mean "separation of church and state."

Opponents of church-state separation argue that Jefferson's letter was a private affair between him and a small group of Baptists, so it shouldn't influence judicial decisions two hundred years later. Granted the letter was private—the point is that it expressed Jefferson's convictions. If you were on trial for a crime and a private letter to a friend was read in court as evidence of your thoughts and attitudes, would it be accepted as valid evidence? Of course! Similarly, Jefferson's letter to the Danbury Baptists tells us what he—the author of the Declaration of Independence and one of the primary Founders of the Republic—thought about church-state separation as it relates to the First Amendment.

Church-state separation has a long history in America since the nation's founding. In chapter 10, I quoted statements by Presidents Andrew Jackson, John Tyler, and Ulysses Grant back in the nineteenth century in support of church-state separation. As recently as 1985, Billy Graham said that Americans "enjoy the separation of church and state, and no sectarian religion has ever been—and we pray God, ever will be—imposed on us."[4]

---

1. A Falwell fax, April 10, 1998; cited in *Church and State*, May 1998, 18.

2. From a November 1993 address by Pat Robertson; cited in *The Religious Right: The Assault on Tolerance and Pluralism in America* (New York: Anti-Defamation League, 1994), 4.

3. This statement is included in a letter Jefferson wrote to the Danbury (Connecticut) Baptist Association. It is a well-known quotation that is available from many sources. One of the easiest to access is Wikipedia, "Thomas Jefferson": http://en.wikipedia.org/wiki/Thomas_Jefferson#Church_and_state; italics added.

4. John Meacham, *American Gospel: God, the Founding Fathers, and the Making of a Nation* (New York: Random House, 2006), 214.

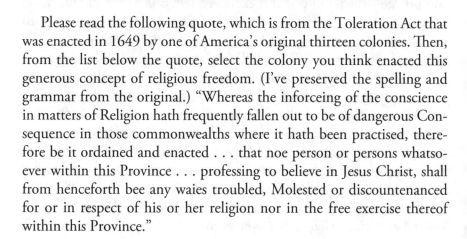

Chapter 15

Catholics in American History: 1776 to 1960— Affirming America

Please read the following quote, which is from the Toleration Act that was enacted in 1649 by one of America's original thirteen colonies. Then, from the list below the quote, select the colony you think enacted this generous concept of religious freedom. (I've preserved the spelling and grammar from the original.) "Whereas the inforceing of the conscience in matters of Religion hath frequently fallen out to be of dangerous Consequence in those commonwealths where it hath been practised, therefore be it ordained and enacted . . . that noe person or persons whatsoever within this Province . . . professing to believe in Jesus Christ, shall from henceforth bee any waies troubled, Molested or discountenanced for or in respect of his or her religion nor in the free exercise thereof within this Province."

❑ Rhode Island
❑ Pennsylvania
❑ New York
❑ Maryland
❑ Virginia

Now, from the list below, select the early American leader who made the following statement: "I have observed that when ministers of Religion leave the duties of their profession to take a busy part in political matters they generally fall into contempt."[1]

❑ George Washington
❑ James Madison
❑ John Carroll
❑ Thomas Jefferson
❑ Cotton Mathers

If you checked Maryland for the first question and John Carroll for the second, you were correct. And your choice is significant, for Maryland was a predominantly Catholic colony, and in 1789, the pope appointed John Carroll as the bishop of Baltimore. Carroll thus became the first American Catholic bishop. For the better part of a millennium, the Catholic Church had dominated European politics, and it had long voiced opposition to church-state separation and religious freedom. Given that history, what had prompted these remarkable Catholic statements?

The answer is simple. Catholics were a tiny minority religion in early America—less than 1 percent of the population at the time of the Revolutionary War. Many early Americans had come to the New World to escape Catholic persecution. Thus, they had a strong prejudice against Catholics that made it extremely difficult for members of that church to find true religious freedom. As a remedy for this problem, in 1649, the Catholic Lord Baltimore established Maryland as a colony where people of all religions, including Catholics, were welcomed. Prejudice against Catholics was still very strong throughout most of the colonies 140 years later, when John Carroll became bishop of Baltimore. Catholics were considered an alien element in the land of the free, which explains Carroll's comment about the importance of the clergy staying out of politics.

What were Catholics to do in the face of these strong anti-Catholic feelings? I will discuss three strategies that Catholic leaders adopted.

"We are Americans!"

Carroll was the leader of American Catholics in the years immediately following the Revolutionary War. One of his primary strategies was to project a sense that Catholics were genuine Americans. This was a major challenge, because the whole point of anti-Catholic prejudice was the idea that members of that church, as subjects of the pope, could not at the same time be loyal subjects of the United States government. People feared that given the chance, Catholics would try to turn America into a theocracy that was loyal to the pope. To allay this fear, American Catholics had to distance themselves from the Catholic philosophy of church-state union and adopt the American spirit of religious freedom.

Another Catholic leader who adopted this policy was John England, who became bishop of Charleston, South Carolina, in 1820. England "worked clearly to communicate the harmony between Catholic principles and the constitutional bases of American government."[2] He quoted the First Amendment to the United States Constitution at the head of the first issue of his *Catholic Miscellany* church newsletter. And the American Catholic hierarchy's *Pastoral Letter of 1837,* which John England wrote, made a remarkable statement: "We [do not] acknowledge any civil or political supremacy or power over us in any foreign potentate, *though that potentate might be the chief pastor of our church.*"[3]

England had good reason to want to demonstrate to the American public that Catholics were loyal to the American government and not to the pope. Irish immigration to the United States was just getting underway in the 1830s. Because the majority of these immigrants were Catholics, Protestants felt threatened, and a militant anti-Catholic backlash soon developed. For instance, Catholics built a convent of Ursulan nuns in Charlestown, Massachusetts, in 1817, for the purpose of training girls between the ages of six and fourteen. All went well for more than fifteen years, but in 1834, a rumor spread that the nuns were mistreating their students, and on August 14, a mob burned the convent to the ground. The authorities didn't intervene. Bishop John England wrote the affirmation quoted in the preceding paragraph three years after this incident.

During the second half of the nineteenth century, Catholic immigration from Europe reached flood proportions, not only from Ireland but also from Germany, Poland, Italy, and Catholic parts of the Balkans. This influx of Catholics fueled a strong "nativist" movement among Protestants, who believed that Catholics held political views that were a threat to the American way of life. Again, a number of Catholic leaders went out of their way to present Catholics to the public as loyal Americans.* Archbishop John Ireland of St. Paul, Minnesota, made the following statement in 1884: "There is no conflict between the Catholic Church and America. I could not utter one syllable that would belie, however

---

*Not all Catholic leaders of the time supported this liberal position. Some felt that the church should insulate itself from the American culture.

remotely, either the Church or the Republic, and when I assert, as I now solemnly do, that the principles of the Church are in thorough harmony with the interests of the Republic, I know in the depths of my soul that I speak the truth."[4]

These are truly remarkable statements, given the strong condemnation of the democratic form of government by the papacy during the nineteenth and early twentieth centuries that I shared with you in chapter 7. Affirming the American experiment in democracy was one way that Catholics tried to present themselves and their church as true Americans during the first 150 years of the nation's history.

Supporting America's wars

Historically, Catholics have also tried to present themselves as loyal Americans by giving strong support to America's war efforts. John Carroll gave enthusiastic support to the American side in the Revolutionary War, and during the War of 1812, "he was unswerving in his defense of the American cause."[5] Catholic author Timothy Byrnes commented, "America's first Catholic bishop understood, as so many of his successors would also understand, that nothing [would be more] effective in establishing the loyalty of American Catholics to their country than enthusiastic patriotism among the hierarchy at a time of war."[6]

During the Civil War, America's hierarchy in the North supported the Northern cause, and the hierarchy in the South supported the Southern cause. Even the Spanish-American War of 1898 garnered strong Catholic support—in spite of the fact that Spain, against which the United States was fighting, was a Catholic nation. Prior to the war, the pope, fearful of the consequence of war to Spanish Catholics, enlisted the aid of Minnesota's Archbishop John Ireland to mediate between the American and Spanish governments. Unfortunately, Ireland's efforts failed, and hostilities between the two countries broke out. However, once the war was underway, "In the tradition of Catholic support of American war efforts, . . . Ireland declared that he was 'for war—for the Stars and Stripes.' "[7] Thus, America's bishops issued a pastoral letter in May 1898 that included the following strongly worded paragraph: "Whatever may have been the individual opinions of Americans prior to the declaration of war, there can now be no two opinions as to the duty of every loyal citizen. . . . We, the members of the Catholic Church, are true Americans, and as such are loyal to our country and our flag and obedient to the highest decrees and the supreme authority of the nation."[8]

The First World War brought American Catholics both problems and a unique opportunity. The problem was the fear of America's Protestant community that Catholics with roots in Germany would be disloyal Americans. The war provided an opportunity for Catholics to demonstrate their loyalty. And they did. The bishops gave their full support to the war, and American Catholic soldiers performed bravely on behalf of their nation on the battlefield.

The church went a step further and organized a national effort to support the war. In 1917, under the leadership of Cardinal Gibbons, the bishops established the National Catholic War Council. The council enabled American Catholics to contribute funds and commit personnel to provide spiritual care and recreational services to those in the service during the war. The church's full support of the war paid off. Anti-Catholicism diminished significantly after World War I.

Timothy Byrnes has pointed out that "during World War II new heights were reached in the identification of Catholicism and American war aims."[9] Archbishop Francis Spellman distinguished himself as an unofficial chaplain to the American military forces overseas, and he served as President Roosevelt's personal representative to the Vatican. To cite Byrnes again, "Nothing pleased Spellman more than this opportunity to simultaneously advance the interests of his church and his nation and to serve as a personification of the compatibility of the two. The wartime sacrifices of Catholics in general so illustrated this compatibility that George Flynn argued that 'Catholic patriotism in the great crusade [WWII] would be so shining that never again would anyone dare to question their Americanism.' "[10]

Thus, a second way that many among the Catholic hierarchy sought to allay the anti-Catholic fears of America's Protestants was by giving unstinting support to all of the nation's wars. A third way was protecting their people through political action.

Political involvement

The flood of immigrants from Europe during the last half of the nineteenth century and the first two decades of the twentieth challenged America's Catholic leadership in two ways: First, they had to provide pastoral support for these various ethnic groups. And second, they had to defend their members against nativist antagonism. This latter challenge was made much easier by the fact that most Catholic immigrants congregated in America's large cities, especially New York, Boston, and Chicago.

This gave the Catholic bishops in these cities enormous political power on the local level, and they often used this power effectively to protect their members from hostile attacks.

When New York's Protestants threatened to riot against Catholics during the 1840s, Bishop Hughes threatened city hall that if even one Catholic church were damaged, his members would burn down the town. Timothy Byrnes made the following significant point: "Hughes stepped with both feet into the political process in order to defend Catholic interests he perceived to be under attack."[11] And, of course, Hughes had a perfect right—indeed an obligation—to do everything he could to protect his people.

Several decades later, Hughes challenged the common practice by teachers in New York City's public schools of reading passages to their classes each day from the Protestant King James Version of the Bible. Hughes protested that this offended Catholic sensibilities. However, school officials turned a blind eye, so Hughes tried to get the state to assist Catholics financially in setting up their own schools. This created a firestorm among Protestants, whereupon Hughes drew up his own slate of candidates for the New York State legislature and urged all Catholics to vote for it. When the bishop's candidates lost, he was left with no choice but to set up his own parochial school system without the benefit of state support.

An incident in Illinois in 1889 turned out much better for Catholics. The Illinois Republican Party managed to push a bill through the legislature stipulating that the requirement of compulsory school attendance could be met only by students who attended schools that were approved by the local school district. Thus, if a public school board didn't approve a Catholic school's curriculum, the students attending those schools would be truants. The bishops in Illinois condemned the law as a violation of Catholic rights, and in the 1892 election, they used their voting power to turn the Republicans out of office. The law was soon repealed—as it should have been!

Catholic political power in the large urban areas grew right along with the growth of the Catholic population. Tammany Hall, the Democratic political machine in New York, is a prime example. While it has been much maligned, Tammany Hall provided immigrants with vital social services. "Catholic politicians . . . understood that . . . their people were concerned with jobs, garbage removal, housing, and a hundred other matters large, and small. The pols [politicians] who organized a city's political subdivisions were, especially through their precinct captains, very much in touch with the needs of the people."[12] Tammany Hall was controlled by Catholics, giving the hierarchy enormous political power. In the large cities, it became nearly impossible for any candidate for political office to win at the polls without the bishop or the archbishop's approval.

To summarize then, for nearly two hundred years following the establishment of the United States as an independent nation, America's Catholics and their leaders made every effort to be seen as loyal American citizens. They did this through strong affirmations of support for America's democratic system and its military conflicts. The only challenge Catholics made to government during this period was at the local level, where they protected their own people from the anti-Catholic prejudice of the Protestant majority. This was an essential policy, given their small numbers in the early years of the republic and the hostility exhibited against Catholics during the nineteenth century as Catholic immigrants swarmed into the country from Europe. However, by the middle of the twentieth century, circumstances had changed dramatically. The effort to be seen as loyal Americans finally paid off, making it possible for Catholic leaders to take a much different approach to the nation and its government, as we shall see.

---

1. Cited in Timothy A. Byrnes, *Catholic Bishops in American Politics* (Princeton, N.J.: Princeton University Press, 1991), 13.

2. Peter Guilday, *The Life and Times of John England* (New York: America, 1927), 1:vii, viii; cited by Byrnes, 14.

3. Ibid., 15; italics added.

4. James H. Moynihan, *The Life of Archbishop John Ireland* (New York: Harper, 1953), 33, 34; cited in Byrnes, 15

5. Byrnes, 13.

6. Ibid., 13.

7. Ibid., 22.

8. Frank Reuter, *Catholic Influence on American Colonial Policies, 1898–1904* (Austin, Tex.: University of Texas Press, 1967), 7; cited by George J. Marlin in *The American Catholic Voter* (South Bend, Ind.: St. Augustine's Press, 2004), 150.

9. Byrnes, 31.

10. Ibid., 30.

11. Ibid., 16.

12. Marlin, 147.

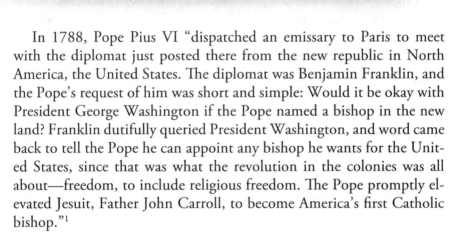

CHAPTER 16

Catholics in American History: 1960 to 2004— Challenging America

In 1788, Pope Pius VI "dispatched an emissary to Paris to meet with the diplomat just posted there from the new republic in North America, the United States. The diplomat was Benjamin Franklin, and the Pope's request of him was short and simple: Would it be okay with President George Washington if the Pope named a bishop in the new land? Franklin dutifully queried President Washington, and word came back to tell the Pope he can appoint any bishop he wants for the United States, since that was what the revolution in the colonies was all about—freedom, to include religious freedom. The Pope promptly elevated Jesuit, Father John Carroll, to become America's first Catholic bishop."[1]

Can you imagine Pope Benedict XVI humbly making a request like that of George W. Bush? But that was then. This is now.

I pointed out in chapter 10 that well into the twentieth century, America's conservative Protestants were strong supporters of church-state separation. They were also sufficiently fearful of any Catholic compromise of that principle that they demanded that John F. Kennedy take a vow favoring church-state separation before they would give him their support in the 1960 presidential election. However, that was about the last significant Protestant apprehension over Catholic political intentions. Kennedy's short presidency erased any lingering anti-Catholicism on the part of most Americans.

Thus, 1960 was a watershed year for American Catholics. Prior to 1960, a major function of the nation's Catholic bishops had been protecting their church and their members from anti-Catholic sentiments, and, during the nineteenth century, from isolated incidents of outright persecution. Since 1960, however, anti-Catholicism has virtually disappeared, with the occasional cases typically treated in the media as the rantings of religious fanatics. Kennedy's vow of support for church-state separation and his popularity as president were major contributing factors to the diminished anti-Catholicism, but several other factors were also involved. We will look at two: Catholic demographics and changes at the Vatican.

Catholic demographics

During the nineteenth and early twentieth centuries, America's Catholics were viewed largely as immigrants, and they were for the most part working-class citizens who were employed in the lower echelons of industry, government, finance, etc. However, for a hundred years prior to 1960, Catholics had been educating their children in their own schools, and following World War II, that education began paying off as Catholics entered the professions and higher positions in government and industry. Also, prior to 1950, Catholics tended to live in ghettos in the inner cities, but following World War II, they started moving into the suburbs, where they made friends with their Protestant middle- and upper-class neighbors. This also broke down prejudices, as Protestants began to realize that Catholics are normal people. In his book *Catholic Bishops in American Politics*, Timothy Byrnes said, "Catholics left the immigrant era behind in the 1960s in what [Bishop Andrew] Greeley termed a 'remarkable success story.' In fact, they emerged from their long immigrant history as one of the best paid, most highly educated population cohorts in the United States. 'If parity with the national performance is a mark of acculturation,' Greeley concluded, 'then American Catholics are now thoroughly acculturated to American society.' "[2]

Changes at the Vatican

Actions at the Vatican also contributed to the lessening of prejudice against Catholics. John XXIII was unusually popular in America during his short reign as pope (1958–1963), as was John Paul II during the final quarter of the twentieth century. And the Second Vatican Council's strong pronouncements in support of the religious freedom of the individual put to rest most remaining Protestant fears about Catholics and church-state separation.

Finally, the Second Vatican Council's *Pastoral Constitution on the Church in the Modern World* revolutionized the church's approach to democratic governments. For 150 years, popes had fulminated against democracies and all but forbidden priests and bishops to become involved in democratic politics. "The Vatican had repeatedly cautioned American bishops not to poison the church through contact with the American culture." Following Vatican II, however, "the bishops were no longer to view American culture as a force against which the church had to defend itself. Rather, they were to view that culture as the very arena in which the church would pursue its mission."[3]

For the previous two hundred years, a number of America's bishops had endorsed the American democratic experiment as compatible with Catholic political thought. The *Pastoral Constitution* didn't go quite that far. Rather, it "envisioned the church as a challenger and critic of modern culture."[4] The *Pastoral Constitution* included a list of issues in contemporary culture that it encouraged the church to focus on—a list that Byrne said "reads like a blueprint of the American hierarchy's political agenda of the 1970s and 1980s."[5]

All this translated into another benefit for the bishops: They could devote more of their energies to political action without having to worry about a Protestant backlash. Even the priestly sexual abuse scandal of the late twentieth and the early twenty-first centuries didn't provoke anti-Catholic prejudice the way it might have three or four generations earlier.

National political action

In the 1960s, the bishops began paying attention to politics at the national level as well as the local. Now that they no longer had to worry about their political stances arousing anti-Catholic bigotry, they began taking a more critical approach to the national government. Thus, whereas in the past they had placed a major emphasis on identifying themselves *with* the policies of the American government, they now began voicing their own moral judgment *against* political issues that conflicted with church teaching. And nobody seemed to mind. As Byrne put it, "Decreased parochialism and diminished episcopal authority [authority of the bishops] led to decreased anti-Catholicism and less strident opposition to the political activities of Catholics and their clerical leaders."[6]

The result of all this was that, during the two decades following Vatican II, the American bishops issued several pastoral letters on topics such as the economy, low-income housing, and farm labor that spelled out Catholic moral and ethical convictions in these areas. In 1976, the bishops also prepared a document titled *Political Responsibility: Reflections on an Election Year.* This document affirmed the bishops' responsibility to take a firm stand on current political issues. A 1971 *Resolution on Southeast Asia* expressed strong disagreement with the conflict in Vietnam. And in a 1983 pastoral letter titled *The Challenge of Peace,* the bishops took a firm stand against the use of nuclear weapons. This pastoral letter was a direct response to Ronald Reagan's platform in the 1980 election that called for a completely new series of nuclear weapons systems. One of the letter's concluding paragraphs stated, "The decisions about nuclear weapons are among the most pressing moral questions of our age. . . . Good ends (defending one's country, protecting freedom, etc.) cannot justify immoral means (the use of weapons which kill indiscriminately and threaten whole societies). We fear that our world and nation are headed in the wrong direction."[7]

We saw in the last chapter that in every previous military conflict, from the Revolutionary War in 1776 to World War II in the 1940s, Catholic leaders took a firm stand in *support* of America's wars. This was one way they presented Catholics to the nation as loyal Americans. The Vietnam conflict was the first war in which the American Catholic hierarchy openly *opposed* an American war, and the challenge to America's nuclear arms build-up was the first time they confronted a major military policy. By this time, they didn't have to prove Catholic loyalty.

Abortion

By far the Catholic hierarchy's most important political initiative during the last half of the twentieth century involved abortion, and that continues to be true in the early twenty-first century. Prior to the United States Supreme Court's 1973 *Roe v. Wade* decision that affirmed a woman's right to have an abortion, just about all political action dealing with abortion happened at the state level, and it was at that level that the Catholic hierarchy had to respond. *Roe v. Wade* brought the debate to the national level. Coincidentally, the National Conference of Catholic Bishops' ad hoc committee on pro-life activities met for the first time the day after the court handed down its abortion decision! The committee immediately condemned the court's ruling and urged that every legal approach for reversing it be explored, including the passage of a pro-life amendment to the United States Constitution.

Nor did the bishops stop with making official pronouncements. In 1975, they published a *Pastoral Plan for Pro-life Activities.* This action "has been called the most 'focused and aggressive political leadership' ever exerted by the American Catholic hierarchy."[8] A brief review of the plan reveals that this is a valid assessment. The *Pastoral Plan* calls for action by Catholics at the levels of the state, the diocese, and the local parish. It lists the responsibilities to be carried out at each level, with the ultimate goal being a reversal of *Roe v. Wade* by the United States Supreme Court and the addition of a pro-life amendment to the United States Constitution.

The *Pastoral Plan* states, "Catholic civil leaders who reject or ignore the Church's teaching on the sanctity of human life do so at risk to their own spiritual well-being. No public official, especially one claiming to be a faithful and serious Catholic, can responsibly advocate for or actively support direct attacks on innocent human life." The document goes on to say, "The abortion decisions of the U.S. Supreme Court must be reversed. . . . Our own commitment will not waver. Our efforts will not cease. We will speak out on behalf of the sanctity of life wherever and whenever it is threatened."

Most Americans are not aware of the extent to which the *Pastoral Plan* and related initiatives of the Catholic hierarchy have contributed to the antiabortion activities of Religious Right Protestants. Timothy Byrne stated it this way:

An adequate account of the political role of evangelicals and fundamentalists in the late 1970s and early 1980s has to include . . . a recognition of the indirect but important role that the Catholic hierarchy played in the new right's strategy.

The bishops set the groundwork for the creation of the pro-family movement in the late 1970s through their role in the creation of the prolife movement during the preceding decade. From the very first rumblings of liberalization of abortion laws in the 1960s, the bishops firmly identified their church and their own moral authority with the right-to-life cause. They were also the source of critical early funding of the right-to-life movement. . . . The bishops did not agree with the new right on many social issues, but when the new right set out to mold the right-to-life movement to new political purposes, it was dealing with a movement *whose original institutional structure and financial resources had come directly from the National Conference of Catholic Bishops.*[9]

Connie Paige wrote, "The Roman Catholic Church created the right-to-life movement. Without the church, the movement would not exist as such today. The church provided from the start the organizational infrastructure, the communications network, the logistical support, the resources, the ideology and the people, as well as a ready-made nationwide political machine otherwise impossible to duplicate. Always, the church contributed money, a great deal of it, either through its own organizations or through direct grants to independent but related groups."[10]

Thus, it is not too much to say that America's right-to-life movement, which is widely perceived by the American public as a fundamentalist Protestant movement, is in reality largely the creation of the American Catholic Church and its bishops. Connie Paige was correct. Without the Catholic Church's support at every level, the pro-life movement as we know it today simply wouldn't exist.

The Catholic voter

One other factor contributed to Catholic political influence in national politics during the twentieth century: the increasing power of Catholics as a voting block. During most of American history, the Catholic hierarchy didn't exercise significant political power on the national level. However, through the ballot box and the votes of individual Catholics, the church had a significant influence on national politics as early as the mid-nineteenth century. As the percentage of Catholics in America has grown from less than 1 percent in 1776 to a little more than 25 percent today, America's political leaders of both parties have become increasingly aware that Catholics constitute a block of voters worth cultivating.

During the early part of the twentieth century, America's Catholics were overwhelmingly Democratic and typically voted for Democratic candidates. The only exceptions were 1952 and 1956, when Catholics supported the Republican Dwight Eisenhower. In 1960, Catholics returned to the Democratic Party, giving their full support to John F. Kennedy, who became the first Catholic to win the presidency of the United States. However, a factor that was little noticed at the time of the 1964 election hinted at the beginning of a trend that would continue to the end of the century. In the election of that year, White Catholics in some parts of New York's boroughs of Queens, Staten Island, Brooklyn, and the Bronx actually gave Barry Goldwater solid majorities.[11] In his book *The American Catholic Voter,* George Marlin concluded, "Myopic reform Democrats could not see that working-class ethnic Catholics in the sixties no longer felt wanted in the Democratic Party."[12]

Catholics voted strongly in support of Ronald Reagan in both 1980 and 1984, and Reagan rewarded their efforts in several ways. The most significant was the establishment of diplomatic relations between the United States government and the Vatican in 1984. Reagan also appointed a number of Catholics to cabinet posts and ambassadorships, including William Casey, head of the CIA; National Security Advisors Richard Allen and William Clark; Secretary of State Alexander Haig; Ambassador at Large Vernon Walters; and Reagan's first ambassador to the Vatican, William Wilson.[13] These were among the key players in Reagan's foreign policy team.

And this team had a significant influence in getting Catholic moral and ethical principles injected into American government policies. Time magazine reported that one of the team's achievements on behalf of their church was to get the administration "to alter its foreign aid program to comply with the church's teachings on birth control. . . . The U.S. withdrew funding from, among others, two of the world's largest family planning organizations: The International Planned Parenthood Federation and the United Nations Fund for Population."[14] William Wilson, the president's ambassador to the Vatican, stated, "American policy was changed as a result of the Vatican's not agreeing with our policy."[15] And it was Catholics in government who brought this about on behalf of their church.

Think about that: The United States government capitulated to Catholic pressure and enforced a Catholic moral dogma! And they achieved this through the efforts of church members who had been appointed to high positions in government. Even fifty years earlier, similar Catholic efforts to influence a government policy would have aroused a storm of protest, and 150 years earlier, it might well have stirred up some violent persecution. But in the mid-1980s, it passed with scarcely a ripple.

Party switching

Another important change occurred in the 1980s: Catholics began switching their votes from the Democratic to the Republican Party.

Between 1980 and 1984, the proportion of Catholics who considered themselves Republican increased from 17 percent to 26 percent.[16] Obviously, this voter shift didn't constitute a mass exodus out of the Democratic Party, but it was significant enough for the Gallup Organization to conclude that "Catholics had become a two-party church," and "no candidate, Democrat or Republican, can take the Catholic vote for granted."[17] A couple of chapters back, we saw that the 1994 mid-term election gave the Republicans strong majorities in both the Senate and the House of Representatives, breaking nearly sixty years of Democratic hold on both houses of Congress. In this election, Catholics supported the Republican candidates by a margin of 52 percent to 48 percent.

George H. W. Bush (Bush I) courted the Catholic vote avidly, and he rewarded it when he won. Within a month after he took office, he included all five American cardinals in meetings at the White House, and two cardinals—Bernard Law of Boston and John O'Conner of New York—spent nights there. Doug Wead, a special assistant to the president, stated that Bush "appointed more Catholic cabinet officers than any other [president] in American history."[18]

As just about every American knows, the 2000 election was so close that the United States Supreme Court ended up settling it in favor of George W. Bush. One of George Bush's first priorities in the months that followed was to cultivate the Catholic vote. Shortly after he was sworn in, he met with Catholic Charities officials to discuss issues they had in the area of tax deductions to charitable organizations. On March 17, Bush celebrated St. Patrick's Day with officials from the Republic of Ireland. In late March, he invited several cardinals and bishops to the White House, where he praised the Catholic educational system. In April, he dedicated the Pope John Paul II Cultural Center in Washington, D.C., where he "spoke passionately of 'the innocent child waiting to be born' "[19]—a theme that was sure to please his hosts. And a few weeks later, Bush was the keynote speaker at the graduation ceremonies for Notre Dame University. George Marlin summarized Bush's support of Catholic interests during his first term: "Throughout his first four years, President Bush initiated and promoted programs and policies that appealed to Catholics. He reversed pro-abortion Clinton executive orders, proposed faith-based initiatives, voucher experiments, and limits on stem-cell research. He also signed into law the ban on partial-birth abortion."[20]

The 2004 election

All this paid off in the 2004 election, which conventional wisdom said Bush would lose—but he didn't. Catholics had a lot to do with that.

Exit polls in November 2004 indicated that 63 percent of Catholics voted in the 2004 election compared to 53 percent of the general population. And Catholics supported George W. Bush over John Kerry by a margin of 52 percent to 47 percent, in spite of the fact that Kerry was a Catholic. Of those who attended Mass once a week, 56 percent voted for Bush. Fifty percent of those who attended Mass less frequently also cast their ballots for Bush.[21] And in the critical state of Ohio, which decided the election, Bush took 53 percent of the Catholic vote to Kerry's 46 percent.[22]

All of which brings us to the real significance of the 2004 election. I pointed out in chapter 13 that the election that year established the Religious Right as a very real power block in American politics that could no longer be ignored or treated as an aberration. That election also demonstrated the political power of America's Catholics, who cooperated with Religious Right Protestants to put Bush back in office in spite of the fact that his Iraq war was highly unpopular with the majority of Americans.

Part of the problem for the Democrats was Kerry's position on abortion and gay rights, which set him at loggerheads with both the Religious Right and the hierarchy of his own church. The hierarchy made it clear that they would rather have a Protestant president who supported their values than a Catholic president who didn't. In fact, several bishops and archbishops stated publicly that Kerry need not appear for Communion in their churches, because he would be refused. One of these bishops, St. Louis Archbishop Raymond Burke, said, "Any legislator who is publicly supporting laws which favor abortion or euthanasia may not present himself or herself for Holy Communion."[23]

And Burke and fellow-members of the hierarchy had the Vatican's support. Because of Kerry's views on abortion, Washington, D.C., Cardinal Theodore McCarrick, chairman of the bishops' taskforce on "Catholics in Political Life," asked the Vatican for guidance on how to relate to Kerry and other politicians who failed to support the church's moral principles. Joseph Cardinal Ratzinger responded that priests and bishops whose congregations include politicians who support abortion or euthanasia should tell the politician that "he is not to present himself for Holy

Communion until he brings to an end the *objective situation of sin*, and [they should warn] him that he will otherwise be denied Communion."[24] Thus, Cardinal Ratzinger, who is now Pope Benedict XVI, gave his approval to Archbishop Raymond Burke's stand against Kerry.[25]

Please notice what Ratzinger said: The politician is to be informed that his failure to support the church's view of abortion or euthanasia *is a sin*. In Christian theology, both Protestant and Catholic, sin will keep a person from receiving eternal life.

In 2002, the Vatican issued a "Doctrinal Note on Some Questions Regarding the Participation of Catholics in Political Life." The introduction of this "Doctrinal Note" says that it is "directed to Bishops of the Catholic Church and, in a particular way, to Catholic politicians and all lay members of the faithful called to participate in the political life of democratic societies."[26] The "Note" states, "A well-formed Christian [read: Catholic] conscience does not permit one to vote for a political program or an individual law which contradicts the fundamental contents of faith and morals."[27] In other words, Catholic lawmakers *must speak out and cast their legislative votes in accordance with church teachings*. The "Doctrinal Note" goes on to say, "John Paul II, continuing the constant teaching of the Church, has reiterated many times that those who are directly involved in lawmaking bodies have 'a grave and clear obligation to oppose' any law that attacks human life. For them, as for every Catholic, it is impossible to promote such laws or to vote for them."[28]

On February 28, 2006, fifty-five of the seventy-three Catholic members of the United States House of Representatives told America's leading bishops that "the primacy of their conscience[s]" led them to support abortion rights, and they asked the bishops if it would not be possible for the church to give them the freedom to vote their conscience in spite of the church's teaching to the contrary. The answer, delivered on March 10, was a firm No.[29]

Please take a moment to reflect on what I have shared in the previous several paragraphs:

- Bishop Burke, with Vatican support, said he would deny Communion to John Kerry because his stand on abortion contradicted Catholic morality.
- Cardinal Ratzinger (who would become Pope Benedict XVI) told America's Catholic bishops that a politician who fails to

vote in harmony with the church's stand on abortion and euthanasia is in a state of sin.

- The Vatican's 2002 "Doctrinal Note on . . . Catholics in Political Life" states that a good Catholic conscience cannot vote for laws that contradict "the fundamental contents of faith and morals"—that is, Catholic faith and morals.
- John Paul II said that "it is impossible" for Catholic legislators to promote or vote for "any law that attacks human life." He meant, of course, any law that attacks human life *as Catholic morality defines it.**
- When fifty-five Catholic legislators petitioned their bishops for permission to vote contrary to Catholic teaching in the U.S. Congress, the answer was a flat and unequivocal *No!*

My question is this: What business have legislators consulting their church leaders for *permission* to vote a certain way? For *guidance?* Yes, absolutely. But for *permission?* In each instance, the Catholic hierarchy told these lawmakers that in their official government duties, they were bound by their church to vote in harmony with their church's teaching on certain issues. Bishop Burke even went so far as to say he would refuse Communion to a politician who dared to voice opinions and to cast his vote contrary to church teaching. As recently as the 1950s and possibly even the 1960s, a position statement like that would have raised a firestorm of protest from America's Protestants. But not in 2004! Today, America's Religious Right Protestants cheered.

You may agree with the values that John Paul II and Bishop Burke were defending. The issue isn't the values. It's whether a church should deny—or threaten to deny—its sacraments to members who fail to support church teaching by their votes in the United States Congress or a state legislature. It's whether a church should order its members who are judges, legislators, mayors, governors, and presidents to support church teaching in their legislative and judicial decisions and refuse them per-

---

*Americans, both religious and secular, hold a variety of opinions about abortion, euthanasia, capital punishment, stem-cell research, and contraception. However, regardless of what others may think, America's Catholic bishops won't be satisfied until all of their moral principles are a part of U.S. law, either as legislation, judicial decree, or Constitutional amendment.

mission to participate in church life if they fail to comply. It's whether a church should pressure legislators to vote a certain way by telling them that the "wrong" vote is a sin.

Back to the Middle Ages

A thousand years ago, Pope Gregory VII excommunicated King Henry IV of Germany when the king defied the pope over the appointment of the bishop of Milan. The king crossed the Alps in the middle of winter and stood in the snow for three days to petition the pope's forgiveness so that he could be reinstated to his throne. We naturally condemn the pope's action as a wholly inappropriate exercise of spiritual authority to achieve a political end. It's a classic example of church domination of the state during the medieval period. Yet the same principle of the relation of the spiritual power to the political power is being played out before our very eyes in twenty-first century America, and we scarcely blink.

It's entirely appropriate for any church to educate its members regarding the church's moral principles. It's also appropriate for the church to *encourage* its members in political office to support the church's moral teachings with their legislative voice and vote. However, *it is totally inappropriate for a religious body to control its members in political office by censuring, withholding the sacraments, or excommunicating those members who speak and vote contrary to church teaching.* This is what Gregory VII did to Henry IV a thousand years ago, and it's what the Catholic hierarchy is doing in America today. But it is as improper today to use spiritual power to force a political outcome as it was improper then.

Protestants in the nineteenth century were deeply concerned about the possibility that Catholic rulers and lawmakers might legislate church doctrine into American law. They worried that the pope, as the head of a foreign government, would use his spiritual power to control the American government. That concern was legitimate, in spite of the unfortunate anti-Catholic bigotry and in some cases outright persecution of Catholics that it led to. In 1960, John F. Kennedy told a group of conservative Protestant ministers in Houston, Texas, that he believed "in an America . . . where no public official either requests or accepts instructions on public policy from the Pope, [the] National Council of Churches or any other ecclesiastical source."[30] Yet today, the very thing that Protestants most feared throughout the nineteenth and early twentieth centuries has become a reality, and very few of them care. In fact, many applaud!

Now, consider this too: The Catholic population in America is continuing to explode through immigration—not from Europe today, but from Mexico, Central America, and the Caribbean. As the percentage of the American population that's Catholic continues to rise, which it inevitably will, what kind of pressure will the hierarchy be emboldened to exert on the nation's politics and its politicians in the future? And to what extent will future Supreme Court justices interpret America's Constitution in harmony with *Catholic* rather than traditional Protestant principles of morality and the relationship of church and state?

The Catholic Church in America truly has done an about-face in the years since 1960. Its political power today is enormous, and it is using that power to challenge the American political system as never before. And Religious Right Protestants now agree with Catholics on a number of key issues regarding morality and the relationship of the church to the state. It is not too much to say, in fact, that, when they unite on an issue, Roman Catholics and Religious Right Protestants are now in a position to elect to office anyone they wish and to enact any legislation their hearts may desire.

So what does the future hold? Seventh-day Adventists have a suggestion.

---

1. Jim Nicholson, "The United States and the Holy See: The Long Road, a Brief History of U.S.-Holy See Relations"; http://vatican.usembassy.it/text/policy/speeches/speech.asp?id=sp020007.

2. Timothy Byrne, *Catholic Bishops in American History* (Princeton, N.J.: Princeton University Press, 1991), 36. Quotes by Andrew Greeley are from *Catholic Schools in a Declining Church* (Kansas City, Mo.: Sheed and Ward, 1976), 74, 47.

3. Byrne, 40.

4. Ibid., 41.

5. Ibid.

6. Ibid., 37.

7. "National Council of Catholic Bishops, "The Challenge of Peace: God's Promise and Our Response—Part 2," para. 332; http://www.osjspm.org/the_challenge_of_peace_2.aspx.

8. Byrne, 58.

9. Ibid., 90, 91; italics added.

10. Connie Paige, *The Right to Lifers: Who They Are, How They Operate, Where They Get Their Money* (New York: Summit Books, 1983), 51.

11. George J. Marlin, *The American Catholic Voter* (South Bend, Ind.: St. Augustine Press, 2004), 59, 60.

12. Ibid., 268.

13. John W. Swomley, "One Nation Under God"; http://www.population -security.org/swom-98-05.htm.

14. "The U.S. and the Vatican on Birth Control," *Time*, February 24, 1992, 35.

15. Ibid.

16. Marlin, 303.

17. Ibid., 306, 307.

18. Swomley.

19. Marlin, 333, 334.

20. Ibid., 334.

21. Center for Applied Research in the Apostolate, "Sixty-three Percent of Catholics Voted in the 2004 Presidential Election," Georgetown University, November 22, 2004; http://www.georgetown.edu/research/cara/Press112204.pdf.

22. Joe Feuerherd, "Cardinal Ratzinger as Presidential Kingmaker," *National Catholic Reporter* online; http://www.nationalcatholicreporter.org/washington/ wnb042105.htm.

23. Rogers Cadenhead, "Bush Courts Catholics," Workbench, http://www .cadenhead.org/workbench/news/2800/president-bush-courts-catholics.

24. Feuerherd, italics added.

25. Ibid.

26. Congregation for the Doctrine of the Faith, "Doctrinal Note on Some Questions Regarding the Participation of Catholics in Political Life"; http://www .vatican.va/roman_curia/congregations/cfaith/documents/rc_con_cfaith_doc _20021124_politica_en.html.

27. Ibid.

28. Ibid.

29. *Christian Century*, April 4, 2006, 17.

30. Cited in Marlin, 254

PART THREE

The Mark of
the Beast

CHAPTER 17

The Mark of the Beast:
Preliminary
Considerations

Back when I was studying at the seminary, I painted houses to earn my living expenses. Painting a house seems easy enough at first thought: Just grab a brush and a bucket of paint and go to work. Not so! Depending on the condition of the previous paint job and of the building itself, as much as 90 percent of a house painter's work is in preparing the surface to be painted. One has to scrape off the old paint and sand the surface down so it's smooth. Holes must be puttied, and the cracks between boards caulked. If there's mildew on the eaves, it has to be killed. Any bare wood has to be primed. Sometimes the building is in need of repairs, which will also have to be primed. Only when this preliminary work is completed can the painter apply the paint.

Similarly, you will find our study of the mark of the beast much easier to understand if we take the time to do some preliminary examination of several background factors. That's the purpose of this chapter.

A mark of which beast?

Revelation 13 presents us with two beasts, one that rises from the sea and the other that rises from the land. To which of these beasts does the mark pertain? Revelation doesn't actually tell us. Obviously, then, before we try to identify the mark of the beast, we must know which beast we're talking about!

Here's a good clue: In verses 12 to 15, which describe the land beast, the word *he* always refers to the land beast, and in each verse, the word *beast* denotes the sea beast:

174

- "*He* [the land beast] exercised all the authority of the *first beast* . . . and made the earth and its inhabitants worship the *first beast*" (verse 12, italics added).
- "*He* was given power to do [signs] on behalf of the *first beast*" (verse 14, italics added).
- "*He* ordered them [the inhabitants of the earth] to set up an image in honor of the *beast who was wounded by the sword and yet lived*" (verse 14, italics added).
- "*He* was given power to give breath to the image of the *first beast*" (verse 15, italics added).

In four of the occurrences of the word *beast*, Revelation identifies it as "the first beast." In the fifth occurrence, Revelation speaks of "the beast who was wounded by the sword and yet lived." There is no doubt, then, about which beast is meant. Now let's examine verses 16 and 17, which again use both *he* and *beast*, this time in connection with the mark: "*He* [the land beast] also forced everyone, small and great, rich and poor, free and slave, to receive a mark on his right hand or on his forehead, so that no one could buy or sell unless he had the mark, which is the name of the *beast* or the number of his name" (italics added).

As in the previous verses, the pronoun *he* in verse 16 clearly refers to the land beast. However, the word *beast* in verse 17 is not identified the way it was in verses 12–15, so it could refer to either the sea beast or the land beast. But three factors connect the mark to the sea beast:

- First, because in verses 12–15, the word *he* always refers to the land beast and the word *beast* always refers to the sea beast, it's reasonable to understand both words as denoting the same entities here.
- Second, verse 15 speaks of an "image *of the first beast*" (italics added) and verse 17 speaks of a "mark . . . *of the beast*" (italics added). In the Greek, the two prepositional phrases are nearly identical and have identical objects ("beast"), which suggests that they're both referring to the same entity.
- Third, it would be strange for the text to read that the *land beast* forced everyone to receive a mark *of the land beast*. If John had meant that the mark was linked to the land beast, it would seem more appropriate for him to have said that the land beast forced everyone to receive a mark of *himself*.

It's reasonable, then, to conclude that the expression "mark of the beast" refers to the sea beast, not the land beast. That, I believe, is how most interpreters of prophecy understand it. It's definitely how Adventists understand it.

The two sides during the end time

Several of Jesus' parables in Matthew provide us with glimpses of the end time, and a common theme runs through them: The world's people at that time will be divided into just two classes—the righteous and the wicked. Jesus used a variety of symbols to represent the two groups. The list below summarizes them:

- The wheat and the tares (Matthew 13:24–30, 36–43).
- The good fish and the bad fish (Matthew 13:47–50).
- The faithful and the wicked servants (Matthew 24:45–51).
- The wise and the foolish virgins (Matthew 25:1–13).
- The faithful and the unfaithful servants (Matthew 25:14–30).
- The sheep and the goats (Matthew 25:31–46).

Revelation also says that during earth's final conflict, the world will be divided into two classes of people: the righteous, who receive the seal of God, and the wicked, who receive the mark of the beast. At the present, there are three classes of people in the world: Those who have made a definite decision for God, those who have made a definite decision against Him, and those who haven't made a decision either way.

Revelation 7:1–4 describes the sealing of God's people. We know them as the mysterious 144,000. We see this group again in Revelation 14:1–5, where they are described as "those who did not defile themselves with women, for they kept themselves pure. They follow the Lamb wherever he goes. . . . No lie was found in their mouths; they are blameless" (verses 4, 5).

On the other hand, those who receive the mark of the beast will worship the dragon (Satan), the sea beast, and its image (Revelation 13:4, 8, 14). And if they persist in their rebellion against God, they will suffer the outpouring of His wrath unmixed with mercy (Revelation 14:9–11).

It appears evident that at the point in history that Revelation 13 and 14 describe, those who are in rebellion against God still have the opportunity to repent, accept Jesus, and declare their loyalty to His commandments. I say this because of three angels that Revelation 14 shows us. The first angel calls on the world's inhabitants to worship God (verses 6, 7), and the third angel warns about the approaching wrath of God (verses 9–11), which is the seven last plagues (Revelation 16). The third angel's message is clearly calling for people to turn away from worshiping the beast and its image lest they receive the mark, so the opportunity to do so still exists at that point.

Obviously, then, whatever the mark is, God is extremely anxious for people everywhere to avoid receiving it!

A spiritual condition

There's an extremely important point about the mark of the beast that we need to understand before we try to interpret it: The mark symbolizes a profound spiritual condition on the part of those who receive it. I pointed out in chapter 2 of this book that Satan rebelled against God in heaven itself and that he involved the human race in his rebellion when he was cast down to our earth. Thus, for the past several millenniums, our planet has been the theater in which the conflict between good and evil has been played out. The last half of Revelation describes the final days of this conflict. The language is highly symbolic and very graphic. But when we read carefully, we can recognize that the issues during the final conflict will bring together everything the Bible has to say about our relationship with Jesus: Have we truly been converted? Do we have faith in God's promises? Are we willing to trust our very lives with Jesus? Are we committed to obeying Him even if it means suffering a martyr's death?

Those who stand firmly for God during the final conflict will have developed this kind of an intimate relationship with Jesus. Their love for Him will be so great and their trust in Him will be so complete that, like the three Hebrews, they would rather die than disobey God. Satan will fail in all his efforts to force them to disobey God's commandments. That's why Revelation says that God's end-time people will "obey God's commandments" (Revelation 12:17; 14:12).

Chapter 12:17 also says that God's end-time people will "hold to the testimony of Jesus." Some Bible versions translate this differently: "bear witness to Jesus." Both translations are correct as far as the Greek is concerned.* For our purpose at this point, the "bear witness" version is the more helpful. God's people who live during earth's final crisis will be so

---

*See *The Seventh-day Adventist Bible Commentary* on Revelation 12:17.

committed to Him that they will witness for Him even under the most intense persecution.

Revelation 14:12 gives a similar insight into the spiritual character of God's end-time people. Immediately after the angel's ominous warning against worshiping the beast and his image, he briefly describes God's people: "Here is the patience of the saints: here are they that keep the commandments of God, and the faith of Jesus" (KJV). Several characteristics stand out in this verse. Obedience to God's commandments is repeated from chapter 12:17. Also, God's people are described as having great patience, and they "keep . . . the faith of Jesus." One conclusion that I believe we can reasonably draw from this verse is that God's people who live during earth's final crisis will have learned a correct balance between faith and works. They will be anxious to obey God completely, yet they will also recognize that their salvation depends solely on Jesus' sacrifice for their sins and His attribution to them of His righteousness.

Revelation 13:16 says that the wicked can receive the mark of the beast either in the forehead or in the hand. That is, they can receive the mark of the beast out of conviction (the forehead—the mind), or they can receive it as a matter of convenience (the hand)—yielding to the beast's spiritual pressure even though they don't believe his propaganda. However, people can receive God's seal only in their foreheads. No one can serve God merely out of convenience.

The spiritual condition of those who receive God's seal is further described in Revelation 14:4, 5: "They kept themselves pure. They follow the Lamb wherever he goes. . . . No lie was found in their mouths; they are blameless." Obviously, these people have developed a very intimate relationship with Jesus!

On the other hand, it's very clear from Revelation that those who receive the mark of the beast will be in total rebellion against God. This is also a profoundly spiritual condition, albeit a negative one. However, while it would be easy to suppose that all those who rebel against God during the final conflict will be atheists and other secular people who openly deny Him, the most deceptive form of rebellion against God is that which passes as a form of *serving* Him. Jesus said that when He returns, many people will say to Him, " ' "Lord, Lord, did we not prophesy in your name, and in your name drive out demons and perform many miracles?" Then I will tell them plainly, "I never knew you. Away from me, you evildoers!" ' " (Matthew 7:22, 23). I propose that many of those who receive the mark of the beast will consider themselves to be upstanding Christians!

False worship in Revelation 13 and 14

Worship is a further indication of the spiritual condition of those who receive the mark of the beast. Worship is one of the major themes in Revelation 13 and 14, and two kinds are described: the true worship of God, and a false worship of the sea beast and its image. Before we attempt to interpret the mark of the beast, it will be helpful to examine what Revelation says about this false worship.

Chapters 13 and 14 mention false worship several times. The first mention is in Revelation 13:4: "Men worshiped the dragon because he had given authority to the beast, and they also worshiped the beast and asked, 'Who is like the beast? Who can make war with him?' " This verse speaks of two entities receiving worship: the dragon and the beast. The dragon, of course, is Satan (see Revelation 12:9), and because the worship described in verse 4 is directed in part to him, it obviously must be a false form of worship.

Revelation 13:8 confirms this conclusion: "All inhabitants of the earth will worship the beast—all whose names have not been written in the book of life belonging to the Lamb that was slain from the creation of the world." The "book of life" contains the names of God's true people (see Revelation 3:5). Thus, the worship of the beast is clearly a false form of worship, because only those whose names are *not* written in the book of life will participate in it. God's true people will refuse to worship the beast.

We also discover a link between false worship and the activities of the land beast. However, there's a difference: While the sea beast *accepts* worship, the land beast *enforces* it. We read about this twice in the last half of Revelation 13: "He [the land beast] exercised all the authority of the first beast on his behalf, and made the earth and its inhabitants worship the first beast, whose fatal wound had been healed" (verse 12). "He [the land beast] was given power to give breath to the image of the first beast, so that it could speak and cause all who refused to worship the image to be killed" (verse 15).

Notice that the land beast "*made* the earth and its inhabitants worship the first beast." It "*cause[d]* all who refused to worship the image [of the first beast] to be killed." In some way, the land beast will force human beings to worship the sea beast. During the medieval period of the papacy,

179

the church made the laws, and the state enforced them. Sometimes the church even excused the imprisonment and execution of "heretics" on the grounds that it didn't punish these people, the state did—though the church had turned them over to the state for that very punishment. Thus, during the medieval period, the state was the enforcement arm of the church.

Revelation predicts the same relationship between church and state for the end time: The land beast, which is a political entity, will enforce the worship of the sea beast, the religious entity. However, this false worship will come with a terrible price tag. Revelation 14:9–11 says, "A third angel followed them and said in a loud voice: 'If anyone worships the beast and his image and receives his mark on the forehead or on the hand, he, too, will drink of the wine of God's fury, which has been poured full strength into the cup of his wrath. He will be tormented with burning sulfur in the presence of the holy angels and of the Lamb. . . . There is no rest day or night for those who worship the beast and his image, or for anyone who receives the mark of his name.' "

This "third angel's message" is the most severe threat recorded anywhere in the Bible that God makes toward human beings. So whatever this "mark of the beast" is, you and I had better learn about it and do everything in our power to avoid receiving it!

Chapter 18

Revelation 13 and the Mark of the Beast

Several years ago, Professor Kevin Warwick walked up to the door of his office at the University of Reading in Reading, England, and the door opened automatically, his office lights switched on, and a voice said, "Welcome, Professor Warwick!" Did someone inside Professor Warwick's office see him approach, open the door, turn on the lights, and call out the greeting? No. Did a hidden camera catch his movements and transmit the information to a monitor in another part of the building, prompting a security guard to flip a switch that opened the door and turned on the lights, and did the security guard then say hello? No.

The story is both more simple and more complex. The week before, Professor Warwick had an inch-long microchip implanted under his skin. A scanner read the information embedded in the microchip as he approached his office, and the scanner sent the command that unlocked the door, turned on the lights, and activated a digital recording that welcomed him.[1]

Today, millions of dogs, cats, horses, and cattle have microchips implanted under their skin. These chips enable veterinarians and animal control officers to identify lost or stolen animals and return them to the rightful owners. Someday, parents may be able to have these chips implanted in their young children, making it possible to identify them should they ever be kidnapped. And adult children may be able to monitor the activities of their aging parents: Did Mom take her medication this morning? Did Dad brush his teeth? And if the parent should fall or wander away from home, the chip could also send a signal to a device that would notify the adult child of the problem. And the day may come when you will no longer need to carry a credit card in your wallet or purse. A scanner at the store will read the information on the chip that's implanted somewhere in your body and authorize the sale. The system would be so secure that you wouldn't even have to sign a sales slip!

The name for this technology is *radio frequency identification.* It sounds great—and it is. However, civil libertarians are already expressing concern over the potential for abuse that the technology poses. Suppose, for example, that in an effort to control terrorism, the government should require every citizen to have a personal identification number recorded on a chip that's embedded under the skin. Theoretically, the government could track you nearly everywhere. And it could monitor and control all your economic activities. That would be great as a way to keep track of terrorists and other criminals who want to harm people. It's not so great for the rest of us. We don't like the idea of government knowing that much about us!

Ever since this technology became feasible, some Christians have speculated that the mark of the beast might be a microchip implanted under the skin. This idea does sound reasonable on a casual reading of the biblical text about the mark of the beast: "He also forced everyone, small and great, rich and poor, free and slave, to receive a mark on his right hand or on his forehead, so that no one could buy or sell unless he had the mark, which is the name of the beast or the number of his name" (Revelation 13:16, 17).

A couple of factors suggest this scenario. First, the mark will be placed on the forehead or the hand, both of which are logical places to implant microchips. Second, the mark, whatever it is, will be used to control people's economic behavior, which a microchip would make very possible.

However, I don't believe that God was predicting microchips under the skin when He gave John his vision about the mark of the beast. What, then, is this "mark of the beast" that Revelation introduces with such ominous language? How can we avoid getting it?

True worship in Revelation 14

Most of the discussion about worship in Revelation 13 and 14 concerns *false* worship. Of the eight times the word *worship* occurs in these two chapters, seven are about the worship of the dragon or the beast and his image, and two of the seven are a dire warning from God against this false worship (Revelation 14:9–11). We examined false worship in the previous chapter.

The eighth occurrence of the word *worship* is in chapter 14:6, 7, where an angel calls on God's people to worship Him. That's obviously true worship, and again, the issue is profoundly spiritual: "Then I saw another angel flying in midair, and he had the eternal gospel to proclaim to those who live on the earth—to every nation, tribe, language and people. He said in a loud voice, 'Fear God and give him glory, because the hour of his judgment has come. Worship him who made the heavens, the earth, the sea and the springs of water.' "

What is this true worship of the true God? We have a good clue in the way the angel mentions the true God. He doesn't actually say, "Worship God." He says, "Worship him who made the heavens, the earth, the sea and the springs of water." So the angel is calling on human beings everywhere to worship God as Creator.

Any interpretation of Revelation needs to take into account that literally hundreds of allusions to the Old Testament occur throughout the book. One occurs in the angel's call to worship "him who made the heavens, the earth, the sea and the springs of water," which is practically a direct quote from the fourth commandment in Exodus 20:11. I've quoted the last part of the commandment on the left side of the chart below and the angel's words in Revelation on the right. Notice especially the italicized words:

Exodus 20:11	Revelation 14:7
" 'For in six days *the LORD made the heavens and the earth, the sea, and all that is in them*' " (italics added).	" 'Worship *him who made the heavens, the earth, the sea and the springs of water*' " (italics added).

Here's the point: The worship of the true God that the angel in Revelation calls for is based on the fourth commandment, which is the Sabbath commandment. Adventists conclude from this that the first angel of Revelation 14 is calling on the world to keep God's Sabbath!

Now put this with the fact that God's end-time people will be a commandment-keeping people: "Then the dragon was enraged at the woman and went off to make war against the rest of her offspring—*those who obey God's commandments* and hold to the testimony of Jesus" (Revelation 12:17, italics added). "This calls for patient endurance on the part of *the saints who obey God's commandments* and remain faithful to Jesus" (Revelation 14:12, italics added).

Both these texts tell us that God's end-time people will keep His commandments. However, this won't be a mere legalistic observance of rules and regulations. Revelation 14:12 says that God's people at this time will both "obey God's commandments" *and* "remain faithful to Jesus"—or, as the King James Version states it, they will "keep . . . the faith of Jesus." I mentioned in the previous chapter that this means God's faithful end-time people will have a clear understanding of righteousness by faith and the correct relationship between law and grace. They will have learned how to make righteousness by faith real in their experience, maintaining their loyalty to God's laws while recognizing that their acceptance by God and their eternal salvation are grounded in Christ's death on the cross, not in their obedience.

The Ten Commandments and worship

Two of the Ten Commandments—the second and the fourth—have to do with worship. Revelation 13 alludes to the second commandment, which forbids the worship of images: The land beast sets up an image in honor of the sea beast and orders the inhabitants of the earth to worship the image. Those who refuse are threatened with death (verses 14, 15). This clearly alludes to the story in Daniel 3 of Shadrach, Meshach, and Abednego, who refused to worship the image King Nebuchadnezzar erected. The enraged king condemned all three of them to death by burning in a fiery furnace. Revelation applies this story to God's end-time people. They, too, will be told that they must worship an image, and they will be threatened with death if they refuse. Obedience to the second commandment is clearly an issue in Revelation 13.

We have seen that obedience to the fourth commandment is an issue in chapter 14 as well. Verses 6 and 7 picture an angel flying in midair and calling on God's people to worship Him as the Creator of "the heavens, the earth, the sea and the springs of water," in harmony with the fourth commandment. This is true worship, in contrast to the false worship of the beast and his image.

So what is this false worship? If true worship in the end time will be characterized by keeping the Sabbath of the fourth commandment, what will characterize its opposite—the worship of the beast and his image? For more than 150 years, Seventh-day Adventists have said the false worship during earth's final crisis will be the observance of Sunday when it is enforced by law.

One of the major differences between Christians in today's world has to do with the choice of a day of worship. The majority of Christians observe the first day of the week, Sunday, while Seventh-day Adventists and a few others observe the seventh day of the week, Saturday. Seventh-day Adventists insist that there is no biblical evidence that God changed the Sabbath from the seventh to the first day of the week. In fact, we believe He still asks His people to observe the Sabbath on the seventh day.* We teach that complete obedience to all of God's commandments—one of the characteristics of His end-time people—requires that we keep the Sabbath according to the commandment. We believe that the observance of Sunday on the part of most Christians, while usually sincere, doesn't meet the specifications of the fourth commandment. This is why we understand the mark of the beast to be the observance of Sunday. However, we also insist that no Christian today is receiving the mark of the beast because of his or her observance of Sunday. *Only when Sunday as a day of worship is enforced by law, with penalties for those who refuse, will those who continue their observance of Sunday receive the mark of the beast.*

As I said in chapter 9, Adventists interpret the land beast of Revelation 13 to be the United States of America, and it's the land beast that enforces the mark of the beast. Thus, we predict that a time is coming when the United States government will enact legislation honoring Sunday as an official day of rest and worship. Eventually, this country will impose harsh penalties on those who refuse to honor Sunday as the Sabbath, and it will lead the entire world into this false worship. Shortly before Christ's return, those who refuse to acquiesce will be threatened with death, and some may pay the ultimate price for their loyalty to God.

Such persecution by the government of the United States sounds incredible. Nevertheless, it's what our interpretation of Revelation 13

---

*For an explanation of why the observance of the Sabbath on Saturday is important, see Appendix B. Appendix C gives the Adventist response to the most common Protestant arguments for the observance of the Sabbath on Sunday.

logically requires, for the land beast threatens death against anyone who refuses to worship in the politically correct manner.

Ellen White and the mark of the beast

Ellen White had a great deal to say about the mark of the beast. She warned that the world is approaching a terrible final crisis, at the conclusion of which Christ will descend to this earth and bring the history of the world's nations to an end. The final crisis that precedes His return will divide the entire world into just two classes—those who receive the seal of God and those who receive the mark of the beast. And the issue that divides them, she said, will be the Sabbath-Sunday controversy: Here are two of Ellen White's more succinct and specific statements:

> The Sabbath question is to be the issue in the great final conflict in which all the world will act a part. . . . Each sabbath institution bears the name of its author, an ineffaceable mark that shows the authority of each.[2]

> The Sabbath will be the great test of loyalty, for it is the point of truth especially controverted. When the final test shall be brought to bear upon men, then the line of distinction will be drawn between those who serve God and those who serve Him not. While the observance of the false sabbath in compliance with the law of the state, contrary to the fourth commandment, will be an avowal of allegiance to a power that is in opposition to God, the keeping of the true Sabbath, in obedience to God's law, is an evidence of loyalty to the Creator. While one class, by accepting the sign of submission to earthly powers, receive the mark of the beast, the other, choosing the token of allegiance to divine authority, receive the seal of God.[3]

All of this, Ellen White said, will come about through the legislation of Sunday by the United States government as an official day of rest and worship:

> When our nation, in its legislative councils, shall enact laws to bind the consciences of men in regard to their religious privileges, enforcing Sunday observance, and bringing oppressive power to

bear against those who keep the seventh-day Sabbath, the law of God, will, to all intents and purposes, be made void in our land; and national apostasy will be followed by national ruin.[4]

The dignitaries of church and state will unite to bribe, persuade, or compel all classes to honor the Sunday. The lack of divine authority will be supplied by oppressive enactments. Political corruption is destroying love of justice and regard for truth; and even in free America, rulers and legislators, in order to secure public favor, will yield to the popular demand for a law enforcing Sunday observance.[5]

When the Protestant churches shall unite with the secular power to sustain a false religion, for opposing which their ancestors endured the fiercest persecution; when the state shall use its power to enforce the decrees and sustain the institutions of the church—then will Protestant America have formed an image to the papacy, and there will be a national apostasy which will end only in national ruin.[6]

Ellen White also suggested that people will urge the passage of Sunday legislation as a way to improve the morals of society. Religious leaders, she said, will "put forth the claim that the fast-spreading corruption is largely attributable to the desecration of the so-called 'Christian sabbath,' and that the enforcement of Sunday observance would greatly improve the morals of society." This claim, she said will especially be urged in America.[7]

Throughout Ellen White's seventy years of service to the Seventh-day Adventist Church, she never deviated from her warning that the world's final crisis will be characterized by a conflict over the law of God, with the primary issue being the Sabbath commandment.

A mark of papal authority

The mark of the beast is a sign or mark of the authority of the sea beast, and the sea beast uses this authority to enforce its worship on the world. Adventists understand the sea beast to represent the papacy during the end time; thus, the mark of the beast will be a mark of the authority of the papacy. In what sense, then, is the mark of the beast a mark of papal authority?

The answer is quite simple. According to Roman Catholic theology, Jesus invested His church with authority so great that it extends even to a license to change God's law. We see a suggestion of this in the prophecy of Daniel 7. I explained in chapter 3 why Adventists identify the little horn in this chapter with the medieval papacy. Verse 25 says that this horn would "think to change *times* and *laws*" (KJV, italics added). Adventists have long maintained that the *law* that the Catholic Church especially changed was the Sabbath commandment, which obviously has to do with *time*, as Daniel's prophecy suggests.

Numerous Roman Catholic authors have claimed that the change of the Sabbath from Saturday to Sunday was a legitimate act of their church, and that in continuing their observance of Sunday, Protestants are following in the steps of the Catholic Church, whose teachings they otherwise so vigorously reject. Following are several examples:

James Cardinal Gibbons: The divine institution of a day of rest from ordinary occupations and of religious worship, *transferred by the authority of the Church* from the Sabbath, the last day, to Sunday, the first day of the week, . . . is one of the most patent signs that we are a Christian people.[8]

The Convert's Catechism of Catholic Doctrine:
Q. Which is the Sabbath day?
A. Saturday is the Sabbath day.
Q. Why do we observe Sunday instead of Saturday?
A. We observe Sunday instead of Saturday because the Catholic Church transferred the solemnity from Saturday to Sunday.[9]

Plain Talk About the Protestantism of To-day *(a book by a Catholic author):* It was the Catholic Church which, by the authority of Jesus Christ, has transferred this rest to the Sunday in remembrance of the resurrection of our Lord. Thus the observance of Sunday by the Protestants is an homage they pay, in spite of themselves, to *the authority of the [Catholic] Church.*[10]

John A. O'Brien (professor of theology at Notre Dame University in the mid-twentieth century): The third commandment [fourth commandment for most Protestants] is: "Remember thou keep

188

holy the Sabbath Day." . . . The word "Sabbath" means rest, and is Saturday the seventh day of the week.

Why then do Christians observe Sunday instead of the day mentioned in the Bible? . . .

The Church received the authority to make the change from her Founder, Jesus Christ. He solemnly conferred upon His Church the power to legislate, govern and administer . . . the power of the keys.[11]

It is this claim by Catholics themselves that has led Adventists to conclude that the change of the Sabbath to Sunday is a mark of Rome's claim to spiritual *authority*. This is one of the important reasons why we continue to maintain that the mark of the beast will be the enforced observance of Sunday during the world's final crisis.

But it's so simple!

Some people may object that the day one keeps is too simple an issue to be Revelation's terrible "mark of the beast." Not necessarily! The Sabbath is one of God's Ten Commandments. This makes it *very important!* Furthermore, God's tests of obedience in the past have been very simple. Witness, for example, the test that He gave to our first parents: "Don't eat the fruit from the tree of the knowledge of good and evil." Some people might protest that God surely wouldn't have rejected Adam and Eve over such a simple thing as eating a piece of fruit from a particular tree! But if God had given Adam and Eve some very difficult test, such as jumping off a high cliff, they could have excused themselves on the grounds that it was too hard. It was the very simplicity of the test that made it so effective.

The test for the three Hebrews facing the enraged Nebuchadnezzar was also utterly simple: Just bow down and worship that image for a few minutes. The Hebrews could have knelt and retied their sandals without worshiping the image. But loyalty to God demanded that they stand straight and tall so that everyone could see them.

This brings us to another characteristic of tests like the mark of the beast: They generally involve an outward sign that has *high public visibility*. There was no question about whom those three young men chose to obey. The whole crowd—probably hundreds and perhaps thousands of people—could *see* them standing straight and tall. Daniel could have left the windows of his house closed when he was threatened with death for worshiping the God of heaven, but he threw the windows open for the world to *see* him on his knees, head bowed, facing Jerusalem. During the early years of Christian history, many of the Christian martyrs were handed a bit of incense and commanded to cast it on a fire in front of a pagan god, but they sacrificed their lives rather than dishonor the God of heaven. All of these tests were both *utterly simple* and *highly visible.*

I propose that the mark of the beast will also involve a choice that is both *very simple* and *highly visible*—and the issue of Sabbath versus Sunday qualifies on both counts. And it's the very simplicity of the issue and its visibility that makes it such an excellent candidate for the mark of the beast. It would be possible, of course, to keep the Sabbath in one's own home, and nobody would be the wiser, just as Daniel could have kept his windows shut and avoided the accusation of breaking the king's decree. But Seventh-day Adventists understand that the issue will be an enforced observance of Sunday, presumably involving church attendance, and those who refuse to comply will be very visible.

Could it really happen?

The Seventh-day Adventist understanding of the mark of the beast has been one of our most controversial teachings during the past 150 years. More than a hundred years ago, one of our critics said that a development such as this in the United States "would be a greater miracle than for God to grow a giant oak in an instant."[12] Another critic called it the "wildest" of our "wild speculations in the prophecies."[13]

So could it really happen?

Most non-Adventist observers say "No." And, indeed, at the present time, it seems incredible to suppose that the United States government would ever pass a law enforcing the observance of Sunday with harsh penalties for nonconformists. For one thing, the United States today is in many ways a very secular nation, and a Sunday law of any kind would not set well with secular people, to say nothing of one with harsh penalties for nonconformists. Nevertheless, Adventists continue to believe that the mark of the beast as we understand it really could happen—indeed, will happen. And in today's world, that idea is much more believable than it was during much of the twentieth century, as we shall see.

---

1. Gail Russell Chaddock, "Microchip Under His Skin," *The Christian Science Monitor,* September 3, 1998; http://www.csmonitor.com/1998/0903/090398.feat.feat.2.html.

2. Ellen G. White, *Testimonies for the Church* (Nampa, Idaho: Pacific Press®, 1901), 6:352.

3. White, *The Great Controversy* (Nampa, Idaho: Pacific Press®, 1911), 605.

4. Ellen G. White, cited in *The Seventh-day Adventist Bible Commentary,* vol. 7 (Hagerstown, Md.: Review and Herald®, 1957), 977.

5. White, *The Great Controversy,* 592.

6. White, *SDA Bible Commentary,* 7:976.

7. White, *The Great Controversy,* 587.

8. James Cardinal Gibbons, "The Claims of the Catholic Church in the Making of the Republic"; cited in John Gilmary Shea et al, *The Cross and the Flag, Our Church and Country* (New York: The Catholic Historical League of America, 1899), 24, 25; italics added.

9. Peter Geirman, *The Convert's Catechism of Catholic Doctrine,* 1957 ed. (St. Louis: B. Herder Book Co., 1930), 50.

10. Louis Gaston de Ségur, *Plain Talk About the Protestantism of To-day* (Boston: Patrick Donahoe, 1868), 225; italics added.

11. Cited in William H. Shea, *Daniel: A Reader's Guide* (Nampa, Idaho: Pacific Press®, 2005), 121, 122; italics added.

12. Theodore Nelson in the introduction to Dudley M. Canright's book, *Seventh-day Adventism Renounced* (Nashville: Gospel Advocate Company, 1914), 23.

13. Dudley M. Canright, *Seventh-day Adventism Renounced* (Nashville: Gospel Advocate Company, 1914), 89.

CHAPTER 19

America and
the Mark
of the Beast

Michael Quitman spent thirty days in a Georgia jail back in 1878. Conditions at the jail were so filthy that in that short time his health broke, and a year and a half later he died. His offense? He had done ordinary work on a Sunday.

Three men, William Dortch, W. H. Parker, and James Stem, were imprisoned in Tennessee in 1885, and they spent several weeks working on a chain gang. Their crime? They had violated their state's Sunday blue law. They had worked on a Sunday.

R. M. King was arrested in Tennessee in 1889 and again in 1890 for nothing more offensive than cultivating corn and hoeing in his potato patch—on a Sunday!

On May 21, 1888, Senator H. W. Blair of New Hampshire introduced a bill in the United States Congress that, had it passed, would have set aside Sunday as a national day of religious worship. Opponents of the bill pointed out that it violated the First Amendment's prohibition against an establishment of religion, whereupon it died. The next year the good senator left the religious language out of the bill and reintroduced it, but it suffered the same fate as the bill he'd introduced the year before.

At first glance, these bits of historical trivia seem like little more than illustrations of America's growing pains toward religious freedom for everyone. However, given the explanation of the mark of the beast that I shared with you in the previous chapter, you can understand, I'm sure, that all the national Sunday law activity between 1888 and 1890 got the attention of Seventh-day Adventists. Back then, they viewed these events as signs of the final crisis and the soon coming of Jesus. End-time fever burned in their brains!

However, the signs didn't last. Sunday blue laws remained on the books of most states in the Union, but by the year 1900, all enforcement of them had died down, and, with an exception here and there, they remained unenforced throughout the entire twentieth century. So why should we expect that at this late date these laws will be dusted off, beefed up, and enforced? And the Adventist scenario calls not just for state Sunday laws but for a national Sunday law. Yet in the more than two hundred years since the founding of the nation, the United States Congress has never passed a national Sunday law. What reason is there to expect that it will do so now?

Church-state separation under attack

Notice the reason why, back in 1888, the Congress refused to pass H. W. Blair's bill setting aside Sunday as a national day of rest: Such a law would have violated the First Amendment's prohibition against an establishment of religion. So, church-state separation kept this proposed bit of legislation out of the American government's law books. I propose that *there can never be a national Sunday law as long as the United States Congress guides its legislation by the principle of church-state separation.* And by now you probably understand one of the basic reasons why a national Sunday law *is* a realistic expectation today: As I pointed out in chapter 14, the principle of church-state separation is under fierce attack by America's Religious Right Protestants. Consider the following statements, which I cited in that chapter:

Pat Robertson: "There is no such thing [as separation of church and state] in the Constitution. It's a lie of the left, and we're not going to take it anymore."[1]

D. James Kennedy: "There is no doubt we can witness the dismantling of [the] diabolical 'wall of separation' that has led to secularization, godlessness, immorality, and corruption in our country."[2]

W. A. Criswell: "There is no such thing as separation of church and state. It is merely a figment of the imagination of infidels."[3]

Francis Schaeffer: "Today the separation of church and state in America is used to silence the church."[4]

These are extremely significant statements by Religious Right Protestants. Unfortunately, as I pointed out in chapter 14, they aren't the only ones who are attacking church-state separation. Consider again the following:

> *William Rehnquist:* "The 'wall of separation between church and state' . . . should be frankly and explicitly abandoned."[5]
>
> *Tom DeLay:* "To claim that our Founding Fathers were for separation of church and state is either rewriting history or being very ignorant of history."[6]
>
> *Jay Alan Seculow:* "There is no 'wall' of separation!"[7]

The attack on church-state separation is also happening in the United States Congress itself. Because the courts keep blocking the way for the Religious Right to achieve their objective of a Christian theocracy in America, various legislators who are sympathetic to Religious Right objectives keep introducing bills into the United States Congress that would restrict the courts from hearing cases dealing with religious issues. For example, in 2005, South Carolina's Representative Gresham Barrett introduced a bill called the "Public Prayer Protection Act." This bill stated, "The Supreme Court shall not have jurisdiction to review, by appeal, writ of certiorari* or otherwise, any matter that relates to the establishment of religion involving an entity of the Federal government or a State or local government."[8] Representative Barrett's bill also stated, "Any federal court decision made before or after the enactment of the law 'is not binding precedent on the court of any State, the District of Columbia, or any commonwealth, territory or possession of the United States.' "[9]

One Web site commented that Barrett's bill "would effectively make the 1st Amendment a historical artifact with no force of law."[10] If the "Public Prayer Protection Act" were to be enacted into law, every decision of the Supreme Court in the history of America that was based on the First Amendment would become null and void.

---

*A writ of certiorari is a written order that an appellate court or the Supreme Court issues to a lower court in order to review its judgment for possible legal error.

194

A similar bill that has been introduced into the United States Congress every year since 1994 is the so-called "Constitution Restoration Act." This bill, if enacted into law, would strip the courts of all legal right to hear First Amendment cases. Significantly, the "Constitution Restoration Act" was written by former Alabama Supreme Court Chief Justice Roy Moore, who fought unsuccessfully to keep a monument of the Ten Commandments in the rotunda of the Alabama Supreme Court building.[11]

In fact, the United States House has already affirmed something of this sort. On Wednesday, July 19, 2006, the House passed a bill that, had it become law, would have barred federal courts from ruling on the constitutionality of the words "under God" in the Pledge of Allegiance. The vote was 260 to 167, which is not exactly a squeaker.[12] Fortunately, the Senate voted against the bill.

I can assure you that if the Congress of the United States should enact any of these bills into law, secularists would immediately challenge the legislation, taking the fight all the way to the Supreme Court. And I'm reasonably certain that the Court, even with Roberts and Alito sitting on the bench, would almost certainly throw it out. But the point isn't that we need to fear an immediate repealing of the First Amendment to the United States Constitution. The point is that a significant segment of the American population is overtly hostile to the principle of church-state separation, and if their opposition continues and grows, church-state separation may indeed someday cease to be a fundamental principle of American legislation and jurisprudence. Years ago, Ellen White predicted that a day will come when "our country [will] repudiate every principle of its Constitution as a Protestant and republican government."[13] The attack on church-state separation by Religious Right Protestants and their effort to bar the Supreme Court from hearing First Amendment cases are chilling moves in the direction of fulfilling Ellen White's prediction.

Back in 1960, America's evangelical Protestant leaders insisted that John F. Kennedy take a vow in support of church-state separation before they would support him in his bid for the presidency. Less than fifty years later, the leaders of those same denominations are in the vanguard of those who *oppose* church-state separation. At the same time, Roman Catholics, who have historically favored church-state union and opposed the separation of church and state, are rapidly gaining political power in the United States. Thus, it is very realistic today to say that the historic

American principle of church-state separation is on increasingly shaky ground. *And this is opening the way for religious laws to be enacted in the United States.* A bill authorizing a national Sunday law probably would not pass in the United States Congress today. But with the foremost legal barrier to Sunday legislation in America being threatened, it easily could pass sometime in the not-too-distant future.

Getting the nation back to God

For most of the past two hundred years, the Judeo-Christian values of America's populace have strongly influenced its laws. At one point or another in our history, the public expression of vulgarity has been forbidden, pornography has been strictly regulated, and homosexual relationships have been illegal. However, these prohibitions have been largely set aside in recent years, and there's a strong sense among Religious Right Protestants that the United States is on a moral slide. Our public entertainment is increasingly filled with violence, sex, and vulgarity. The Internet has multiplied exponentially the spread of pornography. Abortion on demand is killing millions of babies every year. Homosexuality is gaining wide acceptance, with homosexual unions and homosexual marriage becoming more and more common.

At the same time, religious expression is gradually being pushed out of government institutions. In the early 1960s, state-sponsored prayer and Bible reading were outlawed in the nation's public schools. More recently, the Supreme Court has ruled against the posting of the Ten Commandments on government property, and secularists are challenging the religious words in the Pledge of Allegiance and on American coins. Suddenly there's a cry for America to "get back to God." Religious Right Protestants are calling for a "culture war" that will restore the nation to its Christian heritage.

Emphasis on the Ten Commandments

During the past 150 years, many Protestants opposed the Adventist practice of observing the Sabbath on the seventh day of the week with the argument that "the Ten Commandments have been done away with." We still hear that objection now and then. However, today there is a strong emphasis among America's conservative Protestants on the Ten Commandments as the foundation of America's legal system. This has been brought about in large part because of the nation's declining morals. The result is that the Ten Commandments are once again in vogue.

I'm writing the words in this paragraph on Friday afternoon, May 5, 2006. Two days from now is Ten Commandments Day, sponsored by the Ten Commandments Commission. The following quote from the commission's Web page states the reason for its existence:

> Recent court rulings against the Ten Commandments, along with a host of disturbing trends we witness daily throughout our culture, clearly demonstrates [sic] that our nation is moving away from that tradition. These actions have threatened the very fabric and foundation of our culture and faith. The Ten Commandments and all other references to God, which have served as the moral foundation and anchor of our great country, are systematically being removed from public places. Public displays of the Ten Commandments and other symbols of our faith have been a powerful visual testimony to the fact that the United States of America is "one nation under God." Their removal from public places shows that those with a secular humanist agenda are intent on destroying the moral heritage of our nation.
>
> With secular humanists waging their attacks at home and the looming threat from the international radical Islam—people of faith become the line of defense—this is the "Wall of Jerusalem," and you are the watchman God placed.
>
> Those who care about traditional values cannot passively sit by and watch the removal of the very principles that made this country great. The Ten Commandments and what they represent are the heart of all moral code and must be restored to the heart of our society.
>
> We must not let the opponents of traditional values succeed.
>
> The Ten Commandments Commission was founded to counter the secular agenda and help restore the Ten Commandments and Judeo-Christian values to their rightful place in our society.[14]

Seventh-day Adventists have rightly given strong support to this emphasis on the Ten Commandments. After all, we ourselves have stressed the importance of the Ten Commandments for 150 years, even in the face of significant Protestant opposition. Thus, the call for a restoration of the Ten Commandments as the foundation of law and social order is entirely appropriate. After all, Ellen White said, "In His law God has made known the principles that underlie all true prosperity, both *of nations* and of individuals."[15] Certainly, a return to the Ten Commandments would help to restore moral order to a nation that morally is increasingly out of control. And that's precisely why the Ten Commandments Commission was organized. The statement on their Web page says, "[T]he Ten Commandments and what they represent are the heart of all moral code and must be restored to the heart of our society."

The moral reform of society

So, what's the problem? What does all this have to do with Sunday legislation? Please read carefully the following sentence from the Ten Commandments Commission's Web site: "The Ten Commandments Commission was founded to counter the secular agenda and help restore the Ten Commandments and Judeo-Christian values to their rightful place in our *society.*" Notice that I italicized the word *society*. There's a growing emphasis among Religious Right Protestants on changing American *society* and returning it to its biblical roots. The following quotes illustrate the point:

> *Pat Robertson:* "God's plan is for His people, ladies and gentlemen, to take dominion. . . . The Lord says, 'I'm going to let you redeem *society.*'"[16]
> *D. James Kennedy:* Our job is to reclaim America for Christ, whatever the cost. As the vice regents of God, we are to exercise godly dominion and influence over . . . every aspect and institution of human *society.*[17]
> *Paul Weyrich:* "We are talking about Christianizing America. We are talking about simply spreading the Gospel in a political context."[18]
> *Francis Schaeffer:* "Civil government and, therefore, law, must be based on God's Law as given in the Bible. . . . [The state] is to be administered according to the principles of God's Law."[19]
> *Randall Terry:* "Our goal is a Christian nation. We have a biblical duty, we are called by God, to conquer this country."[20]

The problem I see with this emphasis on reforming society, conquering America, and redeeming it for Christ, is that it can easily lead to intolerance of dissenters. As I read the story of the fall of the human race in Eden, I'm impressed by the fact that God allowed His children to disobey Him if that's what they chose to do. I believe that Christians need to grant the same privilege today to those who reject God. Immorality was rampant in the Roman Empire during the first century A.D., including homosexuality and infanticide (the killing of unwanted babies). But nowhere in the New Testament did the apostles suggest that Christians should try to reform society or redeem the Roman Empire by changing its laws to reflect biblical values. The early Christian church didn't set out to convert *society*. It set out to convert *individuals*. Eventually, Christian values reformed Roman *society*, but only as a result of three hundred years of Christians converting *individuals*, one pagan at a time.

The Ten Commandments Commission's statement that I quoted previously stresses the restoration of public morality: "Those who care about traditional values cannot passively sit by and watch the removal of the very principles that made this country great. The Ten Commandments and what they represent are the heart of all moral code and must be restored to the heart of our society." Notice the emphasis on the *moral* reform of society. Years ago, Ellen White said that the moral reform of American society will be one of the arguments advanced by Protestant leaders in their support of a national Sunday law. She said that religious leaders will "put forth the claim that the fast-spreading corruption is largely attributable to the desecration of the so-called 'Christian sabbath,' and that the enforcement of Sunday observance would greatly improve the morals of society."[21]

Some Religious Right leaders are already urging this argument. In his book *Why the Ten Commandments Matter*, D. James Kennedy wrote a chapter on each of the Ten Commandments, showing why they still matter in the twenty-first century. His chapter on the fourth commandment includes a section in which he briefly sets forth the typical Protestant arguments in support of the change of the Sabbath from the seventh to the first day of the week.* Then he says,

> Christians need to understand that keeping the Sabbath [he means Sunday] really does create a more moral climate in our culture. It promotes an awareness that God and His ways and

---

*I respond to several of these arguments in Appendix B.

His laws are important to all of us. Without public morality, our secular laws have less meaning; the result is that lawlessness rises, and our nation sinks into crime, fear, disorder, and injustice.

From the witness of the early Church, from the witness of our disarrayed lives, from the witness of our society as it teeters on the brink of moral collapse, we see that the need to keep the Sabbath is truly urgent.[22]

Of course, Seventh-day Adventists support the renewed emphasis on the Ten Commandments in America! But we also will argue that by ignoring the sacredness that God placed on the seventh day, the vast majority of Christians, wittingly or unwittingly, are actually *breaking* the fourth commandment, which lies at the heart of the Ten. They are breaking the fourth commandment in the name of keeping it! And the danger is that, in the interest of improving public morality, the United States Congress could legalize *Sunday* as a day of rest contrary to the very fourth commandment that it's supposed to honor. Thus, Adventists see both positive and negative aspects to the renewed emphasis on the Ten Commandments.

Could this renewed emphasis on the Ten Commandments lead to legislation that mandates Sunday as an official day for rest and worship?

Dies Domini

On May 31, 1998, Pope John Paul II published an apostolic letter titled *Dies Domini*, which is Latin for "day of the Lord." In this letter he urged upon all Catholics the importance of keeping Sunday holy. John Paul's letter has much to commend it. For example, he pointed out that a correct theology of the Sabbath must take into account that the Sabbath originated at Creation. "In order to grasp fully the meaning of Sunday," he said, "we must reread the great story of creation and deepen our understanding of the theology of 'Sabbath.' "[23] He also pointed out something Adventists have long stressed, that "before decreeing that something be *done*, the [Sabbath] commandment urges that something be *remembered*."[24] And finally, while he applied the fourth commandment to Sunday, John Paul's advice on how to keep the day resembles Adventist recommendations for Sabbath observance. Besides attendance at church services (for him the Mass), he suggested that Christians devote themselves to works of mercy and charity: "Inviting to a meal people who are alone, visiting the sick, providing food for needy families, spending a few hours in voluntary work and acts of solidarity."[25]

However, John Paul's apostolic letter also raises some significant red flags. With respect to Constantine's Sunday law, he said, "Christians rejoiced to see thus removed the obstacles which until then had sometimes made observance of the Lord's Day heroic. They could now devote themselves to prayer in common without hindrance."[26] And regarding our own day, he said, "In this matter, my predecessor Pope Leo XIII in his Encyclical *Rerum Novarum* spoke of Sunday rest as a worker's right *which the state must guarantee.*" He also said, "In the particular circumstances of our own time, *Christians will naturally strive to see that civil legislation respects their duty to keep the Sabbath holy.*"[27]

In chapter 16, I wrote about the great political influence that the American Catholic hierarchy now wields over the United States government. They are determined that *their* understanding of morality, including abortion, euthanasia, and stem-cell research, *will* be enacted as law in this country. At this point, the American Catholic hierarchy is not demanding legislation that protects Sunday as a day for religious rest and worship. However, once these other Catholic moral principles have become the law of the land—and I'm convinced that this is coming—it will be only one step further to demand the legal protection of Sunday. This is especially likely in view of John Paul's apostolic letter *Dies Domini,* which urges governments to protect Sunday as a day of rest and worship.

I also find it interesting that at an April 2005 conference sponsored by the Judeo-Christian Council for Constitutional Restoration, Aryeh Spero, a Jewish rabbi no less, "took the unusual line of contending for the Christian Sabbath, telling the crowd, 'I would suggest that we reinstitute the Sabbath, Sunday, as it was before. Make the day Sunday a day of faith.' "[28] In the context of a conference demanding "Constitutional Restoration," Spero was clearly calling for legislation—even perhaps a constitutional amendment—that would make Sunday a day of religious rest and worship.

Sunday laws in America

As of the early twenty-first century, when Religious Right Protestants and Roman Catholics work together, they have sufficient political power in the United States to elect almost anyone to office whom they wish and to enact just about any legislation that they might wish. Will they eventually demand a law enforcing Sunday as a day of religious rest and worship? Back in the late nineteenth century, Ellen White made a very significant statement. She said that "even in free America, rulers and legislators, in order to secure public favor, will yield to the popular demand for a law enforcing Sunday observance."[29] That statement is ominous in light of the pressure that Catholics and Religious Right Protestants are already putting on America's congressional leaders and state legislators to enact laws that enforce conservative Christian morals.

I'm on the postal and e-mailing lists of several conservative groups, and I'm constantly receiving pleas for me to pressure my congressional representatives on this or that issue. And the Internet has made it extremely easy to do this. E-mails urging people to contact their congressional legislators typically include a link that the recipients of the e-mail can click on that takes them to a Web page where they can fill in a few blanks and, with a click of the mouse, zap off prepared messages to all of their state's senators and/or representatives.

Immigration reform was a matter of intense public debate in America during 2006, and it illustrates the power that Americans—and even non-Americans—have today over national and state legislators. Conservatives form the political base of the Republican Party, which in 2006 controlled the presidency and both houses of Congress. However, a huge Hispanic electorate also exists in the United States, which both Republicans and Democrats are avidly courting. During the first two quarters of 2006, conservative Americans put tremendous pressure on their senators and representatives to enact tough immigration laws. I know, because I was bombarded with frantic e-mails urging me—begging me, pleading with me—to contact my state's congressional leaders in support of protecting our borders and toughening laws against illegal aliens. At the same time, millions of Hispanics all over the country demonstrated and put intense pressure on those same politicians to grant amnesty to illegal aliens. The poor legislators were caught between a rock and a hard spot! As of this writing, it remains to be seen which way Congress will move, but that's beside the point. What I want you to notice is the tremendous pressure that both sides put on Congress. Ellen White's statement that "even in free America, rulers and legislators, in order to secure public favor, *will yield to the popular demand* for a law enforcing Sunday observance" takes on new meaning in light of the popular demands that are being put on Congress from all sides right now on other issues.

So, will the United States Congress at some point in the future enact a law that enforces Sunday as a day for religious rest and worship? That's a question about the future, and from a strictly secular perspective, I obviously can't answer "Yes." Yet even from a secular perspective, I can recognize that the cultural foundation for such a law is rapidly being put in place. And as a Seventh-day Adventist, I don't hesitate to say that a national Sunday law—which we have predicted for 150 years and which has seemed so foolish to so many people during most of that time—is now a distinct possibility. Adventists are confident that it *will* become a reality at some point in the future.

A law that shuts down certain businesses and perhaps bans sports and other entertainment activities in recognition of Sunday as a day for rest and worship would impose certain hardships on Jews and Adventists who observe the Sabbath on Saturday and Muslims whose holy day is Friday. However, the Adventist understanding of the mark of the beast goes far beyond that. We predict that the day will come when seventh-day Sabbath keepers will be severely persecuted for their religious faith, including at some point, even the death penalty.

"Come on!" you say. *"Could that really happen?"*

Stay tuned.

---

1. From a November 1993 address by Pat Robertson; cited in *The Religious Right: The Assault on Tolerance and Pluralism in America* (New York: Anti-Defamation League, 1994), 4.

2. "They Said It! Religious Right Leaders In Their Own Words," http://www.au.org/site/DocServer/They_Said_It.pdf?docID=221.

3. From a CBS interview of September 6, 1984, taped the day after Criswell delivered the benediction at the Republican National Convention; cited in *The Religious Right*, 4.

4. Francis A. Schaeffer, *A Christian Manifesto* (Westchester, Ill.: Crossway Books, 1981), 36.

5. William Rehnquist in *Wallace v. Jaffree*, 1984.

6. *Signswatch*, Winter 2001, 3.

7. *Ministry Magazine* (not the Adventist one), Fall 2004; cited by Rob Boston in "Religious Right Power Brokers: The Top Ten," *Church and State*, June 2006, 13.

8. RedSonja2000, "Dominionist Dream: Repeal the First Amendment," December 16, 2005, Talk to Action, http://www.talk2action.org/story/2005/12/16/103532/64.

9. Ibid.

10. Ibid.

11. Ibid.

12. Jim Abrams, "House Passes Bill Shielding Pledge of Allegiance," *The Idaho Statesman*, July 20, 2006, Main 15.

13. Ellen G. White, *Testimonies for the Church* (Nampa, Idaho: Pacific Press®, 1948), 5:451.

14. "The Ten Commandments Day" http://www.tencommandmentsday.com. Note: The wording on this Web site changes slightly for each year's upcoming Ten Commandments Day. The quote cited here is from the 2006 Ten Commandments Day.

15. Ellen G. White, *Prophets and Kings* (Nampa, Idaho: Pacific Press®, 1917), 500; italics added.

16. Comment by Pat Robertson on *The 700 Club* television program; cited in RedSonja2000, "Dominionist Dream."

17. Cited in "Rise of the Religious Right in American Politics," http://www.theocracywatch.org.

18. *Signswatch*, Winter 2001, 4; statement by Paul Weyrich in August 1980.

19. Francis A. Schaeffer, *A Christian Manifesto* (Westchester, Ill.: Crossway Books, 1981), 100. In these sentences, Schaeffer is stating the views of the seventeenth-century political philosopher Samuel Rutherford (1600–1661), but it is clear from the context that he shares Rutherford's views.

20. *The News Sentinel*, Fort Wayne, Indiana, August 16, 1993; cited in *The Religious Right*, 4.

21. White, *The Great Controversy* (Nampa, Idaho: Pacific Press®, 1911), 587; italics added.

22. D. James Kennedy, *Why the Ten Commandments Matter* (New York: Warner Faith, 2005), 81, 82 in the publisher's prepublication advance reading copy.

23. John Paul II, Apostolic Letter Dies Domini, 1:8; http://www.vatican.va/holy_father/john_paul_ii/apost_letters/documents/hf_jp-ii_apl_05071998_dies-domini_en.html <http://www.vatican.va/holy_father/john_paul_ii/apost_letters/documents/hf_jp-ii_apl_05071998_dies-domini_en.html> .

24. Ibid., 1:16.

25. Ibid., 4:69, 72.

26. Ibid., 4:64.

27. Ibid., 4:66, 67, italics added.

28. Cited by Rob Boston in "Judge Not," *Liberty*, September/October 2005, 23.

29. White, *The Great Controversy*, 529.

Chapter 20

Christian Reconstructionism and Dominionism

If you're like most readers of this book, you probably have no idea what the terms *Reconstructionism* and *Dominionism* mean. *Reconstructionism* is the name of an ultraconservative movement that a man named R. J. Rushdoony started. *Dominionism* is a theological concept that underlies Reconstructionism.

Most readers of this book also probably have never heard of R. J. Rushdoony. Some will be familiar with the name Francis A. Schaeffer. Schaeffer was not a Reconstructionist, but he was a Dominionist in his theology. Both men have had a powerful impact on the thinking of America's Religious Right Protestants. I'll begin with Rushdoony.

R. J. Rushdoony

Rousas John Rushdoony was born on April 25, 1916, in New York City. His parents were refugees from Armenia. In fact, his mother was pregnant when the family fled the genocide in Armenia that was being perpetrated by the Ottoman Turks. Rushdoony was born shortly after they arrived in America. Rushdoony's family didn't remain in New York, though. His father accepted an appointment as the pastor of an Armenian Presbyterian church in Kingsburg, California, so Rushdoony grew up on the West Coast. He was a graduate of the University of California at Berkeley, where he earned degrees in both English and education. He also attended the Pacific School of Religion (also in Berkeley), from which he graduated in 1944. Both UC Berkeley and the Pacific School of Religion were (and are) bastions of liberalism, but Rushdoony didn't accept their liberal philosophy. He learned from them what liberalism means, and he rejected it.

Following his studies in religion, Rushdoony entered the Presbyterian ministry. His first appointment was to a mission among the Chinese in San Francisco. Following that, he accepted an invitation to minister to an Indian tribe in northern Nevada, where he spent eight years.

Rushdoony was an indefatigable reader. He read a book a day, six days a week, for some fifty years! And he didn't just read. He composed a personal index on the back cover of each book.[1] By the end of his life he owned more than thirty-three thousand books that he housed in a large, one-room building that was his own private library.

Rushdoony was also a prolific writer. His first book, *By What Standard?* published in 1959, was an introduction to the views of the Dutch scholar Cornelius Van Til, a professor at Westminster Seminary in Philadelphia, Pennsylvania, whose theology strongly influenced Rushdoony. Over the next two decades, Rushdoony wrote more than a dozen books. In 1965, he moved to Los Angeles, where he established the Chalcedon Foundation (pronounced kal-SEE-dun). In October 1965, he began writing the *Chalcedon Report*, a monthly newsletter that over the years spelled out in detail the religious and political philosophy of Reconstructionism.

Rushdoony's most comprehensive book was the nine-hundred-page *Institutes of Biblical Law*, which was published in 1973. It consisted largely of sermons that he had preached between 1968 and 1972. Rushdoony's *Institutes* applies the legal principles in the Bible to conditions in today's world. He founded his philosophy of law on the Ten Commandments and then made applications of the other laws in the Old Testament, especially those in the Pentateuch, to today's world. He considered that all the Old Testament laws except those that the New Testament specifically abrogates are still in force today. Rushdoony died on February 8, 2001.

Modern secular critics of the Religious Right are very hard on Rushdoony. They lampoon him and speak of him and his Chalcedon Foundation in the harshest terms. It's important to keep in mind when reading these writers that the gospel makes absolutely no sense to them. They are as ready to lampoon you and me and any other evangelical Christian for our beliefs as they are to make fun of Rushdoony for his.

While I share the critics' concern about certain aspects of Rushdoony's philosophy of church and state, I would like first to comment briefly on three areas where I—and I think most Adventists—would agree with him.

Agreement with Rushdoony

First, Rushdoony had a profound interest in Christian education. He believed that the primary responsibility for the education of children rests with the family and the church, not the state. Thus, he was a strong proponent of churches establishing Christian schools, and he was also a strong supporter of home schooling. Rushdoony appeared as an expert witness in many court cases around the United States in which Christian education was being challenged. He also appeared in court cases dealing with home schooling and helped to establish the legitimacy of that form of Christian education. Thus, he made a major contribution toward establishing the legitimacy of Christian education in America. For this, Seventh-day Adventists owe a debt of thanks to Rousas John Rushdoony.

The second area of agreement between Rushdoony and Adventists is in his understanding of the gospel. The Chalcedon Web site includes a link titled "What Chalcedon Believes," which of course is also what Rushdoony believed. The Chalcedon statement of beliefs includes a paragraph on justification that largely coincides with the Adventist understanding. The statement reads in part:

> We believe that sinners are saved *solely* on the ground of Christ's substitutionary, atoning death and law-keeping life, the passive and active obedience of Christ (2 Cor. 5:21; 1 Pet. 2:24). Further, we believe that justification, man's legal acceptance in the sight of God as "not guilty," is appropriated by faith *alone* (Rom. 5:1; Eph. 2:8-10). Because faith itself is a gift of God, no law-keeping or works of any kind that man can perform could in any way secure or contribute to his justification or acceptance before God. God does not cooperate with man in saving him. God saves sinners; He does not help them save themselves. Law-keeping and good works are the essential *results* of justification; they are not the *ground* or means of *appropriating* justification. (1 Cor. 6:9-10; 1 Jn. 1:8). . . . The God who justifies also sanctifies, and sanctification means

progressive obedience to God's requirements, His law of the Old and New Testaments.*[2]

Finally, while I strongly disagree with some of Rushdoony's views on law, his understanding of the relationship of law to grace and the place of law in the plan of salvation is similar to that of Adventists. In the introduction to his book *The Institutes of Biblical Law*, he said, "The purpose of grace is not to set aside the law but to fulfill the law and to enable man to keep the law. If the law was so serious in the sight of God that it would require the death of Jesus Christ, the only-begotten Son of God, to make atonement for man's sin, it seems strange for God then to proceed to abandon the law!"[3]

I believe Seventh-day Adventists can strongly affirm Rushdoony's (and the Chalcedon Foundation's) emphasis on Christian education and their understanding of justification and the relationship between law and grace. And while we may disagree strongly with certain other aspects of their teachings, we should avoid a wholesale attack on them. However, these other aspects *do* cause me serious concern.

My disagreement with Rushdoony

Rushdoony's non-Christian critics tend to scorn him. They ridicule him as a wild-eyed, foolish fundamentalist. That's a dangerous attitude, because Rushdoony was nobody's fool. Even a casual survey of his book *The Institutes of Biblical Law* reveals a careful thinker whose theological and political views formed a very logical, coherent belief system. Rushdoony was also a good writer. He expressed his views clearly. His writing is quite easy to read and understand. I will summarize his belief system as I understand it.

Postmillennialism. Like Augustine fifteen hundred years earlier, Rushdoony was a postmillennialist. He believed that Christ established His eternal kingdom at the time of His resurrection, and the millennium described in Revelation 20 began at that time. Thus, both Augustine and Rushdoony understood the millennium to be figurative of the Christian era, not a literal count of exactly one thousand years. According to this

*I omitted a sentence that says, "God, by His matchless grace in the atoning death of His Son, saves those whom He has chosen." Coming from a Calvinistic perspective, this sounds too much like the predestination that Adventists reject.

scenario, Christ's second coming will occur at some distant point in the future.

Perfecting society. Like Augustine, Rushdoony believed that Christians will succeed in converting the whole world. Jesus will return the second time when the whole world has been Christianized and is prepared to welcome Him. Now here is the key point: *Rushdoony believed that Christians are responsible for perfecting society, including its civil governments, so that Jesus can return.* In his book *The Institutes of Biblical Law*, he said, "Man is summoned to create the society God requires."[4] This is almost identical to Augustine's belief that it is the responsibility of the Catholic Church to Christianize society, including its governments, so that Jesus can return.

Dominionism. Rushdoony was a firm proponent of Dominionism, also called "dominion theology." Dominionism begins with the Eden story in Genesis. When God created Adam and Eve, He commanded them to "have *dominion* over the fish of the sea, and over the fowl of the air, and over every living thing that moveth upon the earth" (Genesis 1:28, KJV; italics added). Rushdoony believed that this dominion mandate is still in force today. He said,

> God's covenant with Adam required him to exercise dominion over the earth and to subdue it (Gen. 1:26 ff) under God and according to God's law-word. This relationship of man to God was a covenant. . . .
>
> The restoration of that covenant relationship was the work of Christ, His grace to His elect people. *The fulfillment of that covenant is their great commission: to subdue all things and all nations to Christ and His law-word.*
>
> The creation mandate was precisely the requirement that man subdue the earth and exercise dominion over it. There is not one word of Scripture to indicate or imply that this mandate was ever revoked.[5]
>
> The purpose of God in requiring Adam to exercise dominion over the earth remains His continuing covenant word: man, created in God's image and commanded to subdue the earth and exercise dominion over it in God's name, is *recalled to this task and privilege* by his redemption and regeneration.[6]

Jesus told His disciples to " 'go and make disciples of all nations, baptizing them in the name of the Father and of the Son and of the

Holy Spirit, and teaching them to obey everything I have commanded you' " (Matthew 28:19, 20). Rushdoony understood this to be a repetition of God's dominion command to Adam and Eve in Genesis. He said, "The redeemed are recalled to the original purpose of man, *to exercise dominion* under God."[7] Thus, in Rushdoony's view of the future, the ultimate fulfillment of Christ's great commission will occur when the world as a whole has come under the dominion of Christ through the efforts of the church, and *a Christian society has been established in every nation.* This, he said, is the preparation Jesus is looking for so that He can return.

Biblical law. Rushdoony didn't believe in the secular state with its laws that are based on human wisdom. "In any culture," he said, "*the source of law is the god of that society.* If law has its source in man's reason, then reason is the god of that society."[8] According to Rushdoony, reason also becomes the *religion* of that society. "The foundations of law are inescapably religious," he said, for "no society exists without a religious foundation or without a law-system which codifies the morality of its religion."[9] Thus, if human wisdom is the religion of a society, then the laws of that society will be based on the religion of human wisdom—that is, humanism and secularism. Rushdoony didn't believe in the American government with its laws that are based largely on secular premises. He believed that secular laws have been "savage in [their] hostility to the Biblical law-system."[10] "*Revealed law* [i.e., biblical law]," he said, "is the need and privilege of Christian society. It is the *only* means whereby man can fulfil [sic] his creation mandate of exercising dominion under God."[11]

In Rushdoony's new Christian world, biblical law will replace secular laws as the foundation for the governing of society. He said, "Civil law cannot be separated from Biblical law, for the Biblical doctrine of law includes all law, civil, ecclesiastical, societal, familial, and all other forms of law."[12] Biblical law, he said, "is therefore the law for Christian man *and Christian society.*"[13] He looked forward to the day—though not in his time—when the whole world will be truly converted and the civil laws of all nations will be based on the Bible.

"Case laws." Rushdoony viewed the Ten Commandments as the foundation for all biblical law. However, because these commandments are brief, God expanded on their meaning by means of the Levitical and other laws of the Pentateuch so that the Israelites could

understand all that the Ten Commandments encompassed. Rush-doony called these additional laws "case laws." This concept is basic to Rushdoony's view of biblical law, so I will quote a paragraph from his book:

> Without case law, God's law would soon be reduced to an extremely limited area of meaning. This, of course, is precisely what has happened. Those who deny the present validity of the [Old Testament] law[s] apart from the Ten Commandments have as a consequence a very limited definition of theft. Their definition usually follows the civil law of their country, is humanistic, and is not radically different from the definitions given by Moslems, Buddhists, and humanists. But, in analyzing . . . the case laws illustrative of the law "Thou shalt not steal," we shall see how far-reaching its meaning is.[14]

The "case law" that Rushdoony referred to was primarily the rest of the civil, religious, moral, and health laws in the Pentateuch, though he also recognized that "the Biblical concept of law is broader than the legal codes of the Mosaic formulation. It applies to the divine word and instruction in its totality."[15] Rushdoony considered all biblical laws to be applicable still during the Christian era unless, like the ceremonial laws, they were specifically abrogated in the New Testament. For example, regarding the Levitical command that a woman was to be "unclean" for several days following the birth of a child, Rushdoony said, "There is no valid reason for the discontinuance of the rite."[16]

Rushdoony also believed that in an ideal world, these biblical "case laws" would be included in the civil laws of nations. Ten chapters in the nearly nine hundred pages of his *Institutes of Biblical Law* are devoted to an analysis of each of the Ten Commandments in light of the "case laws" that pertain to them. Among other things, Rushdoony considered the laws in the Pentateuch that called for the death penalty to be applicable still today. He said, "A godly law-order will restore the death penalty."[17] He even went so far as to call capital punishment an "aspect of man's religious duty."[18] Three times in his *Institutes of Biblical Law* he listed the crimes that call for the death penalty,* and he

---

*See pages 77, 235, 402.

commented on most of them throughout the book.* In Rushdoony's utopia, the civil government would enforce all of these biblical laws. Rushdoony anticipated a day when most of the world's people would be Christians, and biblical law would be the basis for the civil laws of all the world's nations. He believed this would set the stage for the second coming of Jesus.

Analyzing Rushdoony

On careful examination, I find that some of Rushdoony's major premises are quite flawed from a biblical perspective, and they are a setup for the persecution of dissenters.

Dominionism and the Great Commission. As I mentioned earlier, Rushdoony believed that God's command to Adam and Eve to have dominion over the world is still in force, restated for the church by Christ in His great commission. However, he provided no exegetical basis for this conclusion. He simply said it.

This is one area where I strongly disagree with Rushdoony. There is no reasonable exegetical connection between God's "dominion" command in Genesis 1 and His great commission in Matthew 28. In Genesis, God commanded Adam and Eve to " 'have dominion over the fish of the sea, over the birds of the air, and over every living thing that moves on the earth' " (verse 28, NKJV)—in other words, the animal kingdom. Dominion over people was God's role.

In Matthew 28:19, Jesus commanded His followers to *make disciples* of all nations. He didn't give so much as a hint of a suggestion that they were to have *dominion* over all nations.† Rushdoony's "dominion theory" reads far more into Jesus' great commission than its language can sup-

---

*Mosaic laws calling for the death penalty that Rushdoony commented on include idolatry, 66; cursing one's parents, 120; smiting one's parents, 120; kidnapping, 120; enforced slavery, 120; Sabbath breaking, 137 (though he apparently believed this death penalty no longer applies—see 235, 402); homosexuality, 256; bestiality, 256; incest, 399; and adultery, 399.

†The Greek literally says, "Go then make disciples [of] all the nations." If we leave out the word *of,* which translators have added in order for Jesus' words to make sense in English, it might be possible to understand Jesus to mean that the nations themselves are to be made disciples. However, Jesus' next words clearly rule that out. He said, " '. . . baptizing them in the name of the Father and of the Son and of the Holy Spirit.' " It's impossible to baptize a nation. The context is both the discipling and the baptizing of individuals, not of entire nations.

port. Jesus repeated His mandate to His disciples in several other places in the New Testament, and nowhere did He come near implying that it included dominion over civil governments. In Matthew 24:14, He said, " 'And this gospel of the kingdom will be preached in the whole world as a testimony [Greek: *"witness"*] to all nations.' " In Luke 24:48, He told His disciples that they were to be " *'witnesses* of these things' "—that is, of His life, death, and resurrection. And in Acts 1:8, He said, " 'You will be my *witnesses* in Jerusalem, and in all Judea and Samaria, and to the ends of the earth.' " The key word in all of these texts is *witness,* not *dominion.* These texts simply do not support the idea that Jesus intended His followers to have dominion over the world's nations and their civil governments.

A perfect end time. In Rushdoony's optimistic view, as more and more people convert to Christ, the whole world will gradually become Christian, including its civil governments. These governments will be based upon all the biblical laws of the Old and New Testaments, and that will be the signal for Jesus to return.

This notion of a perfect end time flies in the face of the biblical teaching that "there will be terrible times in the last days." (2 Timothy 3:1. In verses 1–5, Paul gave a long list of the evils that people in the end time will be guilty of.) Jesus predicted that shortly before His return the teachings of false christs and false prophets will be so pervasive that even His own elect will be in danger of succumbing to the deception (Matthew 24:23, 24). Peter said that "in the last days scoffers will come, scoffing and following their own evil desires" (2 Peter 3:3). And according to Revelation, with the exception of God's few remnant people, the whole world will follow the sea beast in its rebellion against God (Revelation 13:4, 8). It's the evil sea beast that will be "given authority [i.e., dominion] over every tribe, people, language and nation" in the end time, not God's people (verse 7). The New Testament makes it abundantly clear that the world just before Christ's second coming will be intensifying its rebellion *against* God's laws, not growing in its loyalty *to* them.

Dominionism and persecution. However, my chief concern with Rushdoony's "dominion theory" is that it's a recipe for persecution. While Rushdoony recognized that Christ's mandate to His disciples includes converting *individuals,* in his mind it also included converting *societies* and molding their civil laws into conformity with biblical law. It was precisely this view of the church that led to Catholicism's domination of European politics during the Dark Ages—including its baleful result, the horrible persecution of "heretics" simply because they disagreed with the state religion. I propose that any time Christians switch Christ's great commission from *witnessing to* all nations to *dominating* all nations with biblical laws, sooner or later, the result will be persecution of dissenters. Our mandate is to reform *individuals*, not *society*. Society will be reformed in those cultures in which more and more individuals become Christians. But the mandate will remain always and forever the redemption of *individuals*, not of *society*. The idea that Christians (and the church) are to reform society is a straight path to the persecution of those people in that society who choose not to be reformed.

Now, here's a point I don't want you to miss: Rushdoony published his *Institutes of Biblical Law* in 1973, *at the very time that America's political conservatives were recruiting the country's religious conservatives to their cause. Rushdoony provided these religious conservatives with the theoretical, theological justification they needed to join the conservative political army.* This is not to say that today's conservative Christians have adopted Rushdoony's theology hook, line, and sinker. Most of today's Religious Right Christians are dispensationalist *pre*millennialists who believe in an imminent rapture and the soon return of Christ. They reject Rushdoony's *post*millennialism. Also, most Religious Right leaders reject Rushdoony's extreme application of biblical law—especially his demand for the enforcement of all the Levitical laws that call for the death penalty. Ralph Reed, who during much of the 1990s was the executive director of Pat Robertson's Christian Coalition, criticized Rushdoony's Reconstructionism as "an authoritarian ideology that threatens the most basic civil liberties of a free and democratic society."[19]

However, while Religious Right Christians by and large reject Rushdoony's most extreme views, *they are very attracted to his notion that governments should be Christian and that America's laws should be based on the Bible, thus making America a "Christian nation."*

Francis Schaeffer

Francis Schaeffer was born on January 30, 1912, and he grew up in Germantown, Pennsylvania. Like Rushdoony, he was a Presbyterian. Following his graduation from college, he spent one year studying under Cornelius Van Til at Westminster Theological Seminary in Philadelphia. (Van Til, you will recall, had a major influence on Rushdoony's theology and political philosophy. In fact, Rushdoony's first published book, *By What Standard?* is an analysis of Van Til's theology.) Schaeffer completed his theological training at Faith Theological Seminary in Baltimore, Maryland, from which he graduated in 1938. Following pastorates in Pennsylvania and Missouri, he moved to Switzerland in 1955, where he established a community called *L'Abri*—a French term that means "the shelter."

Schaeffer went on to become one of the most widely respected social, theological, and political thinkers in conservative Christian circles during the second half of the twentieth century. One admirer called him "the last of the relevant and the truly great modern theologians."[20] Schaeffer was not a disciple of Rushdoony. However, both Schaeffer and Rushdoony held dominionist views, the underlying philosophy of which they learned from Cornelius Van Til,* and they both advocated a return of American society, including government, to its Christian roots. The Wikipedia article "Dominionism" comments, "Schaeffer and Rushdoony read each others' writings, and even met. Schaeffer led a study of Rushdoony's writings at Schaeffer's [L'Abri] institute in Switzerland."[21] One of the four main emphases in the teaching of Schaeffer's L'Abri institute is that "because Christianity is true it speaks to all of life and not to some narrowly religious sphere and much of the material produced by L'Abri has been aimed at helping develop a Christian perspective on the arts, *politics* and the social sciences etc."[22]

In his book *A Christian Manifesto,* Schaeffer argued passionately that secular materialists, whose philosophy he claimed now controls the American government, "have no sufficient base for either society or law."[23] He meant that secularism, which is based exclusively on human wisdom, is inadequate as a basis on which to frame a nation's moral laws. He then went on to point out what he considered to be a "sufficient base" for law: "That base was God's written Law, back through the New Testament to Moses' written Law; and the content and authority of that written Law is rooted back to Him who is the final reality. Thus, neither church nor state was equal to, let alone above, that Law. The base for law is not divided, and no one has the right to place anything, *including king, state or church*, above the content of God's law."[24]

---

*Van Til denied having any interest in religio-political movements. See "Dominionism," Wikipedia, http://en.wikipedia.org/wiki/Dominionism#Roots_and _branches.

In Romans 13:1, Paul said, "Everyone must submit himself to the governing authorities, for there is no authority except that which God has established. The authorities that exist have been established by God." From this, Schaeffer argued that "the state . . . is to be administered according to the principles of God's Law."[25] This concept pervades Schaeffer's book. Elsewhere in his book he said, "[Civil] Law is founded on the Law of God,"[26] and "The civil government, as all of life, stands under the Law of God."[27] Schaeffer cited John Knox, who said that the power of kings "is limited by God's word."[28]

In the United States, government is "of the people, by the people, and for the people,"[29] which means that the people formulate their own laws, which may or may not in every respect conform to God's law. However, government "of the people, by the people, and for the people" is what Schaeffer especially objected to. He said, "We live in a secularized society and in secularized, sociological law. By sociological law we mean law that has no fixed base but law in which a group of people decides what is sociologically good for society at the given moment; and what they arbitrarily decide becomes law."[30] That's precisely what "government of the people, by the people, and for the people" means. In America for most of two hundred years, the law has reflected Christian values because most Americans have been Christians. Schaeffer argued that this basis for law changed during the last half of the twentieth century. And in a sense, he was right. Our culture *has* become more secular. Christians themselves tend to think in more secular terms today than they did a hundred years ago, and the nation's laws and the decisions of its courts are gradually coming to reflect this change.

This is precisely what Schaeffer found so objectionable. He argued passionately that "the whole [Judeo-Christian] structure of our society is being attacked and destroyed. It is being given an entirely opposite base which gives exactly opposite results."[31] Thus, according to Schaeffer, America is engaged in a culture war. "These two religions, Christianity and humanism, stand over against each other as totalities,"[32] Schaeffer said. "We should be struggling and praying that this whole other entity—the material-energy, chance world view—can be rolled back with all its results across all of life."[33] "We must understand that there is going to be a battle every step of the way. They [secular materialists] are determined that what they have gained will not be rolled back."[34] "We are at war."[35]

The idea that God's law forms the base for the law of civil government lies at the foundation of all theocracies. Later in his book, Schaffer protested that he was "in no way talking about any kind of theocracy."[36] Technically, he was correct. By definition, a theocracy is a government that is administered by God or by clergy in the name of God. Either way, God's laws become the laws of the state. Thus, while Schaefer may not have had in mind a state run by priests, his statement that he was not demanding a theocracy is contradicted by his demand that God's law must be the basis of civil law.

Again, like Rushdoony, Schaeffer came on the scene as a major evangelical Protestant thinker *at the very time that America's political conservatives were recruiting the country's religious conservatives to their cause. And along with Rushdoony, Schaeffer provided these religious conservatives with the theoretical, theological justification they needed to join the conservative political army.* Schaeffer was even closer to most evangelical Protestants than Rushdoony, because Schaeffer was a premillennialist while Rushdoony was a postmillennialist. Schaeffer was strongly influenced by Rushdoony's Dominionism. He simply adapted it to premillennialism.[37]

A key point that we must not overlook is that both Rushdoony and Schaeffer were convinced that *the laws of the state must be based on the Bible.* Rushdoony said, "Civil law cannot be separated from Biblical law," which "is therefore the law for Christian man and Christian society." And Schaeffer insisted that "the state . . . is to be administered according to the principles of God's law" and "[civil] Law is founded on the Law of God"; "civil government, as all of life, stands under the Law of God."

In chapter 10, I made a key point of the fact that church-state separation means, among other things, that the laws of the state will be based on secular moral principles, not the moral principles of any church or holy book. Rushdoony's and Schaeffer's philosophy of government would destroy church-state separation as we have known it in the United States.

Rushdoony and Schaeffer are actually very similar to fundamentalist Muslims in the kind of government they demand. In his book *A Brief Guide to Islam*, Paul Grieve says, "The secular nation-state based on the Western model is a concept that runs directly contrary to Muslim traditions, which stretch back to the original community of the *'ummah'* [the "faithful"], established . . . by the Prophet in Medina in the seventh century. Here was the ideal Muslim society with no national boundaries *and a merged church and state, ruled by the laws of God.*"[38] A "merged church and state, ruled by the laws of God" is precisely what Rushdoony and Schaeffer demanded. The only difference between Rushdoony and Schaeffer on the one hand and Muslims on the other is that Rushdoony and Schaeffer wanted the American civil government to be ruled by the laws of the Judeo-Christian Jehovah rather than by the laws of the Muslim Allah. They wanted America's laws to be based on the Bible rather than the Koran. They wanted America to be governed by a Christian version of Islamic *Sharia* law!

So what?

I gave a talk based on this chapter to a group of Adventists at the northern California Redwood camp meeting in late July 2006. When I had concluded my remarks, a woman in the back raised her hand. "How do we know that Rushdoony's and Schaeffer's philosophy of government had anything to do with the ideas of today's Religious Right?" she asked.

That's a good question, and there's a good answer.

John W. Whitehead, the president of the Charlottesville, Virginia–based Rutherford Institute,* worked closely with Francis Schaeffer prior to his death, helping him with the research for his book *A Christian Manifesto*, from which I quoted several times in this chapter. Whitehead also met Rushdoony in 1975, and over a period of several years had many in-depth conversations with him.[39] He said, "Rushdoony's writings transformed the way Christians thought about political involvement and essentially laid the foundations for the emergence of a powerful political right wing. As Rushdoony's son-in-law Gary North notes, his writings 'are the source of many of the core ideas of the New Christian Right.' "[40] Whitehead pointed out, "While Rushdoony and Schaeffer are virtually unknown outside Christian right-wing circles, their teachings, co-opted by those with political agendas, have taken on lives of their own."[41]†

---

*The Rutherford Institute is a civil liberties organization that provides free legal services to people whose constitutional and human rights have been threatened or violated.

†John W. Whitehead was a close friend of Francis Schaeffer. In the article in the July/August 2006 issue of *Liberty* magazine that I have cited in this chapter, he said that Schaeffer "disagreed with Rushdoony's dominionist ideas," and "while Rushdoony unabashedly advocated a Christian theocracy, this is a far cry from

In an article about Christian Reconstructionism in *Church and State* magazine, John Sugg[*] wrote, "It would be easy to dismiss the Reconstructionists as the lunatic fringe, no more worrisome than the remnants of the Prohibition Party. But, in fact, they have rather extraordinary entrée and influence with top-tier Religious Right leaders and institutions."[42] His article explains why "Alabama's Ten Commandments judge, Roy Moore, is aligned with this [the Reconstructionist] congregation, and why one-third of Alabama Republicans who voted in the June primary supported him."[43]

Many of today's home-schooling textbooks are by Reconstructionist authors—a fact that is not surprising, given Rushdoony's strong support for the home-schooling movement. Herb Titus, a Harvard-trained attorney and the former dean of Pat Robertson's Regent University law school, is a Reconstructionist; he served as legal counsel to Judge Roy Moore. Jerry Falwell's Liberty University in Lynchburg, Virginia, employs Reconstructionists as professors. Roger Schultz, chair of the university's history department, is a regular contributor to the Reconstructionist journal *Faith for All of Life*. Sugg said that James Dobson "has a warm relationship with many in the [Reconstructionist] movement, and he has admitted voting for Reconstructionist presidential candidate Howard Phillips in 1996."[44]

Reconstructionism has had a profound effect on the thinking of Religious Right Protestants. Notice the emphasis on Christians taking dominion over society in these statements, which are an expansion of those quoted in the preceding chapter:

> *Pat Robertson:* "God's plan is for His people, ladies and gentlemen, to take *dominion*. . . . What is *dominion*? Well, *dominion* is Lordship. He wants His people to reign and rule with Him, . . . but He's waiting for us to . . . extend His *dominion*. . . . And the Lord says, 'I'm going to let you redeem *society*. There'll be a reformation. . . . We are not going to stand for those coercive

---

Schaeffer's views" (pages 9, 8). Perhaps. Whitehead certainly was much better acquainted with Schaeffer than I could ever hope to be. Nevertheless, the quotations that I shared with you in this chapter from Schaeffer's book *A Christian Manifesto* persuade me that his ideas lead to dominionism and theocracy, whether or not he espoused those actual doctrines.

[*]John Sugg is a senior editor of CL Newspapers in Atlanta, Charlotte, Tampa, and Sarasota.

utopians in the Supreme Court and in Washington ruling over us any more. We're not going to stand for it. We're going to say, 'We want freedom in this country, and we want power.' "[45]

D. James Kennedy: "Our job is to reclaim America for Christ, whatever the cost. As the vice regents of God, we are to exercise godly *dominion* and influence over our neighborhoods, our schools, our government, our literature and arts, our sports arenas, our entertainment media, our news media, our scientific endeavors—in short, over every aspect and institution of human *society.*"[46]

Where did Robertson get the idea that "God's plan is for His people . . . to take *dominion*"? Where did Kennedy get the idea that Christians are "to exercise godly *dominion* and influence . . . over every aspect and institution of human *society*"? I haven't talked to either Robertson or Kennedy, but the political philosophy in these statements is a mirror image of the political philosophy of Rushdoony and Schaeffer, and I'm quite certain that's where they got it.

So where is all this dominionism taking us?

We're nearing the end of our story, but there are still a few pieces to be put in place, so keep reading.

---

1. Gary North, "R. J. Rushdoony, R.I.P.," Lew Rockwell.com, http://www.lewrockwell.com/north/north33.html.

2. "What Chalcedon Believes," The Chalcedon Foundation, http://www.chalcedon.edu/credo.php; italics in the original.

3. Rousas John Rushdoony, *The Institutes of Biblical Law* (Phillipsburg, N.J.: P & R Publishing, 1973), 4.

4. Ibid.

5. Ibid., 14.

6. Ibid., 9; italics in the original.

7. Ibid., 3, 4; italics added.

8. Ibid., 4; italics in the original.

9. Ibid., 5.

10. Ibid.

11. Ibid.; italics in the original.

12. Ibid., 4.

13. Ibid., 9; italics added.

14. Ibid., 12.

15. Ibid., 6.

16. Ibid., 12.

17. Ibid., 399.

18. Ibid., 221.

19. Cited in "Dominionism," Religious Tolerance.org, http://www.religioustolerance.org/reconstr.htm.

20. David Hopkins, "Francis Schaeffer: The Last Great Modern Theologian," http://www.next-wave.org/dec99/francis_schaeffer.htm.

21. "Dominionism," Wikipedia, http://en.wikipedia.org/wiki/Dominionism#Origin_of_the_Term.

22. L'Abri Fellowship, http://www.labri.org/history.html; italics added.

23. Francis A. Schaeffer, *A Christian Manifesto* (Westchester, Ill.: Crossway Books, 1981), 26.

24. Ibid., 29; italics added.

25. Ibid., 28, 100.

26. Ibid., 99.

27. Ibid., 90.

28. Ibid., 98.

29. From Abraham Lincoln's Gettysburg Address.

30. Schaeffer, 41.

31. Ibid., 101, 102.

32. Ibid., 54.

33. Ibid., 73, 74.

34. Ibid., 75.

35. Ibid., 116.

36. Ibid., 120.

37. "Dominionism," Wikipedia, http://en.wikipedia.org/wiki/Dominionism#Origin_of_the_Term.

38. Paul Grieve, *A Brief Guide to Islam—History, Faith and Politics: The Complete Introduction* (New York: Carroll and Graf Publishers, 2006), 22.

39. I adapted the details of Whitehead's association with Rushdoony and Schaeffer from the biographical information about him in his article "The Rise of Dominionism and the Christian Right," *Liberty*, July/August 2006, 6.

40. John W. Rutherford, "The Rise of Dominionism and the Christian Right," *Liberty*, July/August 2006, 9.

41. Ibid.

42. John Sugg, "Warped Worldview," *Church and State*, July/August 2006, 13.

43. Ibid., 11.

44. The information about Religious Right ties to Reconstructionism that I have cited in this paragraph is from Sugg's article "Warped Worldview," 11–13.

45. Comment by Pat Robertson on the *700 Club* television program; cited in RedSonja2000, "Dominionist Dream: Repeal the 1st Amendment," Talk to Action, http://www.talk2action.org/story/2005/12/16/103532/64.

46. Cited in "The Rise of the Religious Right in the Republican Party," http://www.theocracywatch.org.

Chapter 21

Dominionism and Triumphalism

Every now and then we hear of a church that claims to be "the only true church." We saw earlier in this book that Catholics do indeed claim this for their church. And they aren't the only ones. Some Protestants also make this claim for their denomination. This claim is one of the characteristics of a philosophy called "triumphalism." This philosophy may also include the belief that "my religion will prevail over yours" or even that "my religion will *conquer* yours."

The Wikipedia online encyclopedia defines *triumphalism* as an "attitude or belief that a particular doctrine, culture, or social system is superior to and should triumph over all others."[1] The Muslim religion is very triumphalistic. Muslims believe that theirs is the only true religion, and many, especially the terrorists, believe that their religion will conquer the world. They believe a day is coming when all people everywhere will be Muslims, and this will usher in the end of the world. That, in fact, corresponds perfectly with Rushdoony's vision for Christianity.

Based on what I just said, you may think that triumphalism is bad. It certainly isn't politically correct in today's Western culture for anyone to claim that his or her religion is the only true religion. However, triumphalism isn't necessarily bad. Christianity is a triumphalistic religion, because Christians believe that they are right and that they have a responsibility to win as many people to Jesus Christ as possible. After all, people's eternal salvation depends on it! We come by our triumphalism from the words of Jesus Himself, who said, " 'I am the way and the truth and the life. No one comes to the Father except through me' " (John 14:6). In other words, if you want salvation, you have to come through Jesus. To this day, many Christians—especially fundamentalist and evangelical Christians—believe that salvation is obtainable only through Jesus—a conviction that Seventh-day Adventists share.

Triumphalism typically drives a sense of mission. The belief that "we're right and everyone else is wrong" and that "salvation is available only through our religion" provides a powerful motivation to convert others to the faith. Again, Jesus Himself said, " 'Go and make disciples of all nations' " (Matthew 28:19).

You may be familiar with the term "manifest destiny," which expressed the nineteenth-century idea that America had a responsibility—almost a divine mandate—to conquer the West. That's civil rather than religious triumphalism. Conservative American politics still contains a triumphalistic strain. George W. Bush is being triumphalistic when he says that he believes America has a responsibility to spread democracy around the world.

A few paragraphs back I mentioned that Catholics tend to be triumphalistic because they believe that the Catholic Church is the only true church. I don't have a problem with that. Catholics have a right to believe that theirs is the only true church. I don't believe it, but I respect it. I also respect Muslims who believe that theirs is the only true religion. After all, there's a triumphalistic streak in Adventism, as you may have recognized by now. We hold certain strong convictions about the final crisis, and we believe it's our mission to warn the world about what we see coming.

Triumphalism's temptation

Triumphalism is a problem when it becomes arrogant, and especially when it seeks to triumph through unethical and abusive methods. The triumphalistic Americans who conquered the western United States treated the Native American people extremely unjustly. Religious triumphalism is particularly dangerous when it links itself up with civil government, because it becomes very easy to use the power of the state to enforce the power-holder's belief system on those who disagree. That was the problem during the Middle Ages, when Catholic leaders persecuted heretics who refused to conform to Catholic doctrines and lifestyle.

In fact, even a casual reading of Revelation 13 makes it obvious that the two end-time beast powers are very triumphalistic. They combine religion and civil government into a single authority that they then use to force the whole world to worship in what they consider to be the correct manner. This is a very wrong expression of triumphalism.

As I said, Adventists are quite triumphalistic, and in fact, triumphalism is the key to our success. We are driven by the sense that we have a message about a stupendous crisis that is coming upon the world, a crisis that will involve spiritual issues that most people don't understand. In fact, the very prophetic interpretation that most people have found so wild and foolish over the years is the message we feel compelled to warn the world about! For Seventh Day Baptists, the Sabbath is simply "the right day to keep." For us, the Sabbath will be *the issue* in the final crisis, and people's eternal destiny will depend on the decision they make about it. That's the eschatological context of our convictions about the Sabbath. It's what has driven our sense of mission these past 150 years. It's why we today have fifteen million adherents and counting.

Rushdoony, Schaeffer, and triumphalism

One of the most significant points to notice in the political philosophy of R. J. Rushdoony and Francis Schaeffer is that both are very triumphalistic, for *by definition, dominionism is triumphalistic.* Again, that's OK, provided that those who hold this philosophy treat others with respect and don't abuse them. But any triumphalistic religion that links up with civil government is in great danger of becoming unethical and abusive in its treatment of those who disagree. That's the problem I see with Rushdoony and Schaeffer. They believed that the laws of civil government must be based upon biblical laws and that Christians bear the responsibility of making this happen by exercising dominion over society. And, as I pointed out in the previous chapter, this political philosophy has had a profound effect on the thinking of Religious Right Protestants. Pat Robertson said, "God's plan is for His people . . . to take *dominion.*" God "wants His people to reign and rule with Him, . . . but He's waiting for us to . . . extend His *dominion.* . . . We want freedom in this country, and we want power."[2] And D. James Kennedy said, "Our job is to reclaim America for Christ . . . [and to] exercise godly *dominion* and influence over . . . government [and] over every aspect and institution of human *society.*"[3]

The dominionism of Rushdoony, Schaeffer, and America's Religious Right is also very triumphalistic—dangerously so in my opinion, be-

Dominionism and Triumphalism

cause, as the quotes by Robertson and Kennedy show so clearly, Religious Right conservatives are determined to take over the American civil government and use it to enforce their moral agenda on the nation. As the nation sinks into moral chaos—which is certainly happening—the triumphalistic dominionism of Rushdoony and Schaeffer seems very attractive to conservative Christians, who see it as the solution to the problem. Unfortunately, it isn't.

Catholics also have a long history of favoring church-state union, and they still view this relationship between the church and the state as ideal. Unfortunately, in the past, Catholic church-state union, combined with Catholic triumphalism, resulted in horrible forms of persecution, such as the rack and burning at the stake. These were perpetrated on dissenters in the name of saving their souls. I do not hesitate to say that *church-state union, which Rushdoony, Schaeffer, Religious Right Protestants, and Catholics look upon with such great favor, is the foundation of all religious persecution.*

I have no doubt whatsoever that if you were to ask them, both Catholics and Religious Right Protestants would assure you that they have no intention of persecuting dissenters. However, notice this: Pat Robertson said, "We want power." I'm reminded of the words of Lord Acton, who said, "Power tends to corrupt, and absolute power corrupts absolutely."[4] In a sinful world, no individual, church, or religion is immune from that principle. I frankly would not want my own Adventist Church to link up with civil authority. It's too dangerous. I fear that sooner or later we would allow our particular brand of triumphalism to lord it over others.

The best insurance any of us can have against persecuting others is to avoid getting our religious belief system entangled with civil government in the first place. That's been the American way since the founding of our nation, which is why we've had very little religious persecution in this country since 1776. *The problem with the political philosophy of today's Catholics and Religious Right Protestants is not with their intentions today. It's with the religio-political system they're determined to set up and the use that others will make of that system once it's been set up.*

Is it possible that the political philosophy of Catholics and Religious Right Protestants might someday lead to persecution in the United States?

Could this really happen?

Well, I've already answered that question, but read on.

8—C. I. R. H.   225

1. "Triumphalism," Wikipedia, http://en.wikipedia.org/wiki/Triumphalism.

2. Comment by Pat Robertson on *The 700 Club* television program; cited in RedSonja2000, "Dominionist Dream: Repeal the 1st Amendment," Talk to Action, http://www.talk2action.org/story/2005/12/16/103532/64.

3. Cited in "The Rise of the Religious Right in the Republican Party," http://www.theocracywatch.org.

4. This is a very well-known quotation. I found it in " John Dalberg-Acton, 1st Baron Acton," Wikipedia, http://en.wikipedia.org/wiki/Lord_Acton.

CHAPTER 22

How Persecution Develops

Constantine was worried, and he had a reason to be. His small army faced a much larger enemy, the forces of Maxentius. The two brothers-in-law (Constantine was married to Maxentius's sister Fausta) were battling for the emperor's throne. Maxentius had been ruling in Rome ever since the death of the previous emperor, Constantius I. However, Constantine was the late emperor's son, and he felt that the throne should be his. And so in October 312, the two men, each with his own army, met at the Milvan Bridge, a short distance from Rome. Maxentius's army was at least four times larger than Constantine's—and some ancient authorities estimate that it was as much as ten times larger. Either way, Constantine was seriously outnumbered, which is why he was worried. How could his small force defeat Maxentius's much larger army? Constantine knew of only one way it might happen.

Back then, everyone assumed that the gods helped whichever side they favored, so naturally, Constantine, who was a pagan, sought the favor of the most powerful pagan god. However, the answer he got was not at all what he expected. In the late evening of October 27, he had a vision of a cross emblazoned across the setting sun. With the cross were the Greek words *En Toutō Nika*, which means, "With this sign you will conquer." Amazing! He was supposed to go to battle in the name of the Christian God! The next morning Constantine ordered his soldiers to inscribe on their shields the Greek letters X and P (the Greek letter for "R" looks like our "P"), which are the first two letters of *Xristos*, the

Greek form of the name *Christ*. Later that same day, Constantine's army defeated Maxentius's army, and Constantine became the emperor of Rome.

Constantine immediately professed faith in Christ, and the following year, 313, he proclaimed the Edict of Milan, which gave freedom to all religions, including Christianity. After nearly three hundred years of on-again, off-again persecution, Christians were finally free to practice their religion without fear of being arrested, jailed, and in some instances put to death. After all, the emperor was now a fellow-believer!

Constantine's conversion was a minor tremor in the "current events" of the time, but over the next hundred years, the tremor grew, becoming a massive earthquake that radically changed the course of world history. H. A. Drake, a professor of history at the University of California in Santa Barbara and author of the book *Constantine and the Bishops*, calls Constantine's conversion and his subsequent support of Christianity "one of the most important transfers of power in Western history."[1] Paganism, and specifically emperor worship, had been the official religion of the empire for the previous several hundred years. The Edict of Milan put paganism and emperor worship on the same level as all other religions. While Constantine was still Pontifex Maximus and thus the official head of the empire's pagan emperor worship, he also was now a Christian, and this gave Christianity an important edge over paganism. By the end of the century, not only had Christianity replaced paganism as the official religion of the empire, but, in some cases, Christians were persecuting pagans as severely as the pagans had persecuted Christians a hundred years earlier!

Early Christians and freedom of conscience

This persecution was a radical departure from traditional Christianity. For nearly three hundred years, Christians had held firmly to the conviction that conversion to the faith had to be the result of the willing choice of each convert. Christianity was a religion of love, not force. Jesus Himself had given the invitation " '*Come* unto me' " (Matthew 11:28, italics added), and in Revelation, He said, "And whosoever *will*, let him take the water of life freely" (Revelation 22:17, KJV, italics added).

The idea that people must choose their religious beliefs freely, without coercion, was reinforced every time Christians were persecuted for their faith. Their tormenters tried to force them to give obeisance to pagan gods, but the Christians said No. Worship must be given willingly or it isn't worship at all. Athanasius, who is famous for his defense of the doctrine of the Trinity at the Council of Nicaea, said it is "not the part of men who have confidence in what they believe, to force and compel the unwilling. . . . The truth is not preached with swords or with darts, nor by means of soldiers; but by persuasion and counsel."[2] Drake points out that Christians at Constantine's time had an "inherent belief that true faith could not be coerced." They "inherited as an article of faith the injunction that enemies must be endured and loved."[3]

Constantine didn't turn against the pagans when he became a Christian, nor did he encourage Christians to persecute pagans.* Though still the official head of the Roman state religion, he also assumed a significant role in Christian affairs. During his reign, he chaired the important Council of Nicaea in 325 as well as other lesser councils. And through it all, he tried to build a climate in which a broad spectrum of religious views could coexist. Constantine would no doubt have been surprised at the American experiment in religious freedom, but he also would probably have approved of it.

Yet a hundred years after Constantine professed his faith in Christ, Christians were persecuting pagans, trying to force them to convert to "the faith." Some pagans even lost their lives at the hands of Christians![†] What happened? How did a religion that began with the conviction that religious belief must be freely chosen become a religion that tried to compel belief? Drake asks, "If Constantine's tolerant and inclusive Christianity succeeded in building a coalition of Christians and pagans in favor of monotheism broadly defined, then why did a more coercive and intolerant form of Christianity come to assert itself by the century's end?"[4] Let's examine the process.

---

*Many historians have assumed that Constantine's acceptance of pagans suggested that his Christianity was more a political strategy than a personal conviction. In his book *Constantine and the Bishops,* H. A. Drake disputes that conclusion. His study has led him to conclude that Constantine was truly a Christian, but that he sincerely wanted a level playing field for all religions in the empire. See Drake, pages 11–27.

†For example, in A.D. 415, a mob of Christians murdered Hypatia, a popular (and reputedly beautiful) female philosopher of Alexandria. See "Hypatia of Alexandria," Wikipedia, http://en.wikipedia.org/wiki/Hypatia_of_Alexandria.

How Christians came to persecute

Constantine ruled the Roman Empire for thirty years, from 307 to 337, and, as I have pointed out, he tried to create a society in which a variety of religious beliefs could coexist. Throughout his rule, Christians maintained their policy that conversion could be only by the willing consent of the convert. Constantine's son Constans, who ruled from 337 to 350, followed his father's policy of tolerance for all religions. During these years Christianity flourished. Converts flocked into the church, and Christians, especially the bishops, gained significant political power.

Constans died in 350 and was succeeded by his brother Constantius II, a more radical Christian who decreed that all pagan temples be closed and that anyone offering sacrifices to pagan gods and goddesses be put to death. Constantius died in 361 and was followed by Julian, who was a pagan by choice. Julian ruled for only two-and-a-half years. During that time, he tried to reinstate paganism as the religion of the empire. In 362, he issued an edict guaranteeing freedom of religion throughout the empire, but he also reintroduced pagan sacrifices and began cutting back the power of the bishops.

Naturally, the bishops were displeased with this reduction in their power. They also felt threatened by Julian's challenge to the Christian society they had created during the fifty years since Constantine converted to Christianity. Julian's rule, while very short, was long enough to generate fears of a reversal to paganism in the minds of Christians. As a result, *extremists in the Christian community who advocated more radical methods of maintaining a Christian society began to gain the upper hand.* And where Constantine had suppressed these radical tendencies, later emperors permitted and even encouraged them.[5] By the end of the century, Christians were severely persecuting pagans.

Comparisons

As accustomed as we in America are to our religious freedom, and as committed as we are to the idea that conversion must result from a personal choice, it's difficult for us to imagine that persecution could ever raise its ugly head in our nation. However, the fact that the Roman Empire and the Christian church changed from religious freedom to religious coercion during the second half of the fourth century should prompt us to recognize that *if it could happen then, it can happen now,* and *if it could happen there, it can happen here.* A couple of comparisons between then and now do indeed give us pause to ponder the direction some of us are taking.

First, we today easily feel as threatened by the pagans of our day—we call them atheists and secularists—as Christians in the fourth century felt by Julian's paganism. A favorite term today is "culture wars." We rail against our "pagans" just as they railed against theirs. I receive some of the most hostile postal mail and e-mail from Christians who castigate secularists bitterly for their moral convictions. And I have to wonder, *How would these religious zealots treat secular people should they gain the positions of political power in the United States that they seek?* A comparison with similar Christian zealots during the second half of the fourth century A.D. gives me serious cause for concern.

Second, Religious Right Protestants and Catholics are as intent on building a Christian society today as Christians were back then. Early in the fifth century (the century beginning with the year A.D. 400), Augustine wrote his book *The City of God* to argue that Christianity would ultimately triumph over paganism in Roman *society*. Today, Religious Right Christians are pushing hard for the ultimate triumph of Christianity over secularism in American *society*.

Catholics have been in the business of molding nations into *Catholic societies* for the better part of two millenniums, and they're very good at it. Unfortunately, where they have truly succeeded, intolerance of dissenters has often raised its ugly head. Again, you may protest that the bold statements in support of freedom of conscience that came out of Vatican II should prevent Catholics from ever persecuting anyone again. However, in chapter 8, I called attention to the qualifying phrases in those statements that, under the right (or wrong) circumstances, could even now give legitimacy to coercion.

It's also very evident that certain unique moral principles of the Catholic Church could at some point become "the law of the land" in the United States. I've pointed out in previous chapters that America's twenty-first-century Catholic hierarchy is putting tremendous pressure on Catholic legislators and judges to write laws and issue judicial rulings that are in harmony with Roman Catholic moral teaching. This is simply a lesser form of the spiritual pressure that popes used against rulers in order to dominate European politics during the Middle Ages—one result of which was the most severe persecution of dissenters. When Catholic moral teaching becomes law in the United States, as I suspect it eventually will, what consequences will result to those whose conscientious convictions lead them down a different moral path?

Religious Right Protestants are also campaigning hard to make biblical law the foundation of the nation's legal system. They want Congress and the various states to enact laws that are based on the Bible, and they want judges to interpret national and state laws according to the Bible.

I suggest that all of us, moderate Christians as well as those further to the right, need to pause and take a long look into the future. We need to ask ourselves where the path we are taking will lead us. Richard Evans, in his book *The Coming of the Third Reich*, raised several questions about the citizens of Germany during the years leading up to Hitler's takeover of their nation that we need to be asking about the Religious Right in America today. Notice especially the italicized words at the end of the following quote: "How was it that an advanced and highly cultured nation such as Germany could give in to the brutal force of National Socialism so quickly and so easily? Why was there such little serious resistance to the Nazi take-over? How could a party of the radical right rise to power with such dramatic suddenness? *Why did so many Germans fail to perceive the potentially disastrous consequences of ignoring the violent, racist and murderous nature of the Nazi movement?*"[6]

Admittedly, the Religious Right in America today is much more benign than Hitler's storm troopers were in pre-Nazi and early Nazi Germany. Yet the voices of intolerance are there, and the seeming benignity of the Religious Right's cause simply masks the dangerousness of the direction it is headed. Are we today, like the Germans in the years leading up to World War II, failing to perceive the potentially disastrous consequences of ignoring the intolerant, coercive nature of Religious Right Christians in their proclamation of a culture war and their demand to turn America into a society that is based on biblical principles? I propose that if an insignificant party of the radical right could rise to power with such dramatic suddenness in Germany, the same thing could, under the right circumstances, happen in America today.

The Bible predicts universal persecution

For those who still question the idea that religious persecution will ever come to America, I will offer one more reason for my certainty: Jesus Himself predicted it. To be sure, He didn't name America. He simply

232

said that His followers will be " 'handed over to be persecuted and put to death, and you will be hated by *all nations* because of me' " (Matthew 24:9, italics added). Need I remind you that America is a nation that must be included in Jesus' prediction? This is particularly true in view of the fact that Jesus spoke these words in response to His disciples' question about signs of His return. Thus, we can expect that Jesus' prediction will especially be fulfilled in the days immediately prior to His second coming.

Several statements in the last half of Revelation confirm this prophecy of end-time persecution by "all nations." They make it very clear that God's people all over the world will be severely persecuted shortly before Jesus returns:

- "He was given power to make war against the saints and to conquer them. And he was given authority over every tribe, people, language and nation" (Revelation 13:7).
- "He [the land beast] was given power to give breath to the image of the first beast, so that it could speak and cause all who refused to worship the image to be killed" (Revelation 13:15).
- "I saw that the woman was drunk with the blood of the saints, the blood of those who bore testimony to Jesus" (Revelation 17:6).

Even without identifying the particular political powers represented by the sea beast and the land beast in Revelation 13 or the harlot in chapter 17, it's obvious that Revelation predicts worldwide persecution in the months and perhaps years leading up to Jesus' second coming. Most conservative Christian interpreters of prophecy understand that we are living in the final days of this earth's history. Therefore, we should *expect* that the United States, which today is the world's only superpower, will be intensely involved in that end-time persecution. The question shouldn't be *whether* but *how*. We should, in fact, be alert to recognize trends in both the United States and other parts of the world that signal the approach of that persecution. That has been one of my primary motives in writing this book. Thus, I make no apology for the historic Adventist prediction that religious intolerance will arise in America someday. Under the right circumstances, it *could* happen, and trends that are already well developed in this country suggest both that it *will* happen and *how* it will happen.

Many conservative students of prophecy interpret the intolerant beast powers in Revelation as representing atheism and secular humanism. Tim LaHaye's Left Behind novels, for example, depict the antichrist as Carpathia, an evil, atheistic leader of the United Nations. Adventists see Revelation 13 differently. We understand the two evil beasts of that chapter to represent Christian political powers that will exercise dominion over the whole world during the final crisis. Is it possible that Christians in the United States might someday persecute those with whom they disagree?

Could that really happen?

One more piece of the puzzle remains to be put in place.

---

1. H. A. Drake, *Constantine and the Bishops: The Politics of Intolerance* (Baltimore, Md.: The Johns Hopkins University Press, 2000), xv.

2. Cited by Drake, 407.

3. Drake, 402.

4. Drake, 408.

5. For a more complete discussion of this issue, see Drake, 437–440.

6. Richard Evans, *The Coming of the Third Reich* (New York: Penguin Press, 2004), xxii; italics added.

CHAPTER 23

The Final Crisis

I want to make something very clear, so, although I've said it in previous chapters, I'll repeat it: I don't believe anyone in today's Christian world, whether Protestant, Catholic, or Orthodox, has any notion of persecuting anyone. When Pope John Paul II apologized to the world several years ago for the persecution that his church inflicted on Jews, Protestants, Muslims, and others in ages past, he meant it. When the cardinals and bishops gathered in Vatican II issued their official statement in support of religious freedom back in the mid-1960s, they meant it. If you were to ask Pat Robertson, D. James Kennedy, Jerry Falwell, and other Protestant Religious Right leaders in the United States whether they have it in their heads to torture those who disagree with them, I am sure they would respond with a most vehement No! And they'd mean it.

President George W. Bush has repeatedly stated very publicly that he wants to see democracy and freedom spread around the world. I can assure you that religious persecution is not a part of his agenda. A group of Seventh-day Adventist religious liberty leaders spent forty-five minutes with President Bush in the Oval Office on April 4, 2006. Jan Paulson, the president of the Seventh-day Adventist world church, said Bush "disclosed how passionately he feels about religious liberty; freedom of conscience, freedom to worship, freedom to think."[1]

My concern, as I have stated in previous chapters, is with the direction I see Catholics and Religious Right Protestants taking. In a crisis, trends that are worrisome today can outgrow even our worst fears. It's entirely possible for people who wouldn't think of harming a gnat to-day to perpetrate some of the most awful abuses tomorrow, during a crisis.

There's a good example of this in the news as I write these words. A group of U.S. Marines is charged with murdering civilians in Haditha, Iraq. As of this writing, these charges have not been brought before a court of law. However, regardless of the final verdict, I suspect that these young men are basically decent Americans who under normal circumstances would never have committed such a crime. But if indeed they did, the crisis of war obviously "got to them." Something in their minds snapped, and they committed atrocities that they wouldn't think of doing under normal circumstances. The Bible predicts that the world will be faced with a terrible crisis immediately before Jesus returns, and it's in the context of this crisis that laws will be enacted and persecutions perpetrated that seem unthinkable today.

How people respond to crisis

Several years ago, I read a book called *The Addictive Organization*. I've had quite an interest in addiction the past several years, but I'd always thought of addiction as something that happens to people. It had never occurred to me that organizations could be addictive. However, the authors, Anne Wilson Schaef and Diane Fassel, made a good case for their proposal. One of the ways they suggested for identifying a dysfunctional, addictive organization is to note the way its managers handle crises. Here's how they described the management style of an addictive organization: "In [times of] crisis we allow people to take over and enact unusual procedures. Crisis feeds on the illusion that control can bring the situation under control. Crises are used to excuse drastic and erratic actions on the part of managers. . . . Individuals have fewer responsibilities in crisis as management gathers power to ride out the problem. When crisis is the norm, management tends to assume an unhealthy amount of power on a daily basis."[2]

One good way to tell whether an organization is addictive is to observe how its managers handle crises. If top management consults with the lower-echelon supervisors and works out a joint strategy for solving the problems, the organization is probably quite healthy. On the other hand, if top management takes control away from lower-level managers, tries to micromanage the organization, and in the process makes some rather dumb decisions, the organization is probably quite dysfunctional and addictive. And even when you don't know whether the organization is facing a crisis, you can still suspect it's addictive if you see top management grasping for control, micromanaging, and making rash decisions.

I propose that this helps us understand the behavior of the two beast powers in Revelation 13. Even without interpreting the symbols, anyone reading that chapter can immediately recognize that the behavior of these two beasts isn't normal. Something is driving them to act in a very erratic manner. They are the world's "top management," they are frantic for control, and they are exhibiting some extremely unhealthy behavior to get it. The sea beast is persecuting God's people and grasping for political control of the whole world, and the land beast is threatening to kill anyone who refuses to worship the sea beast and its image. These two beast powers are doing what Schaff and Fassel told us addictive organizations do when they're in a crisis: They're grasping for an inordinate amount of power, and they're feeding "on the illusion that control can bring the situation under control." The behavior of these two beasts leads us to suspect that there's a crisis going on in the background, though Revelation 13 doesn't say one word about a crisis.

Fortunately, other parts of Revelation provide some excellent clues. Chapter 7:1–4 pictures "four angels standing at the four corners of the earth, holding back the four winds of the earth to prevent any wind from blowing on the land or on the sea or on any tree" until a seal is placed on the foreheads of God's people—the mysterious 144,000. These winds are symbolic of nature's destructive forces, because once God's servants are sealed and the four winds are allowed to blow, the land, the sea, and the trees will be harmed. In other words, the world's ecology will be devastated. We get a further glimpse of this crisis in chapter 16, which describes seven terrible plagues that will fall on the earth at the very end of time: People will break out with terrible skin sores (verse 2), the water in the oceans and streams will turn to blood (verses 3, 4), and the sun will burn so hot that it scorches people with fire (verse 8). In chapter 18, we discover that these plagues shatter the world's economy. The kings and the merchants of the earth "will weep and mourn" because no one buys their goods anymore (verses 9, 11) and the sea captains " 'will throw dust on their heads with weeping and mourning' " at the sight of the devastation that the plagues have caused (verses 17–19).

COULD IT *REALLY* HAPPEN?

Nature has devastating power when it's unleashed. We saw examples of this with the tsunami in the Indian Ocean in December 2004 and hurricanes Katrina and Rita in August and September 2005. God is holding these forces in check now, as the image of angels holding back the four winds in Revelation 7 suggests. But when He releases them, the devastation will be global.* Sufficient resources were available that the world was able to respond reasonably well to the destruction caused by the tsunami and hurricane Katrina. But imagine multiplying the destruction caused by these events a hundred times over. The world's coping systems would be totally overwhelmed.

The Old Testament prophet Daniel described the world's final crisis in chapter 12:1. He said, " 'At that time Michael, the great prince who protects your people, will arise. There will be a time of distress such as has not happened from the beginning of nations until then. But at that time your people—everyone whose name is found written in the book—will be delivered. Multitudes who sleep in the dust of the earth will awake: some to everlasting life, others to shame and everlasting contempt' " (Daniel 12:1, 2). According to Daniel, the worst time of distress the world has ever known will happen immediately before the resurrection of the righteous at Christ's second coming. That's precisely when the two beast powers of Revelation 13 will come on the world scene.

We get another clue about the severity of the final crisis from some words of Jesus in Matthew 24:21, 22. His disciples had asked Him about signs of the end, and one of the things He told them was that a time of great distress would come on the world " 'unequaled from the beginning of the world until now—and never to be equaled again' " (verse 21). Jesus was simply paraphrasing the words of the prophet Daniel. He then went on to say, " 'If those days had not been cut short, *no one would survive*' " (Matthew 24:22, italics added). Please notice the italicized words. The coming time of distress will be so severe that it will threaten the very survival of the human race. If God didn't put a stop to the devastation, human beings would become the next extinct species! That's a terrible, *terrible* crisis!

We get further evidence of the final crisis in Luke's version of the signs of the end. He said that because of the signs in the sun, moon,

---

*Opinions differ among theological thinkers over the degree to which God will be responsible for the natural disasters of the final crisis.

and stars, " 'nations will be in anguish and perplexity. . . . Men will faint from terror, apprehensive of what is coming on the world' " (Luke 21:25, 26). The people in the world will realize that their survival is hanging by a thread, and they will react very predictably: They will panic.

How crisis affects our thinking

Fear causes people to do things that in their right minds they would never dream of doing. And I propose that the fear Jesus predicted—nations in anguish and perplexity and the entire human race fainting from terror—is the crisis that lies behind the scenes in Revelation 13. This chapter isn't describing the sane, rational religious and political climate that the Western world knows today. It describes a world—an entire planet—that's in a panic and reacting horribly, yet predictably, to the final crisis.

Several years ago, I read a book called *Disasters and the Millennium* by Michael Barkun, a professor of social science at the University of New York in Buffalo. Barkun studied the effect that disasters can have on people's attitudes. One of his most significant conclusions was that "disaster creates conditions peculiarly fitted to the rapid alteration of belief systems."[3] Here are several similar statements: "Disaster produces the questioning, the anxiety, and the suggestibility that are required [for change]; only in its wake are people moved to abandon old values of the past."[4] "Disaster, by removing the familiar environment, removes precisely those frames of reference by which we normally evaluate statements, ideas, and beliefs. Belief systems which under nondisaster conditions might be dismissed, now receive sympathetic consideration."[5] "A disaster population suffers a temporary sense of incapacity, vulnerability, and confusion. The collapsed social structure renders traditional authority relationships less effective and traditional statuses less meaningful.

"The disaster victim, for whom the ordinary cues and landmarks of living have been removed, is left passive, receptive to suggestion, and in need of a substitute environment. He requires a new configuration of social relationships and values to explain his new predicament."[6]

In a disaster situation, ideas to which in the past people would never have given a second thought and from which they might even have recoiled in horror now seem reasonable and proper. In the face of disaster, the majority of people become more passive and open to new authority relationships and new social systems. So, global crisis provides a perfect opportunity for the world's political leaders to consolidate their power in order to bring the situation under control. And that, I propose, is the crisis that lies in the background of Revelation 13.

Nobody is thinking about persecuting people today regarding the day they keep—certainly not in America! It's ludicrous to suggest that anyone is even contemplating such an idea. However, trends in the United States that are already quite well developed concern me even now. In a crisis, these trends could easily prompt the world's political and religious leaders to do things that we today would find inconceivable.

A death decree?

There's one other issue we need to deal with. Seventh-day Adventists claim that the mark of the beast is the observance of Sunday when it is enforced by law and that eventually those who persist in keeping the seventh day of the week as the Sabbath will be threatened with death. Would the world, even in a panic, react that drastically? The Bible describes another aspect of the final crisis—spiritualism—that will make this possible.

Please keep in mind the spiritual context of the final crisis that I set forth in chapter 2 of this book. Satan and his angels rebelled against God in heaven, and when God cast them out, they came to our earth, where they have been waging a spiritual war against God ever since. *The final crisis will be their last stand.** Satan will be trying to get as many people to side with him as he possibly can, and two of his primary tools will be force and deception. We've been discussing his use of force. Jesus also warned of Satan's deception. He said, " 'False Christs and false prophets will appear and perform great signs and miracles to deceive even the elect—if that were possible' " (Matthew 24:24). One of Satan's defining character traits is deception, and the deceptions of these end-time false christs will be so subtle that even God's own people will be in danger of being deceived.

Paul also warned of Satan's end-time deception. He said, "The coming of the lawless one will be in accordance with the work of Satan displayed in all kinds of counterfeit miracles, signs and wonders, and in

---

*Satan's final stand will actually take place at the end of the millennium, but his last stand in the history of our present world will be during the final crisis, just before Christ's second coming.

every sort of evil that *deceives* those who are perishing. They perish because they refused to love the truth and so be saved. For this reason God sends them *a powerful delusion so that they will believe the lie* and so that all will be condemned who have not believed the truth but have delighted in wickedness" (2 Thessalonians 2:9–12, italics added).

Paul left no doubt about the demonic source of this deception. He attributed it to "the lawless one"—Satan. And he said that it will be a "powerful delusion."

Revelation 13 also comments on this delusion. John said that in his vision, the land beast "performed great and miraculous signs, even causing fire to come down from heaven to earth in full view of men. Because of the signs he was given power to do on behalf of the first beast, he *deceived* the inhabitants of the earth" (Revelation 13:13, 14, italics added). Notice that Jesus, Paul, and John all said that the end-time delusions of Satan will include miracles—supernatural occurrences that astound the human race and cause them to believe a lie.

John gave us one more bit of information about these false miracles. Speaking of the sixth plague, he said, "Then I saw three evil spirits that looked like frogs; they came out of the mouth of the dragon, out of the mouth of the beast and out of the mouth of the false prophet. They are spirits of demons performing miraculous signs, and they go out to the kings of the whole world, to gather them for the battle on the great day of God Almighty" (Revelation 16:13, 14).

Just before the end of time, Satan's evil spirits—his miracle-working demons—will actually rally the world's political and military leaders for earth's final battle, which Revelation calls Armageddon (verse 16).

Seventh-day Adventists believe it's in the context of this demonic deception that world leaders will issue a death decree against those who keep God's commandments, including the fourth one. Ellen White predicted that during the final crisis, Satan will reveal himself personally, visibly to the human race, and he will claim to be Christ:

> As the crowning act in the great drama of deception, Satan himself will personate Christ. The church has long professed to look to the Saviour's advent as the consummation of her hopes. Now the great deceiver will make it appear that Christ has come. In different parts of the earth, Satan will manifest himself among men as a majestic being of dazzling brightness, resembling the description of the Son of God given by John in the

Revelation. Revelation 1:13-15. The glory that surrounds him is unsurpassed by anything that mortal eyes have yet beheld. The shout of triumph rings out upon the air: "Christ has come! Christ has come!" The people prostrate themselves in adoration before him, while he lifts up his hands and pronounces a blessing upon them, as Christ blessed His disciples when He was upon the earth. His voice is soft and subdued, yet full of melody. In gentle, compassionate tones he presents some of the same gracious, heavenly truths which the Saviour uttered; he heals the diseases of the people, and then, in his assumed character of Christ, he claims to have changed the Sabbath to Sunday, and commands all to hallow the day which he has blessed. He declares that those who persist in keeping holy the seventh day are blaspheming his name by refusing to listen to his angels sent to them with light and truth. This is the strong, almost overmastering delusion.[7]

This satanic delusion is what Adventists understand will lead the world to issue a death decree against those who keep the seventh-day Sabbath. Today's Protestants and Catholics obviously have no such thoughts in their heads and understandably react with horror at the idea that they ever would. But when Seventh-day Adventists talk about the coming persecution of God's people because of the day they keep, we aren't talking about today's normal times. We're talking about a final crisis in which desperate satanic forces are making their last stand in the six-thousand-year history of the conflict between good and evil. We're talking about the short period just before Jesus comes that Daniel said will be the worst time of distress the world has ever known. We're talking about a time when the human race will be in a panic and demonic forces will be working their miracles to deceive. We're talking about a time of trouble so severe that Jesus said no one would survive it if God didn't cut it short. *This is the crisis Adventists believe the world will face.*

We are also talking about a time when, under the pressure of the final crisis with its severe natural disasters, *religious fanaticism* will lead human beings to advocate ideas and actions that today are the furthest thing from their minds. You will recall that one of the factors in the fourth-century transformation of Christianity from a religion of freedom to a religion of coercion was fanatical Christians who gained the upper hand in church and state. And, unfortunately, that kind of fanaticism is even now beginning to show its ugly head in America. Please note the following two quotes:

> *Gary North, Reconstructionist and founder of the Institute for Christian Economics:* "So let us be blunt about it: we must use the doctrine of religious liberty to gain independence for Christian schools until we train up a generation of people who know that there is no religious neutrality, no neutral law, no neutral education, and no neutral civil government. Then they will get busy in constructing a Bible-based social, political and religious order *which finally denies the religious liberty of the enemies of God.*"[8]
>
> *Randall Terry, founder of Operation Rescue and a Republican candidate for the Florida State Senate in the 2006 primary election:* "I want you to just let a wave of intolerance wash over you. I want you to let a wave of hatred wash over you. Yes, hate is good. . . . Our goal is a Christian nation. We have a biblical duty, we are called by God, to conquer this country. We don't want equal time. We don't want pluralism."[9]

Those are fighting words. They're fanatical words. Yet they're extreme only in degree as compared to the views of Pat Robertson, Jerry Falwell, D. James Kennedy, and others in the Religious Right. I'm reminded of the words of Roland Hegstad, who for many years during the second half of the twentieth century was the director of the Religious Liberty department of the Seventh-day Adventists' General Conference. "Persecution doesn't come from bad people trying to make other people bad," Hegstad said. "It comes from good people trying to make other people good." He's right. And, unfortunately, that's precisely the mind-set of many of today's Religious Right leaders. I don't doubt their sincerity. But in their desire to make America a godly nation, they're good people who want to make other people good. And that's the problem.

I'd hate to see the day when people of that mind-set gain control of the American government. Yet the Adventist understanding of Revelation 13 leads us to conclude that this is precisely what *will* happen. The United States will be intimately involved in the persecution of the final conflict. This shouldn't surprise us given the fact that Jesus said that before His second coming, "all nations" will hate and persecute God's people (Matthew 24:9). The deceptions of the end time will cause even the United States to break its foundational principle of religious freedom. And Adventists see trends in this country that are even now leading toward that very development. It goes without saying that those who support this trend at the present time don't have any notion of persecuting people who keep the Sabbath on Saturday. What they don't realize is that in their bitter opposition to church-state separation, they are laying the foundation for that very persecution to happen during a future crisis. This persecution will happen under circumstances that differ dramatically from today's relatively peaceful world and under the direction of fanatical leaders who don't hold the same convictions about freedom of religion that they do.

The papacy

In chapter 3, I pointed out three conclusions that we can reasonably draw from the description of the sea beast in Revelation 13:

- *"He [the sea beast] was given authority over every tribe, people, language and nation" (verse 7).* This means that it will achieve political control of the whole world.
- *"The whole world was astonished and followed the beast. Men . . . worshiped the beast and asked, 'Who is like the beast? Who can make war against him?' " (verses 3, 4).* The world will acknowledge the sea beast's spiritual leadership and will pay it homage.
- *"He was given power to make war against the saints and to conquer them" (verse 7).* The sea beast will persecute those who oppose its authority.

If the sea beast is an end-time power, and if it represents the papacy, as Adventists have traditionally taught, then the papacy will fulfill each of these specifications in the final days of earth's history. Incredible as this may seem, keep in mind that the Vatican has historically aspired to global dominance. Pius XI, who was pope from 1922 to 1939, said, "The Empire of our Redeemer embraces all men," and "The whole of mankind is subject to the power of Jesus Christ."[10] Pius also objected strongly to the modern secular state that for some two hundred years has made it impossible for the papacy to exercise global dominance. Referring to the ending of the political dominance over Europe that the papacy had held during the medieval period, he said, "The Empire of Christ over all nations was rejected. The right which the Church has from Christ Himself, to teach mankind, to make laws, to govern peoples in all that pertains to their eternal salvation, that right was denied. Then gradually the religion of Christ [Catholicism] came to be likened to false religions and to be placed ignominiously on the same level with them. It was then put under the power of the State [instead of the state being put under the power of the church] and tolerated more or less at the whim of princes and rulers."[11]

Obviously, Pius XI would have liked to see the papacy's political authority over all the world's civil governments restored. The Catholic author George La Piana summed up the papal ambition in these words: "By its own claim the Roman Catholic Church . . . [is] a totalitarian church expecting to conquer the world on the principle that it is the exclusive divine agency of salvation, the exclusive organ of divine grace, and the exclusive channel of the divine spirit."[12]

The title of the book by Jesuit author Malachi Martin that I referred to in early chapters also reveals the Vatican's global ambitions: *The Keys of This Blood: The Struggle for World Dominion Between Pope John Paul II, Mikhail Gorbachev, and the Capitalist West.*[13] Martin's book, which was published in 1990, begins with the bold assertion that a one-world government is only decades away, and John Paul was competing with Gorbachev and the capitalist West for domination of that government. "The chosen purpose of John Paul's pontificate," Martin said, "is to be the victor in that competition, now well underway."[14] According to Martin, the Vatican wants to dominate the world politically in order to bring order out of its moral chaos. Of course, once the world submits to the Vatican's moral/political dominance, the persecution of dissenters will follow naturally, as it always does when church and state are truly united.

So, how do we factor in the bold statements in support of freedom of conscience that came out of Vatican II? In chapter 8, I pointed out several clauses in the Vatican II document on religious freedom that, given the right—or wrong—circumstances, could lead to the suppression of dissent. But the events of the final crisis that I have described in this chapter are what will ultimately bring the dire predictions of Revelation 13 to their complete fulfillment, including Revelation's prediction about the end-time role of the papacy, Protestantism, and the United States government. Malachi Martin would agree, for near the end of his book he stated clearly that John Paul "is waiting . . . for an event that will fission [divide] human history, splitting the immediate past from the oncoming future. It will be an event on public view in the skies, in the oceans, and on the continental land masses of this planet. It will particularly involve our human sun. . . .

"Fissioning it will be as an event, in John Paul's conviction of faith, for it will immediately nullify all the grand designs the nations are now forming and will introduce the Grand Design of man's Maker. John Paul's waiting and watching time will then be over. His ministry as the Servant of the Grand Design will then begin."[15]

Martin said that John Paul expected some kind of natural disaster to bring about papal dominance of the world.* That agrees exactly with the Adventist conclusion, which I've outlined in this chapter, that severe natural disasters that overwhelm the world's ability to cope will bring about the final crisis. It isn't too farfetched to imagine that the world's people would turn to a religious authority to help rescue them from the catastrophic consequences of unprecedented global natural disasters. And what better religious authority than the only one that already has global influence and respect?

This brings us back to another variation on the question I've asked repeatedly throughout this book: How realistic is the Adventist prediction that the papacy will gain political control of the world someday and then that control will result in the persecution of dissenters?

Could this really happen?

For more than 150 years, Adventists have steadfastly maintained that it *will* happen in the final days of this earth's history.

---

*Martin said that John Paul expected to see this prediction fulfilled in his lifetime. Obviously, that didn't happen. However, the prediction should be understood more broadly as the future role of the papacy rather than as the future role of any one pope.

1. "World Church: Adventist Leaders Meet with United States President at the White House," Adventist News Network, http://news.adventist.org/data/2006/03/1144177860/index.html.en.

2. Anne Wilson Schaef and Diane Fassel, *The Addictive Organization* (San Francisco: Harper Collins Publishers, 1988), 160.

3. Michael Barkun, *Disasters and the Millennium* (New Haven, Conn.: Yale University Press, 1974), 113.

4. Ibid., 6.

5. Ibid., 56.

6. Ibid., 55, 56.

7. Ellen G. White, *The Great Controversy* (Nampa, Idaho: Pacific Press®, 1911), 624.

8. *Christianity and Civilization*, Spring 1982, italics added.

9. *The News-Sentinel*, Fort Wayne, Indiana, August 16, 1993; cited in Anti-Defamation League, *The Religious Right: The Assault on Tolerance and Pluralism in America* (New York: Anti-Defamation League, 1994), 4.

10. Pius XI, Encyclical Letter, "On the Feast of Christ the King," par. 18.

11. Ibid., par. 24.

12. George La Piana and John Swomley, *Catholic Power vs. American Freedom* (Amherst, N.Y.: Prometheus Books, 2002), 20.

13. Malachi Martin, *The Keys of This Blood: The Struggle for World Dominion Between Pope John Paul II, Mikhail Gorbachev, and the Capitalist West* (New York: Simon and Schuster, 1990).

14. Ibid., 15, 17.

15. Ibid., 639.

CHAPTER 24

Putting the Pieces Together

One of my favorite pastimes is putting together jigsaw puzzles. Not that I do it all that often, you understand; I'm enough of a workaholic that I find it hard to make the time for something that's just plain fun! Nevertheless, on those rare occasions when I do sit down to a jigsaw puzzle, I scarcely notice the hours as they pass.

I typically start with the edge. I've noticed that most people do, since these pieces, being flat on one side, are the easiest ones to identify. Once the edge is pretty much in place, it's time to begin putting together the inside, and that's the real challenge. Fortunately, the puzzle manufacturers print a handy miniature version of the picture on the box that gives a good idea of what the completed puzzle will look like, and I always check this picture for patterns that might show up on the pieces. Maybe there's a red barn in the picture, or a crystal-clear creek, or a section with a lot of yellow daisies. Most landscapes also have some sky at the top. I hunt for all the pieces with these colors and patterns and put them in bunches off to one side. It's easier to find matching pieces within these patterns than it is to try to match up a table filled with pieces that have no relationship to each other. In due time I've put together several of the larger parts of the picture, and I drop them into place where they belong in the frame that's made by the edge pieces.

This is an analogy of what we've been doing in this book. In chapter 1, I gave a broad outline of the Adventist understanding of end-time events, particularly our interpretation of the two beast powers and the mark of the beast in Revelation 13. We can compare this to looking at the picture on the box of a jigsaw puzzle. In succeeding chapters, I explained our interpretation of the sea beast, the land beast, and the mark of the beast, and I pointed out how history and current events have fulfilled or are in the process of fulfilling our understanding of these prophetic symbols. We can compare these themes to the major parts of our imaginary jigsaw puzzle. In this chapter, I'd like to fit these major parts of the puzzle together to make a completed picture. Obviously, this will involve some repetition, but I think we need to do it in order to view the picture as a whole. Each of the subheads in the remainder of this chapter is one of the major parts of the picture that we've been assembling.

The threat to church-state separation

Church-state separation is the foundation of religious liberty. When the laws of the state are based on religious rather than secular moral principles, sooner or later, persecution of dissenters always results. This is not to say that the laws of the state will disagree with religious principles. In many cases the two will be the same. It is to say that when legislators frame the laws of the state, they should consult the common sense of the people, not the holy books the people carry with them to their churches, synagogues, or mosques. Unfortunately, recent trends in the United States threaten to reverse the historic American principle of church-state separation.

Catholics, who have been relatively silent during the recent American culture war on the matter of church-state separation, nevertheless have historically favored church-state union. They come by their political philosophy of church-state union quite naturally. Paganism was already the state religion at the time Constantine became a Christian. It didn't occur to anyone back then to separate religion from government. So, following Constantine's conversion, Christianity gradually replaced paganism as the state religion, and nobody saw any problem with that arrangement. It's just the way things were done. It continued to be the way things were done for the next fourteen or fifteen hundred years, until the Enlightenment broke the power of religion over government and created the secular nations we know today that separate religion from government.

The reaction of the popes to this change was understandable: They didn't like it. Nobody likes change—especially those changes that challenge our authority and upset the way things have been done for

249

a millennium and a half! So, the popes fulminated against church-state separation. But there was precious little they could do about it; the nations of Europe had become secular, and they had gained enough power that they could throw off the political power that the papacy had exercised over them for hundreds of years. The French Revolution was the climax of that trend—the straw that finally broke the Catholic camel's back. This is the "fatal wound" that struck the sea beast of Revelation 13 after some 1,260 years of dominance in European political affairs (the forty-two months of verse 5).

However, the papacy didn't change its view of its relationship to civil government. To this day, Catholics view Christianity as the only true religion and their church as the only true Christian church, with the pope as its controlling head. Even now, in the ideal Catholic state the authority of the pope would be respected as supreme not only in religious affairs but also in political affairs. After all, just as the soul is superior to the body, so the church is superior to the state. Consequently, the state should be subject to the church, at least in regard to issues relating to theology and morals.

What about freedom of conscience? Granted that for hundreds of years the papacy condemned the idea that each person is free to believe and worship according to the dictates of his or her conscience. But didn't Vatican Council II bring a remarkable change in the Vatican's understanding of religious freedom?

That council did affirm that "the human person has a right to religious freedom," and "no one is to be forced to act in a manner contrary to his own beliefs." Each person, the council said, is to "enjoy immunity from external coercion as well as psychological freedom," and this "religious freedom has its foundation . . . in [the person's] very nature." However, I pointed out in chapter 8 a number of statements in the Vatican II document on religious freedom that could compromise these positive declarations. In any case, the primary threat to religious freedom in the Vatican's political philosophy today is its continued support of church-state union, for Vatican II did not abandon that principle, and church-state union is one of the foundation stones of religious persecution.

And now Religious-Right Protestants are also on a roll toward church-state union, for they are attacking the principle of church-state separation viciously. Pat Robertson has declared that church-state separation "is a lie of the left, and we aren't going to take it anymore,"[1] and "[the courts] are taking our religion away from us under the guise of separation of church and state."[2] Jerry Falwell said, "Separation of church and state has long been the battle cry of civil libertarians wishing to purge our glorious Christian heritage from our nation's history,"[3] and W. A. Criswell, former senior pastor of the Dallas, Texas, First Baptist Church, declared that church-state separation "is merely a figment of the imagination of infidels."[4]

Another recent threat to church-state separation is the demand by Rousas Rushdoony and Francis Schaeffer that America's civil laws be based on the Bible and the law of God. Rushdoony said, "Civil law cannot be separated from Biblical law." Biblical law "is therefore the law for Christian man and Christian society."[5] And Schaeffer insisted that "the state . . . is to be administered according to the principles of God's law" and "[civil] Law is founded on the Law of God."[6] Rushdoony and Schaeffer are simply demanding an American version of Muslim *Sharia* law. Other voices, though perhaps expressing it more moderately, are echoing the same sentiment. The Ten Commandments Commission wants to "help restore the Ten Commandments and Judeo-Christian values to their rightful place in our society."[7] Paul Weyrich wants to "Christianize America."[8] Pat Robertson wants Christians to "redeem society."[9] And D. James Kennedy wants to "reclaim America for Christ."[10]

Throughout most of American history, Protestants, including evangelical and fundamentalist Protestants, have given strong support to church-state separation. As recently as 1960, they refused to endorse John F. Kennedy for president until he took a vow in support of church-state separation. But now a significant block of Protestants is joining Catholics in their opposition to church-state separation. Catholics today number about 25 percent of the American population, and Religious-Right Protestants are close behind. These two groups, should they ever unite, could easily destroy church-state separation in America. And for all their declarations in support of freedom of religion, with church-state separation out of the way, *religious freedom would eventually give way to religious persecution.*

You may wonder about the mid-term election in 2006, which broke the control that the Republican Party had held over the United States Congress for the previous twelve years. Didn't that weaken the power that the Religious Right had exercised over American politics during those twelve years? Of course it did, but that's really quite irrelevant to the point I've been making. Political power is constantly shifting from one side to the other, and we should avoid at any one time making too much of a shift in either direction. My point is that the Religious Right arose in the last quarter of the twentieth century as a powerful political force in American politics that even the secularists can no longer ignore. It's a power that, given the right circumstances, could reemerge at any time, and in a crisis could lurch far more to the extreme right than most of today's Religious Right leaders themselves would want to see.

Way back in 1964, when Barry Goldwater was running for president, I predicted that the Republican Party would probably be in control of the American government when America fulfills its prophetic role as Adventists understand it. The rise of the Religious Right in American politics since then makes that prediction even more reasonable today than it was at that time.

The new evangelism

Christianity has always been a religion of evangelism. Jesus Himself commanded His followers to " 'go and make disciples of all nations' " (Matthew 28:19). For two thousand years, Christians have traveled all over the world winning souls for Jesus. Billy Graham's evangelistic crusades in the second half of the twentieth century are a prime example of Christian evangelism at its best. This is traditional biblical evangelism.

However, the new "evangelism" of America's Religious Right Protestants and Catholics is much different. While biblical evangelism seeks to win *individuals* to Christ, today's Religious Right evangelism is fighting to shape entire *societies* "for Christ." In genuine biblical evangelism, which seeks to *win* people to Christ, each person is free to choose whether to become a Christian. But in a nation that is deliberately being molded into a Christian society that is governed by God's law, those who choose not to become Christians and those Christians who believe differently from the national definition of God's law will inevitably feel like outcasts, and sooner or later, pressure will be brought to bear on them to conform to the will of the majority. I feel certain that the effort by today's Religious Right Protestants and Catholics to shape America into a Christian society will eventually almost certainly be felt by dissenters as coercive, just as the pagans in the fourth century felt the coercion of Christians trying to create a "Christian society" in the Roman Empire.

I'm reminded of the words of Roland Hegstad that I shared with you in the previous chapter. "Persecution," Hegstad said, "doesn't arise from bad people trying to make other people bad. It arises from good people trying to make other people good." That's what easily happens—almost inevitably happens—when Christians focus a major share of their "evangelistic" efforts on creating a *Christian society* instead of following Christ's mandate to simply preach the gospel, make disciples, baptize, and teach *individuals* (see Matthew 24:14; 28:19, 20).

And today's Religious Right Protestants *do* want to change *society*. I referred to the following quotes a few paragraphs back in the context of church-state separation, but they apply equally to the Religious Right's "new evangelism." According to Pat Robertson, "The Lord says, 'I'm going to let you redeem *society*.' "[11] D. James Kennedy's vision is for Christians to "reclaim America for Christ, whatever the cost. As the vice regents of God, we are to exercise godly *dominion* and influence over . . . every aspect and institution of human *society*."[12] And the Ten Commandments Commission "was founded to counter the secular agenda and help restore the Ten Commandments and Judeo-Christian values to their rightful place in our *society*."[13]

It's true, of course, that very few people in the Religious Right today are talking about persecuting dissenters. However, Christian Reconstructionist Gary North wants Christians to "get busy in constructing a Bible-based social, political and religious order which finally *denies the religious liberty of the enemies of God*."[14] And Randall Terry, the firebrand founder of Operation Rescue, wants you to "just let a wave of intolerance [and hatred] wash over you. . . . Our goal is a Christian nation. . . . We are called by God, to conquer this country."[15]

Granted that Gary North and Randall Terry are among the more radical voices in our society. However, coercion arose in the fourth century because the more radical elements of that era's Christian society gained the upper hand. Furthermore, Gary North and Randall Terry are only slightly more radical than Pat Robertson and D. James Kennedy. These men are all voicing ideas that down the road could easily lead to coercion in the name of making other people good.

The new evangelism—the effort to convert *society* rather than *individuals*—is a powerful threat to religious freedom.

Dominionism

Closely allied to the new evangelism is the concept of "dominionism," which proposes that Christians are to purify America and ultimately the whole world by holding "godly dominion" over society and government.

Dominionism was proposed explicitly during the last half of the twentieth century by R. J. Rushdoony and implicitly by Francis Schaeffer.

Like Augustine fifteen hundred years ago, Rushdoony believed that the millennium began with Christ's first coming rather than His second coming. Augustine reinterpreted Daniel's prediction about the stone that struck the image on the feet, applying it to the Christian church rather than to Christ at His second coming. Thus it became the responsibility of the church to " 'crush all those kingdoms and bring them to an end' " and establish God's eternal kingdom on earth (Daniel 2:44). Rushdoony's postmillennialism proposes essentially the same thing. "Man is summoned," he said, "to create the society God requires."[16] Rushdoony equated Christ's great commission with God's charge to Adam and Eve to subdue the earth and "have dominion over the fish of the sea, and over the fowl of the air, and over every living thing that moveth upon the earth" (Genesis 1:28, KJV). Thus, Christ's great commission to " 'make disciples of all nations' " (Matthew 28:19) now becomes a mandate to conquer the world politically. Where Augustine viewed the Catholic Church as the stone that would destroy all earthly kingdoms, Rushdoony assigned the task to Christianity as a whole. Otherwise, their views are identical. That's dominionism, even though Augustine didn't use the term.

While Francis Schaeffer didn't use the term "dominion" quite the way Rushdoony did, his basic philosophy resembles Rushdoony's. "The state," he said, "is to be administered according to the principles of God's law."[17] He wanted America's laws to be "founded on the Law of God."[18] "The civil government," he said, "stands under the law of God,"[19] and the power of kings "is limited by God's word."[20] Rushdoony's and Schaeffer's dominionism has profoundly influenced today's Religious Right Protestants and their call for fundamentalist Christians to take dominion of our society and its institutions, including the government.

The point is this: Dominionism—the idea that Christians are to hold godly dominion over society and its governments—is simply another name for church-state union. Church-state union is the foundation of all persecution. And America's Religious Right Protestants want dominion.

Breaking the cooperation of secularism and religion

The concept of church-state separation is a uniquely secular proposition. It came about during the eighteenth century as a result of the Enlightenment's opposition to the clerical domination of Europe's governments. The French Revolution, which at one point outlawed all religion, was the most extreme form of this secular opposition to church-state union.

The Enlightenment also profoundly affected the American Revolution and the Constitution that resulted from it. However, in America, church-state separation took a significantly different approach. America's secular leaders—Thomas Jefferson, George Washington, James Madison, John Adams, and Benjamin Franklin, to name a few—were keenly aware of the contribution that religion can make to a stable society. Madison, for instance, said, "Belief in God [is] essential to the moral order of the world,"[21] and George Washington said, "Reason and experience both forbid us to expect that national morality can prevail, in exclusion of religious principle."[22]

However, the regard of Madison, Washington, and their fellow-patriots for religion doesn't mean that they were interested in a union of church and state. To the contrary, they believed that the best way to protect religion was to separate it from government. Thus, Madison said, "Religion flourishes in greater purity without than with the aid of government"[23] and "The number, the industry, and the morality of the Priesthood, & devotion of the people have been manifestly increased by the total separation of the Church from the State."[24] And Thomas Jefferson envisioned "a wall of separation between church and State."[25]

It's extremely important to understand that *the American brand of church-state separation was the result of a unique cooperation between secularism and religion.* While in Europe two hundred years ago, secularism and religion tended to be at each other's throats, in America, each recognized the contribution that the other could make to a stable society and a democratic government. Americans have by and large supported this cooperation between the religious and the secular throughout most of our history. Notice that I said "*most* of our history," for today the Religious Right is at war against secularism. Francis Schaeffer claimed that secular materialists "have no sufficient base for either society or law."[26] He argued passionately that "these two religions, Christianity and humanism [secularism], stand over against each other as totalities,"[27] and thus "we should be struggling and praying that this whole other entity—the material-energy, chance world view—can be rolled back with all its results across all of life."[28]

Schaeffer said, "We are at war."[29] He meant, of course, that religious people in America are at war with secularists. This is the same thing as the "culture war" that Religious Right Protestants sometimes speak about. It's a war between the Christian religion and secularism. In his book *American Gospel*, Jon Meacham noted that "God did not give us easy answers" to "the issues that divide us." But he pointed out one answer that has served America well throughout its history. This answer, which "has much to recommend it, is simply conversation between those who disagree. . . . *Conversation in such matters generally trumps combat.*"[30]

Unfortunately, today's secularists and religionists aren't conversing. They're fighting. And there doesn't seem to be much chance that they'll start conversing anytime soon.

Now please note this: *Cooperation between religion and secularism is being seriously threatened today by the culture war of Religious Right Protestants.* Yet this cooperation between religion and secularism—this conversation, as Jon Meacham put it—is what has made possible America's separation of church and state and the religious freedom that results from it. Church-state separation and religious freedom are profoundly threatened the moment Christians and secularists break their historic cooperation, refuse to converse, and instead start warring against each other.

At this point, it looks like a battle to the finish, with one side winning and the other side losing. The only question is which side will come out on top. If the Adventist understanding of prophecy is correct, you know the answer.

Summary

For 150 years, Seventh-day Adventists have identified the sea beast of Revelation 13 as the papacy and the land beast as the United States of America. We have also identified the mark of the beast as the enforced observance of Sunday as a day of rest and worship. Based on this interpretation, we have drawn the following conclusions:

- The papacy, which was a political powerhouse in Europe for hundreds of years during the Middle Ages, received what appeared to be a fatal wound when the modern secular states of Europe and America separated religion from government.
- However, during earth's final crisis, the papacy will recover from that fatal wound and become a global political powerhouse, en-

forcing its doctrines and moral principles with the persecution of dissenters similar to its persecution of dissenters in medieval history.

• The United States of America will also become a persecuting power, cooperating with the papacy, especially in the enforcement of Sunday as a day of religious rest and worship—the mark of the beast.

These predictions have seemed wild and foolish throughout most of our history, which is why I have repeatedly asked the question, Could what we've predicted based on our understanding of Revelation 13 really happen? I trust that by now—given the trends in today's world that I've outlined in this book and given the Bible's prediction of a global crisis brought on by natural disasters that will overwhelm the world's ability to cope—you can understand why Adventists believe the answer is Yes. We believe not only that all this *could* happen but that it *will happen.*

1. From a November 1993 address by Pat Robertson, cited in Anti-Defamation League, *The Religious Right: The Assault on Tolerance and Pluralism in America* (New York: Anti-Defamation League, 1994), 4.

2. Pat Robertson on his television program *The 700 Club*, July 19, 2005, cited by Rob Boston in "Religious Right Power Brokers: The Top Ten," *Church and State*, June 2006, 10.

3. Cited by Rob Boston in "Religious Right Power Brokers: The Top Ten," *Church and State*, June 2006, 14.

4. From a CBS interview of September 6, 1984, taped the day after he delivered the benediction at the Republican National Convention, cited in Anti–Defamation League, *The Religious Right: The Assault on Tolerance and Pluralism in America*, 4.

5. Rousas John Rushdoony, *The Institutes of Biblical Law* (Phillipsburg, N.J.: P & R Publishing, 1973), 4, 9.

6. Francis A. Schaeffer, *A Christian Manifesto* (Westchester, Ill.: Crossway Books, 1981), 28, 100, 99.

7. "The Ten Commandments Day," http://www.tencommandmentsday.com. Note: The wording on this Web site changes slightly for each year's upcoming Ten Commandments Day. The quote cited here is from the 2006 Ten Commandments Day.

8. *Signswatch,* Winter 2001, 4; statement by Paul Weyrich in August 1980.

9. Comment by Pat Robertson on *The 700 Club*, cited in RedSonja2000 "Dominionist Dream: Repeal the 1st Amendment," Talk to Action, http://www.talk2action.org/story/2005/12/16/103532/64.

10. Cited in "The Rise of the Religious Right in the Republican Party," http://www.theocracywatch.org, italics added.

11. See endnote 5.

12. See endnote 6.

13. See endnote 7.

14. *Christianity and Civilization*, Spring 1982, italics added.

15. *The News-Sentinel*, Fort Wayne, Indiana, August 16, 1993; cited in *The Religious Right: The Assault on Tolerance and Pluralism in America*, 4.

16. Rushdoony, *The Institutes of Biblical Law*, 4.

17. Francis Schaeffer, *A Christian Manifesto* (Westchester, Ill.: Crossway Books, 1981), 28, 100.

18. Ibid., 99.

19. Ibid., 90.

20. Ibid., 98.

21. Joseph Laconte, "Faith and the founding: the influence of religion on the politics of James Madison," *Journal of Church and State*, September 22, 2003, 7; cited by Mark R. Levin in *Men in Black: How the Supreme Court Is Destroying America* (Washington, D.C.: Regnery Publishing, Inc., 2005), 249.

22. *Address of George Washington, President of the United States, . . . Preparatory to His Declination* (Baltimore, Md.: George and Henry S. Keatinge, 1796), 22, 23.

23. James Madison in a letter to Edward Livingston, July 10, 1822, cited in "Pure Religion," *Liberty*, December 2005, 13.

24. *Church and State*, April 2006, 24.

25. "Separation of Church and State in the United States," Wikipedia, http://en.wikipedia.org/wiki/Separation_of_church_and_state_in_the_United_States.

26. Schaeffer, 26.

27. Ibid., 54.

28. Ibid., 73, 74.

29. Ibid., 116.

30. Jon Meacham, *American Gospel, God, the Founding Fathers, and the Mercy of a Nation* (New York: Random House, 2006), 83, 84; italics added.

CHAPTER 25

How Should We Respond?

So, how should we respond to what I've shared with you in this book? I will mention four areas of response that I believe are the responsibility of everyone who believes even some of what they've read in these pages.

Protect religious freedom

Every now and then I hear some Adventist say, "Why not just let the forces that would destroy our freedom take over? This will hasten Jesus' second coming." That's very wrong thinking. We need to do everything we can to protect the religious freedom we have in America for as long as possible. Speaking in this very context, Ellen White said on one occasion, "It is our duty to do all in our power to avert the threatened danger."[1]

What can you and I do to "avert the threatened danger" of religious persecution?

The first thing we must do is to become informed about the issues. I've tried to present them in this book as clearly as possible, but there's still a lot more we can all learn. I suggest that you read the following three books. As you become familiar with the field, you'll learn about other books.

- Levy, Leonard W.. *Original Intent and the Framers' Constitution.* *New York: Macmillan,* 1988.
- Meacham, Jon. *American Gospel: God, the Founding Fathers, and the Making of a Nation.* New York: Random House, 2006.

• La Piana, George and John Swomley. *Catholic Power vs. American Freedom.* Edited by Herbert F. Vetter. New York: Prometheus, 2002. (The first part by George La Piana is especially helpful.)

It's also a good idea to get on the mailing list of some of the secular organizations in America. I suggest the following:

• Americans United for Separation of Church and State, http://www.au.org
• People for the American Way, http://www.pfaw.org/pfaw/general/*
• American Civil Liberties Union, http://www.aclu.org/

I also suggest that you become familiar with the thinking of Religious Right activists. For that, I recommend getting yourself on the mailing list of the following:

The Christian Coalition, http://www.cc.org
The American Center for Law and Justice, http://www.aclj.org
The Moral Majority Coalition, http://www.moralmajority.us/

The best way to get on the mailing lists of these organizations, both secular and religious, is to send them an occasional donation. They keep sending me requests for donations, and I send them enough money now and then to stay on their mailing lists.

One of the most important things you can do to defend religious liberty is to be aware of the religious liberty issues that are being debated in the United States Congress and in your state legislature. You'll be informed about much of this from the postal mail and the e-mail communications you receive from both the secular and conservative religious organizations I mentioned above. However, awareness isn't enough. You need to take action. When there's an important issue concerning religious freedom, let your senators and representatives know of your convictions. Postal letters, e-mails, and phone calls are all simple ways to communicate.

---

*People for the American Way and the American Civil Liberties Union deal with a variety of civil rights issues, including issues of religious liberty and church and state.

Finally, be sure you vote your convictions at election time. You'll have to balance your convictions about religious freedom and church-state separation with other issues as you decide how to cast your vote. But don't just vote a party line. Be an informed voter.

Prepare for the inevitable

A large cluster of tornados hit Oklahoma in the summer of 1999. I remember reading in my newspaper about a woman who, several years earlier, had turned one of the closets in her home into a storm shelter by building a cinderblock wall around it. When she and her family heard a tornado warning on their TV, they all hid in the storm shelter. Moments later, a tornado demolished their house—but they survived just fine. This woman had no idea when—or even whether—a tornado would destroy her home, but she prepared ahead of time for the possibility, and when it came, she was ready.

If what I have shared with you in this book is correct, the world faces a terrible crisis. This crisis will consist of severe natural disasters, warfare, and perhaps terrorism. The world's economy will be shattered, bringing on incalculable hardship. I believe we can also expect a great religious revival. People the world over will realize that God is trying to get our attention, and they will turn to Him in large numbers. Unfortunately, this will also be a time of intense demonic activity, and the falsehoods that the demons perpetrate on the world will lead many people astray. Religious persecution will follow for those who refuse to adopt the politically correct modes of worship.

The woman in Oklahoma City didn't know whether a tornado would ever hit her home, but she prepared just in case. We today don't have to wonder whether a storm is coming. We *know* it, because the Bible *predicts* it. Back in 1896, Ellen White wrote, "The storm is coming, relentless in its fury." Then she asked the key question: "Are we prepared to meet it?"[2] What preparation, then, should we be making? I will suggest three ways to prepare.

Spiritual preparation. Your most important preparation will be spiritual. It's easy for me to say that you'll need a close relationship with Jesus. Many people talk about a relationship with Jesus, and they're right, of course. But what does that mean? How can you develop that relationship with Jesus?

It goes without saying that you need to study your Bible and pray. Regarding Bible study, I need to advise you that "a little word from the

Lord for today" won't do. The quick reading of a page from a morning devotional book isn't *study*. You need to take the time to study in an organized way. If you're following a regular Bible study plan such as a Sabbath School quarterly, then keep it up. Personally, I like to go through books of the Bible. I have a Bible program on my laptop computer that gives me access to half a dozen versions of the Bible. I can turn to any text in the Bible within seconds, and the text appears on my screen in all six versions, including Greek or Hebrew (depending on which Testament I'm in). I write my own commentary a verse at a time right on my computer. It usually takes me two or three weeks just to go through one chapter.

It's also important to have a good foundation in the basic teachings of the Bible—what theologians call "doctrine." Some people seem to think that doctrine is unnecessary, that "having a relationship with Jesus" is all that matters. The problem with this notion is that your doctrine will affect your relationship with Jesus. Justification and sanctification are doctrines. Law and obedience are doctrines. Sabbath is a doctrine. Each of these makes a major contribution to your relationship with Jesus, and the better you understand them, the closer the relationship you'll have with Him. So I recommend that you find a way to study the basic teachings of the Bible and Christianity. The book *Seventh-day Adventists Believe** is a good way to study Seventh-day Adventist doctrines. If you want to go deeper into Adventist teachings, a good resource is the *Handbook of Seventh-day Adventist Theology*, which is volume 12 in the Seventh-day Adventist Bible Commentary series.[3]

I especially urge you to learn all you can about righteousness by faith. This will be extremely important to understand when you are under the spiritual pressures of the end time, because Satan will tempt you to believe that you are lost and your case is hopeless. But he will have a much harder time doing that if you have a good understanding of righteousness by faith. Be sure you learn the difference between justification and sanctification. Paul went into great detail about both in the first eight chapters of Romans. Several years ago, I wrote a book explaining these chapters. The title is *Forever His: How to Have a Joyful and Unbroken Relationship With Jesus*.[4] I recommend that you get a copy and study it carefully.

---

*You can order this book and others by Adventist publishers that I refer to later in this chapter by calling 1-800-765-6955. You can also order online at http://www.adventistbookcenter.com.

Prayer is also a vital part of your spiritual preparation for the final crisis. Again, this can't be just a two-minute conversation with God in which you ask Him to "protect you from harm and danger today." We all need to do that, of course. But prayer is much more than that. To begin with, you need to spend time on your knees with God. Your mind will wander. Mine does. So does everyone else's. Just keep bringing it back. Some people prefer to pray sitting down, others lying down. Some prefer to pray with their eyes open, others with their eyes closed. God doesn't care about these matters. He's just interested in you spending time talking to Him and listening to Him. So whether it's kneeling, sitting, or lying down, and whether it's with your eyes open or closed, do what works best for you. *Just be sure you do it.*

Overcoming character defects. My second suggestion for preparing spiritually to survive the coming crisis is to overcome your character defects, because these are the issues in your life that will cause you to yield your convictions under the threat of persecution. Any addiction is based on a character defect, and we all have them: addictions to food, sex, pornography, work, alcohol, tobacco, narcotics, gambling, TV, the Internet—the list goes on and on.

So, how can you deal with a character defect? Several years ago, I wrote a book called *Conquering the Dragon Within*[5] that goes into detail about how to overcome addictions and other character defects. I'll give you a brief explanation here. The most important concept to keep in mind as you struggle with any addiction or character defect is that your wrong behavior isn't the basic problem. The basic problem is your wrong desire. James said: "When tempted, no one should say, 'God is tempting me.' For God cannot be tempted by evil, nor does he tempt anyone; but each one is tempted when, by his own evil desire, he is dragged away and enticed. Then, after desire has conceived, it gives birth to sin; and sin, when it is full grown, gives birth to death" (James 1:13–15).

Whatever the temptation that you yield to, if you didn't *want* to do it, you *wouldn't* do it. So if you get rid of the desire, you'll basically get rid of the temptation, and with that you'll get rid of the wrong behavior. My book *Conquering the Dragon Within* has a number of practical suggestions for dealing with wrong desires and the wrong behaviors they prompt you to commit.

One other suggestion that I will share here is to thank God for the victory while you're still under temptation. You can say something like this: "Thank You, Father, that by His death on the cross Jesus broke the power that this temptation has over my life. Thank You that through Jesus the victory is already mine." You should say this prayer even while the temptation is burning in your brain and you feel that its power is about to overwhelm you. Saying the prayer is an act of faith, and righteousness is "by faith." This prayer has been one of the most powerful strategies I've found for overcoming temptation.

Physical preparation. Part of your spiritual preparation for the final crisis is to stay physically fit. The rules are simple; you've heard them before: A balanced diet (with an emphasis on fruits, nuts, legumes, and vegetables), plenty of water, aerobic exercise, fresh air and sunshine, and adequate rest. Also, it's a good idea to get a yearly physical examination, including your teeth and eyes.

However, there is one form of physical preparation I recommend that you not try to make. A number of years ago a young man approached me after church one day and asked if I thought it would be a good idea for him to purchase a cabin in the mountains as an escape for the time of trouble. I told him that, if he could afford it, buying a cabin in the mountains was a good idea as a vacation opportunity for his family. However, I advised him *not* to buy the cabin as a preparation for the time of trouble. Neither do I advise storing up food or money for the time of trouble, and I certainly don't recommend storing up guns and ammunition! God will provide for your needs during the time of trouble, and He will protect you from your enemies.

Share your convictions

Suppose that I had absolutely certain information that sometime in the next five years your house would burn to the ground—however, I couldn't give you a date; it might be any time during those five years. How would you want me to relate to this information? I might hesitate to warn you of the impending danger, because you'd think my prediction was foolish. Which would you prefer—that I not tell you in order to avoid looking stupid or that I tell you and let you decide how to relate to the information?

That's the issue Seventh-day Adventists have faced for 150 years. About a hundred years ago, one commentator said that the United States' renouncing its historic support of religious freedom "would [require] a greater miracle than for God to grow a giant oak in an instant."[6] Another said, "Of all the wild Advent speculations in the prophecies, [our prediction about Sunday laws] deserves to stand among the wildest."[7] However, a number of trends in the American religious and political world—trends that began during the last quarter of the twentieth century and continue to the present—all point in the direction of the fulfillment of our prediction.

So what is our responsibility? What is the responsibility of anyone who recognizes the danger in these trends? Should we share what we know? The answer is Yes, of course, just as it would only be right of me to share the bad news of your house burning down in the next five years—and horribly wrong of me not to tell you for fear you'd think me foolish. I will discuss three issues that you need to keep in mind as you share with others what I've outlined in this book.

Always show respect. A strong "nativist" anti-Catholicism developed in the United States during the nineteenth century, when immigrants were pouring into the country from the various Catholic nations of Europe. The fear was that these Catholics would be more loyal to their pope than they would be to America's political institutions. This anti-Catholicism resulted in some unfortunate occasions of persecution. Today, though, we are seeing played out in American politics what the nativists most feared: Catholic politicians who are being told by the Vatican that they are sinning if their votes in the United States Congress don't line up with Catholic moral principles. So how should those of us who recognize the problem respond?

The nativist reaction during the nineteenth century was very bigoted, which is why it resulted in occasional flare-ups of persecution. *That is entirely inappropriate.* Bigotry never solves problems. It only makes them worse. Therefore, one of the first principles to keep in mind as we contemplate the question "How shall we respond?" is this: Always show respect. We must respect everyone: Catholics, Religious Right Protestants, and secularists, for we don't want a repeat of the nativist attitudes of the nineteenth century. It's possible to disagree passionately and still show respect. I've tried to model that kind of respect in this book. I want to shun bigotry like the plague. To the extent that I've failed, please blame my humanness.

Share Jesus first. Bible prophecy won't save anyone. The mark of the beast is about the antichrist, not the real Christ. There's no saving grace in talking about Sunday laws. I do believe in prophecy. It has its place. But the most important aspect of the Christian religion is Jesus, not prophecy. Therefore, one of the first principles for sharing any prophecy is that you don't start there. You start with Jesus. You start with the plan of salvation. You start with a concern about people's souls and seeing them saved in God's kingdom.

A major purpose of Bible prophecy, especially those prophecies dealing with the end time, is to help people understand the challenges to their faith that they will experience during the world's final crisis. That's why Bible prophecy is important. By warning people of what lies ahead, we give them an opportunity to prepare spiritually so they won't lose the salvation they gained during more peaceful times. But they must receive that salvation first in order to make the spiritual preparation they'll need to preserve their salvation during a later crisis. And it goes without saying that you can't share a Jesus you don't know. This means you must develop your own relationship with Jesus so that you can share Him with others.

Share intelligently. What arithmetic lessons did your first-grade teacher give you? Probably very simple lessons in addition and subtraction. If my memory serves me correctly, I didn't learn multiplication and division until the third or fourth grade, and I didn't study algebra and geometry till I was in high school. The point is this: You start with the simple and move to the complex. It would be a mistake for teachers to start first-graders off with algebra and geometry. Those subjects wouldn't make sense to them. They need the background provided by the simpler problems in mathematics as a foundation for understanding the more complex tasks.

The same is true in presenting Bible prophecy to those who aren't familiar with it. Prophecy is quite complex, and the most complicated parts won't make sense to those who have no biblical background for understanding them. They'll think you're foolish, and the truth is that you would be. The foolishness wouldn't lie in your prophetic understanding. It would be in the way you jump into the most complex part before you've laid the foundation people need in order to make sense of it.

People need to know Jesus first. They need to understand the broad range of biblical teachings. Before studying the Adventist understanding of the mark of the beast, they need to understand the biblical teaching about the Sabbath. Once you're ready to lead them into the prophecies, begin with something simple like the image of Daniel 2. From there you can take up the four beasts of Daniel 7. With this background, people should be prepared to understand Revelation 13 and 14.

Love the secularists

America's Religious Right Protestants see themselves involved in a "culture war" against secularism. And the secularists are fighting the Religious Right just as hard as the Religious Right is fighting the secularists. This development troubles me deeply. In the previous chapter, I explained my concern that this culture war is breaking the historic cooperation between religious people and secular people that has made such a vital contribution to America's religious freedom. Today's secular forces still defend the principle of church-state separation, and on that, I support them. Fortunately, the conservative Religious Right is not the only religious power in America. There are still many Protestants and Catholics in America who favor the traditional cooperation between religion and secularism, and we need to support them. That's one of the things you and I can do to defend religious freedom.

However, the Religious Right's attack on secularism troubles me for another reason too. Jesus commanded His followers to love their enemies, not hate them (Matthew 5:44). But it's impossible to love our enemies and at the same time engage them in a culture war. War promotes hatred, not love, and hating our enemies is the inevitable result of shifting Christ's great commission from winning individuals to reforming society.

It's impossible to win people to Jesus when we're at war with them. People are drawn to Jesus through faithful Christians, but we can't draw people while we're fighting them. The new evangelism of the Religious Right, converting a *society* to Jesus, is actually counterproductive to the real mission Christ has given us, which is to win *individuals* to Him by loving them. The early Christian church lived in a culture that was far more hostile to its interests than our American culture is, yet within three hundred years the church conquered that culture. It did so not by focusing on the culture but by focusing on the real mission, which was winning individuals to Jesus.

Francis Schaeffer said, "We should be struggling and praying that this whole other entity—the material-energy, chance world view [secularism]—can be rolled back with all its results across all of life."[8] "We must understand that there is going to be a battle every step of the way. They [secular materialists] are determined that what they have gained will not be rolled back."[9] Those are fighting words, not soul-winning words.

Some may protest that unless we fight for our freedom, the secularists will take it away from us. If that should happen, we must remember that

Christians had little freedom for the first three hundred years of the movement, yet without freedom, they still conquered the empire. Christians don't win by fighting. We win by loving. And we win by losing. Does that last statement sound strange to you? Remember that everyone standing around the cross that Friday afternoon thought Jesus had lost. But what looked like a terrible loss was a great victory. Revelation says that in earth's final crisis, the sea beast will "make war against the saints and . . . conquer them" (Revelation 13:7). Yet a short time later, those saints will be joining Christ at His second coming. *Christians win by losing.* God has not called us to fight secularists. He has called us to love them, and even though they oppress us, He will be with us clear to the end (Matthew 28:20).

Christians *are* engaged in a war. Revelation says "the dragon was enraged at the woman and went off to make war against the rest of her offspring" (Revelation 12:17). However, "our struggle is not against flesh and blood." It isn't against people. Them we are to love. Our struggle is "against the rulers, against the authorities, against the powers of this dark world and against the spiritual forces of evil in the heavenly realms" (Ephesians 6:12).

Yes, Christians are engaged in a war. Let's be sure we're fighting the right enemy.

1. Ellen G. White, *Last Day Events* (Nampa, Idaho: Pacific Press®, 1992), 126.

2. White, *Maranatha* (Hagerstown, Md.: Review and Herald®, 1976), 108.

3. Raoul Dederen, ed., *Handbook of Seventh-day Adventist Theology,* Commentary Reference Series, vol. 12 (Hagerstown, Md.: Review and Herad®, 2000).

4. Marvin Moore, *Forever His: How to Have a Joyful and Unbroken Relationship With Jesus* (Nampa, Idaho: Pacific Press®, 2004).

5. Moore, *Conquering the Dragon Within: God's Provision for Assurance and Victory in the End Time* (Nampa, Idaho: Pacific Press®, 1995).

6. Theodore Nelson in the introduction to Dudley M. Canright's book, *Seventh-day Adventism Renounced* (Nashville: Gospel Advocate Company, 1914), 23.

7. Ibid., 89.

8. Francis A. Schaeffer, *A Christian Manifesto* (Westchester, Ill.: Crossway Books, 1981), 73, 74.

9. Ibid., 75.

Epilogue

I like wild, foolish predictions. The more wild and foolish they are, the better I like them. Why? Because the wilder and more foolish a prediction seems when it's first given, the more of an impression it will make when it comes to pass.

Of course, there's always the possibility that my prediction won't come to pass. In that case, my prediction isn't the only thing that's wild and foolish—I am too! That's the risk anyone takes who makes a prediction. Therefore, it's always wise to be sure that our predictions have a reasonable, rational foundation in the best facts available at the time we make them.

Correctly understood, the Bible's prophecies provide a sound basis on which to predict the future. In this book, I've shared with you the biblical foundation for the Adventist understanding of Revelation 13 and the events in the world that are leading to its fulfillment.

Are our predictions wild and foolish? Or . . . *could it really happen?*
I leave it with you to decide.

Reflections on "Original Intent" and "Judicial Activism"

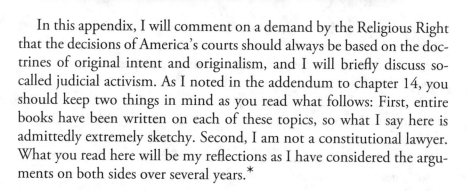

In this appendix, I will comment on a demand by the Religious Right that the decisions of America's courts should always be based on the doctrines of original intent and originalism, and I will briefly discuss so-called judicial activism. As I noted in the addendum to chapter 14, you should keep two things in mind as you read what follows: First, entire books have been written on each of these topics, so what I say here is admittedly extremely sketchy. Second, I am not a constitutional lawyer. What you read here will be my reflections as I have considered the arguments on both sides over several years.*

Original intent

"Original intent" is a view of judicial responsibility that states that judges—especially the United States Supreme Court judges and lower federal court judges—should base their decisions on what the Framers of the Constitution intended. A related term is "originalism," which states that the Constitution has a fixed meaning that was established at the time of its passage, and it must be interpreted strictly according to that

---

*Two books dealing with original intent, one on each side of that topic, have helped me understand the issues involved: *Original Intent and the Framers' Constitution,* by Leonard W. Levy (Chicago: Ivan R. Dee, Publisher, 1988), and *Original Intent: The Courts, the Constitution, & Religion,* by David Barton (Aledo, Tex.: WallBuilders, 2000). Levy is a constitutional historian. Barton is a layman who founded the Religious Right organization WallBuilders in Aledo, Texas. Of the two books, I find Levy's to be by far the more persuasive.

meaning today. Originalists and the supporters of original intent don't view the Constitution as a document that states broad principles, the interpretation of which can evolve with time. When a case comes before the Court, the judges must ask, What did the Framers understand it to mean? What did the Constitution mean relative to this issue when it was created? Judges must always seek to base their decisions on these determinations.

Some judges—though probably a minority—believe in the principles of originalism and original intent. For example, Supreme Court nominee Robert Bork* made the statement that "originalism seeks to promote the rule of law by imparting to the Constitution a fixed, continuous, and predictable meaning."[1] Bork also said, "Judges are not to overturn the will of legislative majorities absent a violation of a constitution right, *as those rights were understood by the framers.*"[2] Religious Right activists are extremely critical of judges who don't rule according to originalism and original intent. Mark R. Levin, in his book *Men in Black*, said, "To the extent that [the principle of originalism] is compromised, both liberty and the rule of law are jeopardized. The judiciary, operating outside its scope, is the greatest threat to representative government that we face today."[3]

What about original intent? What about originalism? Are these valid principles for Supreme Court justices to follow as they make their decisions? My first comment is that both of these are valid principles for judges to *consider* as they make their decisions. Levy said, "In most cases original intent should be followed when clearly discernible, and it is always entitled to the utmost respect and consideration as an interpretive guide."[4] The question is whether judges should ever and always be *bound* by a fixed meaning of the Constitution and the intentions of the Founders. For several reasons, the answer is No.

Who were the Framers? Before judges can base their decisions on what the Framers *intended,* they first have to decide who the Framers *were.* Do we limit them to the members of the Constitutional Convention who met in Philadelphia between May 25 and September 17, 1787? Or should we add the members of the state ratifying conventions that gave final approval to the Constitution? And are there others whom we should consider? Both of these views have their proponents.

---

*Bork's nomination by President George H. W. Bush was so controversial that Bork eventually withdrew his name from consideration.

In fact, David Barton, in his book *Original Intent,* argues that the Founders should include the following:

- the fifty-six signers of the Declaration of Independence;
- the most significant military leaders (he says three dozen or so) who fought for independence;
- the fourteen presidents who governed America between 1774 and 1779;*
- the fifty-five men who made up the Constitutional Convention;
- the delegates to the state conventions that ratified the Constitution;
- the ninety members of the first Congress, who created the Bill of Rights;
- the earliest members of the Supreme Court;
- the members of George Washington's cabinet during his two terms.[5]

That's quite a list! And it's way too long. Obviously, the delegates to the convention that created the Constitution must be included as Framers, and it's reasonable to include the delegates to the state conventions that ratified the Constitution, because presumably they had read the document and gave their consent to it; there would have been no Constitution without them. I believe we have to restrict our definition of "the Framers" to these two groups.

How do we know what they intended? Once we determine who the Framers *were,* we then have to find out what they *thought,* what they *intended.* Levy points out that "we cannot answer any question concerning the intent of the Framers without first determining whether evidence exists that will provide an answer."[6] But where do we turn for that evidence? Almost no records were kept of the proceedings of the Constitutional Convention. If the convention had been held today, every speech would no doubt have been audio and perhaps even video recorded, and the intent of the delegates would have been plain for everyone to see. But handwriting was the only way to record proceedings back then, and handwriting is much too slow to keep up with normal speech. Thus, it was impossible to make completely accurate

---

*Prior to the adoption of the Constitution, each president of the Continental Congress, of which there were fourteen between 1774 and 1779, essentially served as president of the nation.

records of what was said at the Constitutional Convention. Further-more, the only one who came even close to keeping a record of the proceedings was James Madison, and he didn't publish his notes till some fifty years later, by which time he had to resort to his memory to fill in any gaps. Also, by that time, his own judgment had matured; he had even changed his mind on some significant Constitutional issues, and this could have colored his thinking as he prepared his record of the convention for publication.

The proceedings of the state ratifying conventions are even more sparse and far more problematic. Pennsylvania's state convention has the best reporting available. Levy says, "No other states' debates have yet been so fully reported, or, rather, reconstructed from newspapers and tracts."[7] Notice carefully what Levy said: Our record of Pennsylvania's debates has to a great extent been "reconstructed from newspapers and tracts." The problem is that newspapers and tracts are not official min-utes. They are the reports of the proceedings of the Pennsylvania conven-tion by newspaper reporters and others, and this is a rather unreliable source for determining the opinions of the Founders. Eldridge Gerry, who was a delegate to the Pennsylvania convention, later complained that the " 'debates of the State Conventions, as published by the short-hand writers were generally partial and mutilated.' "[8]

Beginning in 1827, a man by the name of John Elliott published *The Debates in the Several State Conventions, on the Adoption of the Federal Constitution.* However, his *Debates* "unreliably report the proceedings of only five states, plus some fragments from others."[9] And his reporting of Pennsylvania's proceedings was particularly flawed because he quoted only the speeches by James Wilson and Thomas McKean, both of whom were Federalists who favored ratification. He ignored all of the oppo-nents of ratification. It's no wonder that Levy says, "The extant records [of the Constitutional Convention and the state ratifying conventions] are simply not sufficiently ample, a fact rendering a jurisprudence of original intent quite impossible."[10]

No unanimous voice. A major flaw with the doctrine of original intent is the assumption that the delegates to the Constitutional Convention and the state ratifying conventions were all of one mind about the mean-ing of the document they produced. But it's simply unrealistic to expect fifty-five people in one room all to agree about everything in a document as complex as the United States Constitution. And getting unanimity of opinion in thirteen state conventions is much less likely. If you have access to C-Span on cable TV, spend an hour watching the proceedings of the United States Senate. You'll see a huge diversity of opinion. The same would certainly have been the case with respect to the Constitutional Convention and the state ratifying conventions.

Levy points out that "[original] 'intent' is unsatisfactory because it implies a single or uniform frame of mind, or purpose, or understanding on the part of the Framers of the Constitution and even of the ratifiers of the Constitution. 'Original intentions' would have been a far better term."[11] The Framers, Levy said, "disagreed on many crucial matters." Finally, Levy points out that "for several decades after the ratification of the Constitution the fading memories of those who had attended the Philadelphia Constitutional Convention supplied the main evidence of the Framers' intent. Even when those memories were fresh, the Framers disagreed vehemently about what the Convention had meant or intended."[12]

Because of these conflicting views in the minds of the Framers of the Constitution, an obvious problem with the doctrine of original intent is that, by choosing who one quotes, it's possible to make the Framers say just about anything one wishes. And even then, the source one cites may be more a reflection of some reporter's flawed notes, his imperfect memory, or his personal bias about what the Framer said, than an accurate representation of what the Framer in question actually meant.

Originalism. One of the chief issues with respect to the Constitution is whether it has a fixed meaning for all time or whether it's a "living document," the meaning of which evolves with time. Those who advocate a fixed meaning are originalists. They are also called "strict constructionists," because they wish the Constitution to be interpreted according to exactly what it means and nothing more. Those who advocate a more flexible interpretation view the Constitution as a "living document" that is adaptable to many circumstances and situations. Religious Right activists are almost without exception strict constructionists.

A major problem with the strict constructionist understanding is that the Framers could not possibly have anticipated all of the myriad situations that Congress would have to grapple with or that would be brought to the Supreme Court as the years rolled by. For that very reason, the Framers appear to have intentionally left many parts of the Constitution ambiguous so that its interpretation would be adaptable to a variety of situations. And circumstances *do change.* Levy aptly states that "the Framers and ratifiers cannot speak from their graves to run our lives by settling the constitutional issues of our time. We live in a world of supersonic aircraft, recombined DNA, robots, computers, microwaves, a global village ecology, interplanetary exploration, and an interdependent world economy. Our particular problems of constitutional law cannot be settled by the wisdom and insight of those who framed and ratified the Constitution, even though we observe their intent on many crucial and fundamental matters."[13]

Even if we could resurrect the Framers from their graves and ask them to resolve our problems according to their own original intent, they wouldn't speak with one voice. I pointed out a moment ago that they were as deeply divided in their day as we are in ours, and were they alive to debate our issues, they would be as deeply divided over them as we are.

Judicial activism

The proponents of original intent often complain that today's judges "legislate from the bench." Another term for this is *judicial activism.* This objection is based on the idea of originalism—that the Constitution has a fixed meaning for all time, and that it is the responsibility of judges to determine that meaning and frame every decision in harmony with that predetermined meaning. Judges who render decisions that are outside this original meaning of the Constitution are said to be "judicial activists" who are "legislating from the bench." That is, rather than interpreting the law, they are creating it. According to this view, it is the responsibility of the legislative branch of government to *create* laws. The only responsibility of the judiciary is to *interpret* laws, including the Constitution.

There are two or three major problems with this view. The first is the mistaken belief that judges can somehow interpret law without at the same time creating it. A number of years ago I got a traffic ticket, and I decided to challenge it in court. Unfortunately, the judge ruled against me. Whether I liked it or not, the judge's decision had the force of law for me. I had to pay the fine. Every judicial decision from the least to the greatest is enforceable as law. *It is law.*

The Religious Right objects that judges make decisions in areas that the Constitution doesn't address. Religious Right activists often say that today's judges *create* rights that don't exist in the Constitution. Supreme Court nominee Robert Bork, for example, stated, "Judges may look to the text, structure, and history of the Constitution, *but are prohibited from inventing extra-constitutional rights.*"[14] However, to return to an argument I posed a moment ago, today's justices are asked to address issues that the Framers had no notion of. To quote Levy again, "Justices who look to the Constitution for more than a puzzling if majestic phrase might just as well turn to the comic strips for all the practical guidance they will find on how to decide most of the great cases that involve national public policy, whether the question relates to legislative apportionment, use immunity, pornography, nonunanimous jury verdicts, racial segregation, affirmative action, electronic eavesdropping, the regulation of utility rates, child labor, subversive activities, warrantless searches, the curtailment of crop production, the seizure of steel mills, a lawyer at lineups . . ."[15] Levy's list goes on and on, but you get the point. Levy concludes by saying, "The Constitution contains not one word about these or most of the subjects of considerable import with which the Court must deal. That fact, paradoxically, is a great strength of the Constitution, accounting in part for its longevity and vitality, because it allows for evolutionary adaptation to new needs."[16]

Religious Right activists sometimes respond that in the absence of constitutional guidance, the Court should allow the citizens of the nation to decide the issue through amendment rather than through a judicial decision that creates a new law. However, this would be an extremely cumbersome way to settle the myriad issues that are brought before the Court. Twenty-seven amendments to the Constitution have been ratified in the 217 years (as of this writing) since the United States government under the Constitution came into existence (March 4, 1789). Of these, ten were in the Bill of Rights, leaving seventeen amendments to be ratified over the succeeding years. That's one about every thirteen years. Imagine the difficulty the nation would face if every decision of the Supreme Court that couldn't be based on the actual wording of the Constitution had to be decided by constitutional amendment! All manner of issues would simply go unresolved. Forbidding judges to rule about issues the Constitution doesn't address would create horrible and intolerable national chaos.

One of the problems with the charge of judicial activism is that to a great extent, whether someone believes that a judge has "legislated from the bench" depends on whether that particular observer likes or dislikes the decision the Supreme Court made. After all, if the Constitution doesn't speak to a particular issue, then the judges are just as guilty of "legislating from the bench" in those situations where the Religious

Right is happy with the decision as in those cases where they are unhappy. But the only ones they complain about are the decisions they don't like.

In its haste to call for a downgrading of the authority of the Supreme Court, the Religious Right overlooks the fact that in any human organization, the buck has to stop at someone's desk. Someone has to have the final say in situations where people lower down in the pecking order disagree. Very early in its history, the Supreme Court assumed that responsibility, and it has remained a foundational operating principle of the American government ever since.

Furthermore, in the American system, certain rights are "unalienable," to quote the Declaration of Independence—meaning that these rights cannot be trumped by majority vote. Sometimes clashes that inevitably occur between individuals threaten unalienable rights. Religious Right activists, for instance, are fond of saying that the rights of the majority are being undermined by the minority. But in our system of government, it sometimes has to be that way. And in the American government, the Supreme Court has the responsibility to make the tough decisions when people on two sides of an issue can't resolve their conflicting interests themselves. In her book *In God We Trust*, author Kathryne Page Camp asks, and answers, a provocative question: "Does the Supreme Court always get the answer right? Of course not. Supreme Court Justices are human. But someone has to decide, and the founding fathers created a system of checks and balances that gives the judicial branch the final say. And imperfect though the system may be, most citizens of the United States are unwilling to trade it for any of the systems existing in other countries. That means that the Supreme Court is stuck with the job, and America must live with its answers."[17]

Unfortunately, some Americans are increasingly unwilling to live with the answers. By characterizing the Supreme Court justices as "fools," "white-robed Ku Klux Klan members," and other derogatory terms, they are undermining one of the foundational branches of our government that has kept Americans of all persuasions free for more than two hundred years. My concern is that these voices are growing in number and increasing in volume. Where will it all end?

In conclusion, I will share with you what Leonard W. Levy considers the Framers' foundational intention to be: "The majestic opening of the Preamble [to the Constitution], 'We the People,' summons forth the still radically democratic idea that the government of the United States exists to serve the people, not the people to serve the government. That is fundamental to the Framers' original intent, as is the related idea that government in the United States cannot tell us what to think or believe about politics, religion, art, science, literature, or anything else; American citizens have the duty as well as the right to keep the government from falling into error, not the other way around."[18]

---

1. Mark R. Levin, *Men in Black: How the Supreme Court Is Destroying America* (Washington, D.C.: Regnery Publishing, Inc., 2005), 13.

2. Ibid.; italics added.

3. Ibid.

4. Ibid., x.

5. David Barton, *Original Intent: The Courts, the Constitution, & Religion* (Aledo, Tex.: WallBuilders, 2000), 123, 124.

6. Leonard W. Levy, *Original Intent and the Framers' Constitution* (Chicago: Ivan R. Dee, Publisher, 1988), 284.

7. Ibid., 289.

8. Ibid.

9. Ibid.

10. Ibid., 285.

11. Ibid., xiv, xv.

12. Ibid., ix.

13. Ibid., 298, 299.

14. Levin, 13; italics added.

15. Levy, 352.

16. Ibid., 353.

17. Kathryn Page Camp, *In God We Trust: How the Supreme Court's First Amendment Decisions Affect Organized Religion* (Grand Rapids, Mich.: FaithWalk Publishing, 2006), 5.

18. Levy, x.

Why the Sabbath Is Important

I pointed out in chapter 1 that the Seventh-day Adventist Church has grown to some fifteen million members today, whereas the Seventh Day Baptist denomination, a member of which introduced the seventh-day Sabbath to us 160 years ago, has remained relatively static at fifty thousand. One of the primary reasons for this difference is that, as I pointed out in chapter 1 and as you have seen in this book, Adventists have included an eschatological component in their teaching about the Sabbath. However, this in itself doesn't make the Sabbath an important biblical teaching. So why is the Sabbath important? That's the question I will deal with briefly in this appendix.

The Sabbath is important simply because it's part of the Ten Commandments, which are the foundation of Judeo-Christian morality. Both Revelation 12:17 and 14:12 tell us that God's end-time people will "obey God's commandments," and this obviously has to include the Sabbath commandment.

Of course, Christians who observe the Sabbath on Sunday also recognize the importance of the Sabbath because of its inclusion in the Ten Commandments. D. James Kennedy, senior pastor of the Coral Ridge Presbyterian Church in Fort Lauderdale, Florida, said, "From the witness of the early Church, from the witness of our disarrayed lives, from the witness of our society as it teeters on the brink of moral collapse, we see that the need to keep the Sabbath is truly urgent."[1]

One of the most common arguments for Sunday observance is that it doesn't matter which day a person keeps as long as it's one day in seven.

This line of reasoning assumes that all days are alike and the Sabbath can roam around among them. However, the Bible doesn't say that the Sabbath is just like every other day. When God created the Sabbath in Eden, He "*blessed* the seventh day and made it *holy*" (Genesis 2:3, italics added). And the fourth commandment says, " 'For in six days the LORD made the heavens and the earth, the sea, and all that is in them, but he rested on the seventh day. Therefore the LORD *blessed the Sabbath and made it holy*' " (Exodus 20:11, italics added). The Sabbath is different because it's holy time, set apart by God Himself for a special purpose. Therefore, we simply cannot say that it doesn't make any difference which day a person keeps, because the day God commanded us to keep really *is* different from the other six days of the week. It's *holy* time.

When God designates a particular thing and gives a command about it, He means *that one thing* and not something else. Can you imagine Adam and Eve saying, "Oh well, there are lots of trees in the Garden. As long as we choose one tree out of the many, it doesn't make any difference which one is the tree of the knowledge of good and evil." I hardly think God would have accepted that line of reasoning!

When Moses approached the burning bush in the Sinai desert, the Bible says that God told him, " 'Take off your sandals, for the place where you are standing is *holy ground*' " (Exodus 3:5, italics added). Can you imagine Moses interrupting God and saying, "You know that grove of trees on the other side of the mountain where I worship You each morning? That's my holy ground. Please meet me there," and then running off to the other side of the mountain? Do you think God would have accepted that? Of course not! Similarly, when God designates a particular day of the week as holy, He means *that* day and not some other day.

Some people argue that there have been too many calendar changes in the past several thousand years for us to be sure which day is the Sabbath. However, as strictly as the Jews have kept the Sabbath throughout history, this is highly unlikely. Jesus kept the same day the Jews kept in His day, and we know that the weekly cycle has remained unbroken during the two millenniums since.

The New Testament speaks of the abrogation of the ceremonial laws of the Israelite temple service. Hebrews 9 and 10 make that clear. It also bears witness to the end of the Jewish ritual of circumcision. However, there is no indication whatsoever in the New Testament that God removed the sacredness of the Sabbath or that He switched it to Sunday.

Some commentators have argued that the seventh day is a ceremonial aspect of the Sabbath commandment. However, the Levitical ceremonial laws abolished in the New Testament dealt with the temple rituals, which pointed forward to Christ's life, death, and resurrection. The Sabbath, on the other hand, was established at Creation, and the Sabbath commandment points back to Creation. There is nothing ceremonial about it.

Some Christians say, "I worship God every day." Seventh-day Adventists reply "Good! You should. We're glad you do." Other Christians say, "Every day is the Sabbath." Adventists respond that if every day is the Sabbath, then no day is the Sabbath, for the same God who set aside the seventh day as holy time also commanded us to work the other six days.

The bottom line about the Sabbath is that it is holy time, set aside by God Himself, and we humans are not authorized to change His moral code, the Ten Commandments. Therefore, Adventists continue to observe the Sabbath on the seventh day, as God commanded.

---

1. D. James Kennedy, *Why the Ten Commandments Matter* (New York: Warner Faith, 2005), 81, 82, in the publisher's prepublication advance-reading copy.

Does the New Testament Authorize a Change in the Day of Worship?

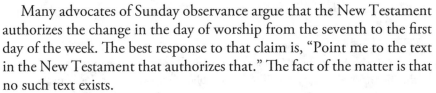

Many advocates of Sunday observance argue that the New Testament authorizes the change in the day of worship from the seventh to the first day of the week. The best response to that claim is, "Point me to the text in the New Testament that authorizes that." The fact of the matter is that no such text exists.

As you are no doubt aware, Paul taught that Gentiles need not be circumcised in order to accept Jesus and become Christians. Unfortunately, not everyone agreed with him. Conservative Jews persecuted him bitterly for his teaching about circumcision. At one point he even said, "As for those agitators, I wish they would go the whole way and emasculate [castrate] themselves!" (Galatians 5:12). The Jews in the New Testament era attached even greater significance to the Sabbath than they did to circumcision. Thus, any change of the Sabbath from Saturday to Sunday would have stirred up an even greater hornet's nest than the abolition of circumcision did, and this would certainly be reflected in the New Testament. But the New Testament is totally silent about any such controversy. This is one of the strongest arguments against the idea that the New Testament witnesses to a change of the day for observing the Sabbath.

Nevertheless, advocates of Sunday observance do point to several New Testament texts to justify their practice. I will examine these texts here.

Acts 20:7

Advocates of Sunday observance point to two "first day" texts in the New Testament as evidence that a trend in that direction had already started in the first century. One of these texts is Acts 20:7, which tells of a meeting Paul conducted on the first day of the week at a church in a town called Troas.* Acts 20:7 says, "On the first day of the week we came together to break bread. Paul spoke to the people and, because he intended to leave the next day, he kept on talking until midnight."

At the time of this meeting, Paul had completed his third preaching tour around Asia Minor and southeastern Europe, and he was on his way back to Jerusalem. From verse 25, we learn that this was the last time he expected to be in that part of the world. Thus, this would be the last opportunity for the Christians in Troas to hear him.

The significant point to note is that this meeting began on a Saturday night and continued until sunup on Sunday morning (see verse 11). Luke called it a first-day meeting because according to Jewish reckoning, the seventh day ended and the first day began at sundown. The New English Bible actually says "Saturday night" rather than "the first day of the week."

So, is this text evidence that a trend toward Sunday observance had already begun in the New Testament church? If that were true, it would place an apostolic stamp of approval on Sunday keeping. However, the facts in this case suggest that, far from indicating a New Testament *trend* toward Sunday keeping, this meeting was an *exception* to the usual practice.

The clearest evidence for this is that the meeting lasted all night. People back then weren't accustomed to all-night preaching services any more than they are today! But they were willing to endure one in this case because Paul was leaving the next day, and they knew they would never see him again. Luke called attention to the fact that it occurred on the first day of the week, not because it was typical, but because this was one of several *unusual* factors about this particular gathering.

1 Corinthians 16:1, 2

This text says, "Now about the collection for God's people: Do what I told the Galatian churches to do. On the first day of every week, each one of you should set aside a sum of money in keeping with his income, saving it up, so that when I come no collections will have to be made."

---

*Troas was in Asia Minor (modern Turkey), just south of the Hellespont, the narrow body of water that divides Europe from Asia Minor.

A famine was raging in Palestine when Paul wrote these words, and Paul was collecting a relief offering from the churches in Europe and Asia Minor to help the famine-stricken Christians. That's why he told the Christians in Corinth to set money aside.

Some Christians claim that Paul was instructing the believers in Corinth to take up a collection during their weekly church service. If that were correct, then this would indeed provide evidence for Sunday observance in the New Testament.

However, a careful reading of the Greek rules out this interpretation. Paul said, literally, that on the first day of the week each one of the Corinthian Christians should "by himself let him put, storing up whatever he is prospered."

Paul's words "by himself let him put" mean that he was instructing the Christians in Corinth to save up their money *at home*, not *in church*. The Greek words "by himself" are the equivalent of the English "at home." The Spanish edition of the highly respected Jerusalem Bible actually says, *"Reserve en su casa"*; that is, "Reserve [or set aside] at home."

Revelation 1:10

This verse says that John was "in the Spirit on the Lord's day" (KJV). People who are searching for biblical support for their practice of observing Sunday claim that "the Lord's day" means Sunday. But they're reading into the text a conclusion that the text itself does not state. To the contrary, Jesus—who everyone agrees kept the Sabbath on the seventh day—claimed to be Lord of the *Sabbath*—the day which the Jews were observing (Mark 2:27, 28). And Isaiah—who wrote his book when the last day of the week was the only one any of God's people had ever heard of keeping—called the seventh-day Sabbath " 'the LORD's holy day' " (Isaiah 58:13). So if there is a biblical definition of "the Lord's day," it would have to be the seventh day of the week, not the first.

Colossians 2:16, 17

The advocates of Sunday observance frequently use this text. I'll begin by quoting it: "Therefore do not let anyone judge you by what you eat or drink, or with regard to a religious festival, a New Moon celebration or a Sabbath day. These are a shadow of the things that were to come; the reality, however, is found in Christ."

The Greek word translated "Sabbath" in Colossians 2:16 is *sabbatōn*. This is the same word, whether singular or plural, that's translated "sabbath" everywhere else in the Greek Old and New Testaments.* Nothing in the word itself indicates whether it refers to the weekly Sabbath or the yearly ceremonial sabbaths described in the Old Testament.

There are two ways to view this text, neither of which provides an adequate basis for concluding that the New Testament church was observing the first day of the week. The traditional Adventist response to this text is that the "Sabbath" Paul mentioned in Colossians 2:16 was the yearly sabbaths of the Jewish temple ritual (their ceremonial law), not the weekly seventh-day Sabbath. Some commentators have argued that because *sabbatōn* in Colossians 2:16 is plural, it refers to the weekly Sabbath. However, the plural of *sabbatōn* is used elsewhere in the New Testament of a single Sabbath (see for example Matthew 28:1). We cannot determine whether *sabbatōn* refers to weekly Sabbaths or ceremonial sabbaths on the basis of the Greek form of the word. We have to determine that by the context. So let's examine the context.

Paul mentioned two points in Colossians 2:16 that can help us decide whether the sabbath(s) he referred to was the weekly Sabbath or the yearly ceremonial sabbaths. The first is that "sabbath" was the last of several issues the Colossian Christians apparently were judging each other about. The others were choices of what to eat and drink, religious festivals, and new moon celebrations. All of these were a part of the Jewish ceremonial system.

Second, Paul said that all of these "are a shadow of the things that were to come; the reality, however, is found in Christ." So, Paul wasn't talking just about what people ate and drank at their regular mealtime. He had in mind eating and drinking that foreshadowed Christ. He also had in mind the observance of religious festivals and new moon celebrations that pointed forward to Christ.

We know, of course, that the ceremonial law required the Jews to bring a variety of food and drink offerings to the temple as a part of their worship (see for example Leviticus 7:12–18 [food offerings] and Leviticus 23:13 and Numbers 15:10 [drink offerings]). It also mandated the observance of various holy days throughout the year (Leviticus 23:4–44), and the new moon was to be celebrated on the first day of each month (Numbers 10:10; 28:11).

---

*The Old Testament was originally written in Hebrew and Aramaic but was translated into Greek a couple centuries before Christ.

All of these were indeed "a shadow of the things that were to come"—that is, of Christ's life, death, and resurrection. That's why Paul said, "The reality . . . is found in Christ." When Christ came, He fulfilled all these shadows or types, including animal sacrifices, and they ceased to exist. This is consistent with the statement in Hebrews that the entire sanctuary ritual was "a copy and *shadow* of what is in heaven" (Hebrews 8:5, italics added).

The weekly Sabbath has never been a shadow of anything. The fourth commandment presents the weekly Sabbath as a memorial of Creation: " 'For in six days the LORD made the heavens and the earth, the sea, and all that is in them, but he rested on the seventh day. Therefore [that's why] the LORD blessed the Sabbath day and made it holy' " (Exodus 20:11). Even at the time God gave the Ten Commandments, Creation was an event in the distant past and not a shadow of Christ, whose coming was still future. This rules out the sabbath in Colossians 2:16 being the weekly Sabbath.

On the other hand, all of the ceremonial sabbaths pointed forward to Christ, just as Paul said. Thus, in Colossians 2:16, Paul was referring to the yearly ceremonial sabbaths of the Hebrew tabernacle service, not the weekly Sabbath of the fourth commandment.

What I have just given you is the traditional Adventist response to those who claim that Colossians 2:16, 17 is evidence of the New Testament change of the Sabbath from Saturday to Sunday. But a different response is also possible, on the assumption that Paul really did have in mind the weekly Sabbath.

Paul's basic purpose in writing Colossians was to condemn certain false teachers and advise the Colossian church members to resist the ascetic practices these teachers were urging on them. Commentators generally agree that these false teachers were not the conservative Jewish Christians who followed Paul everywhere he went, insisting that Gentiles had to become Jews and submit to all the Jewish ceremonial laws before they could become Christians. Rather, these were Gnostic teachers who insisted on an ascetic lifestyle. This is evident from chapter 2:20, 21, 23, where Paul said, "Since you died with Christ to the basic principles of this world, why, as though you still belonged to it, do you submit to its rules: 'Do not handle! Do not taste! Do not touch!'? . . . Such regulations indeed have an appearance of wisdom, with their self-imposed worship, their false humility and their harsh treatment of the body, but they lack any value in restraining sensual indulgence."

If Paul indeed had the weekly Sabbath in mind when he wrote Colossians 2:16, then these false teachers obviously were condemning the Colossian Christians who chose to observe the day. Paul doesn't say so, but given their strict ascetic tendencies, the false teachers may have been insisting on very legalistic rules of Sabbath keeping. Whatever the details, Paul said, "Don't let them pass judgment on you for your Sabbath keeping."

So, Paul wasn't forbidding Sabbath keeping in Colossians 2:16. He wasn't telling the Colossian Christians that the Sabbath had been done away with and didn't need to be kept any longer. There isn't a hint of that in this text. Rather, if the Sabbath in this text does indeed refer to the weekly Sabbath, it's obvious that the Colossian Christians were already keeping the day, and Paul's advice was, "Don't let these false teachers pass judgment on you for that." Colossians 2:16, 17 thus becomes an argument in *favor* of Sabbath observance in the New Testament, not an argument *against* it.

There's a practical lesson in this for Christians today. Many of us also have varying convictions about the Sabbath, and it's important that we take Paul's advice seriously and avoid judging each other regarding our choices.

If you found this book helpful, you'll want to read these other books by the same author.

Forever His
Marvin Moore

This is a book for sinners. It's for those who worry that their repeated failures disqualify them from having a relationship with Jesus. If this describes you, Moore has some good news from the book of Romans. You can have a joyful and unbroken relationship with Jesus right now. And being "perfect" has nothing to do with it!
Paperback, 192 pages.   0-8163-2006-3   US$13.99

The Crisis of the End Time
Marvin Moore

A storm is coming. This is the big one. Sadly, many Adventists are growing weary with those who insist the end is near. Still others fear the approaching tempest and wait joylessly for the time of trouble and the close of probation.

With compelling evidence from Scripture and the Spirit of Prophecy, Moore suggests that the greatest crisis in human history is about to break upon us, and more importantly, how we can keep our relationships with Jesus during earth's darkest hour.
Paperback, 256 pages.   0-8163-1085-8   US$13.99

The Coming Great Calamity
Marvin Moore

Are you prepared for your world to be shaken to its very foundations?

Religion will control the governments of our world just before Jesus comes again. The Bible predicts it. But something drastic will have to happen between now and then. Everything could happen in the twinkling of an eye—in response to calamities beyond anything humanity has ever experienced. Forewarned is forearmed.
Paperback, 190 pages.   0-8163-1354-7   US$10.99

Order from your ABC by calling **1-800-765-6955**, or get online and shop our virtual store at **http://www.AdventistBookCenter.com**.
  • Read a chapter from your favorite book
  • Order online
  • Sign up for e-mail notices on new products

Prices subject to change without notice.